D0919929

Direct Response Television

The Authoritative Guide

Frank R. Brady ■ J. Angel Vasquez

Printed on recyclable paper

Library of Congress Cataloging-in-Publication Data

Brady, Frank
Direct response television: the authoritative guide/
Frank Brady, John Angel Vasquez.
p. cm.
Includes bibliographical references and index.
ISBN 0-8442-3548-2
1. Television advertising. 2. Television—Production and
direction. 3. Advertising media planning. I. Vasquez, John Angel.
II. Title.
HF6146.T42B65 1996
65914'3—dc20 94-17786
CIP

Published by NTC Business Books, a division of NTC Publishing Group
4255 West Touhy Avenue
Lincolnwood (Chicago), Illinois 60646-1975, U.S.A.

Manufactured in the United States of America.

4 5 6 7 8 9 ML 9 8 7 6 5 4 3 2 1

From Frank, to my daughter, Tania who always told me I should write a book.

Thanks to my mom, Ruth, I have vision. Love, Angel

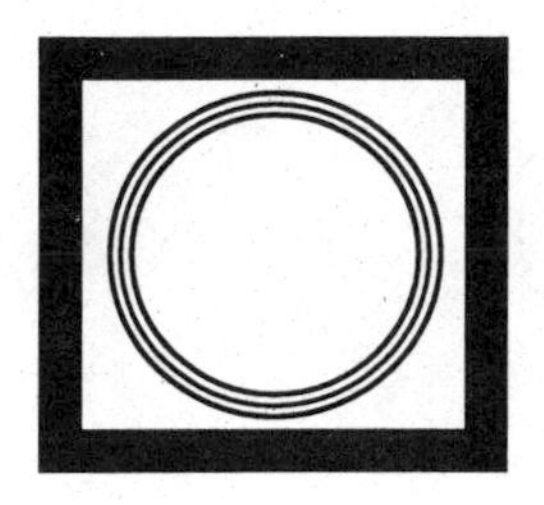

Table of Contents

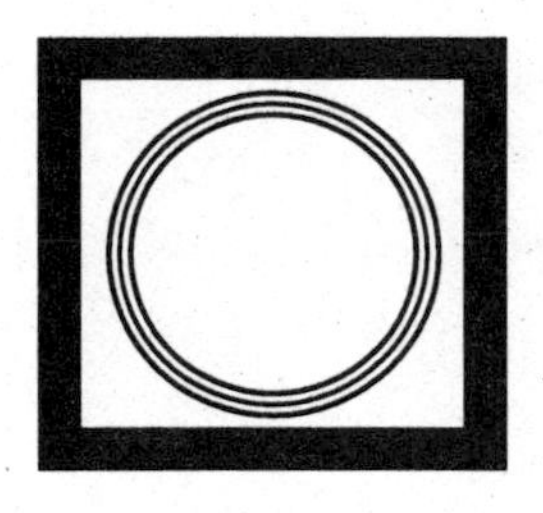

Acknowledgments

Thanks to our colleagues, friends, and wives, without whose advice and encouragement this book would not have been written.

Claudia Almoslino
Jennifer Brady
Chekitan Dev., Ph.D.
Tim Devitt
Carl Fremont
Stu Hyatt
Dennis Martin
Dan McGillick
Diane Okrent

Thanks, also, to our editors at NTC, first for believing this book might be good, then for making it better.

Carole Bilina
Betsy Lancefield
Richard Hagle
Anne Knudsen

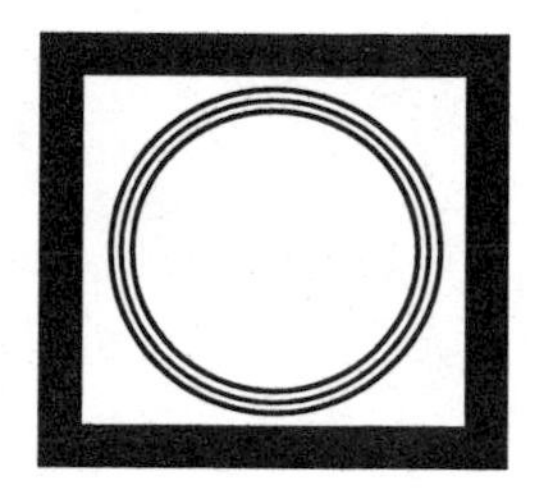

Introduction

If you're like many direct marketers, you're perfectly at home in direct mail and print, but you may be reluctant to sell on television. If so, it's probably for one of two reasons:

1. You've never done it before.
2. You *have* done it before.

Obviously, the first reason is valid. Unfortunately, the second is too. The fact is, when many direct response (DR) advertisers finally muster up the courage (and the budget) for TV, they do it all wrong and never try it again. Whichever group you're in, *Direct Response Television* can help you. Whether you've never done DR TV, or done it badly, we're going to show you the right way to do it.

We're also going to show you the right way to do it *within your budget.* We've worked with companies that range in size from small-budget start-ups to Time-Warner, CBS-Sony, BMG, and other giants of DR TV. So we're able to show you how both the "little guys" and the "big guys" do it successfully.

We've divided the book into four sections: *Your Marketing Strategy, Creating Your Commercial, The Economics of Direct Response Television,* and *Producing Your Commercial.* Everything is modular. If you think you already know the information in a particular section or chapter, review the end-of-chapter checklists to be sure.

Wherever possible we've illustrated key points with examples. We've also provided you with checklists, worksheets, and sample forms: everything you need—and need to know—every step of the way. In Appendixes A–D at the end of the book, we've included a "Glossary," a "Recommended Reading" list, and a list of "Associations and Organizations," and other practical information.

Direct Response Television is designed to help you minimize the downside risk and maximize the upside potential of DR TV. In other words, make money. If it helps you, please let us know.

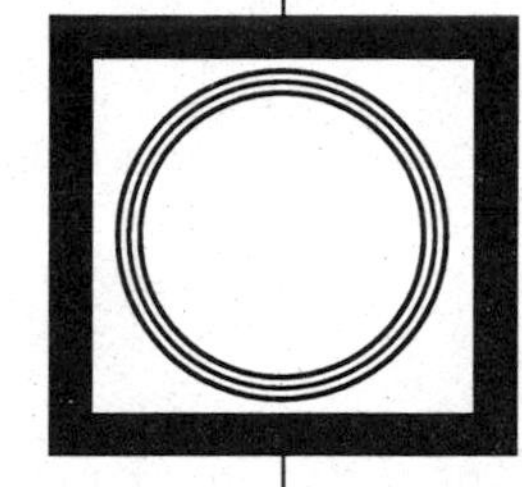

SECTION ONE

Your Marketing Strategy

What Direct Response Television Can Do for You

What exactly is direct response (DR) television? Who is using it? How is it being used? What are its advantages and disadvantages? The answers in this chapter will give you the information you need to help you decide if DR TV is right for you.

What Is Direct Response Television?

Ask most people what DR TV is and they'll say, "Those long commercials with an 800 number that try to sell you something." That's correct, as far as it goes. For years, traditional direct marketers such as Time-Life Books, Sports Illustrated, and CBS Videos have been on TV. But today, even Fortune 500 packaged goods companies are trying it.

Fresh Feliners, a division of Colgate Palmolive, gave away a free sample through direct TV. So did Tempo antacid. Manufacturers Hanover Trust invited home owners to a seminar. And Ford offered a brochure for a new car. The list goes on. More and more companies are discovering the power of DR TV. Emerging technology, such as interactive television and 500-channel access, should make it more powerful—and more appealing to businesses—in years to come.

The Strengths of Direct Response Television

What makes DR so strong? Direct response television gives you a cost-efficient channel of distribution, great flexibility, measurable media, and the ultimate mass-communication tool—all at the same time.

An Efficient Channel of Distribution

If you have a product or service to sell, how do you get it to the consumer? If you expect to get shelf space in a store, you're going to need a sales force or give away a percentage of your profits to a broker or distributor. You can try to be included in a catalog, but that takes time and, again, you're forced to share profits.

With DR TV, you're the master of your own destiny. You're the one taking the product to market, and you're not giving anyone a share of the pie. Your product will probably get to market more quickly. And, after a successful run on TV, you may be able to get in-store distribution on more favorable terms. Your direct response commercial is also creating consumer awareness and establishing your product image.

Great Flexibility

A commercial is inherently more flexible than print or mail. You can change your advertising the day of the shoot. You can't do that the day of the press check. You can also change your commercial *after* the fact if you must. You can change your media, too. Once you're in a magazine or in the mail, you're committed. But within a day you can put more money against a particular TV station, cut back on spending, or cancel the commercial altogether.

Measurable Media

Like direct mail, DR TV response rates can be precisely measured. However, TV is quicker. Instead of waiting weeks for results, you get an answer in days. This can be an advantage to a direct marketer. It is also one reason why general image TV advertisers have been discovering direct.

After they are aired, general image commercials are measured by day-after recall testing. For instance, the Burke Test finds out if people saw a particular commercial and what they remember about it. The ideal is when viewers remember the brand and the key selling message.

But finding out if the commercial had an effect on sales can take months. Packaged goods advertisers normally put new television creative in a test market for six months. If the results are good, they may run the creative in another test market for another six months. Why so much testing?

To reduce the possibility that outside factors are affecting the results. Just a few of the things that can skew test results are: distribution, pricing, competitive pressure, competing sales forces, and the ups and downs of the economy.

In a DR test, you start to get results the first day. Your test is completed in two weeks! And the answers aren't ambiguous. You *know* people saw your commercial. You *know* they understood your key selling message. You *know* they believed it. Why? Because they called.

You know even more than that. If you tested different pricing, offers or creative, you know which work the best. So you have a good idea if you're going to make money and how much. All in two weeks!

The Ultimate Mass Communication Tool

Television is the most efficient way to sell large amounts of mass-market products to vast numbers of people. This is what separates TV from print and mail. If you're like many direct marketers, you may be comfortable thinking of mail as *the* channel of distribution and *the* measurable media vehicle. And if you have a niche product and a segmented customer base, you probably should *not* be on TV. However, if you have a product that appeals to a mass market, you should be considering TV as part of your media mix.

Television has a greater reach than any other medium. It is more persuasive than any other medium. As postal rates continue to rise, it has become more economical than mail. And new technologies have made DR TV production costs comparable with mail packages. Direct response television has the potential to make you more money than any other advertising medium. Its only disadvantage is that because viewers truly "call now," they're acting on impulse.

We've seen why DR TV can be so effective. Next, we'll take a look at some of the ways it's being used today.

Ways To Use Direct Response Television

Further proof of the effectiveness of DR TV is the fact that it works in so many ways.

Direct Selling

The first uses of DR TV were to sell products. You may have seen the early commercials for Veg-O-Matic and Ginsu Knives. Today, the selling of products and services is by far the number one use of DR TV. It will be the focus of this book.

Support

Direct response television is often used to support other direct marketing efforts. For instance, a commercial may tell viewers to check their mail for a special offer. Or to look for an insert in the Sunday paper.

How is it possible to tell if support TV is working? The first way is to do a split test. Market A gets only the direct mail package. Market B gets the mail *and* the TV. As long as the markets are equivalent, B should show a lift in mail response. And the lift should more than pay for the cost of producing and running the support TV.

The second, and even more definitive, way to test support TV is to use what has become known in DR as the "Gold Box." Buried away somewhere in an ad or a mail piece is a little box or circle. It's so unobtrusive, not 1 person in 1,000 would notice it. But the support commercial says that when you respond to the offer, if you mark the Gold Box with an "X," you get an extra CD, an extra book, or whatever. Again, do a market test. Simply counting the responses marked with an "X" tells you how much the support TV helped.

Lead Generation

Direct response television can be a most cost-effective way to generate large numbers of sales leads. Typically, a commercial generates interest in a product or service and offers an 800 number for the viewer to learn more. When the viewer calls, a telemarketer captures his or her name, address and telephone number. The telemarketer may ask other questions to further qualify the prospect. This information is passed on to the sales force. Fulfillment information is often *not* sent directly to the prospect. Instead, a salesperson or agent will phone the prospect and offer to deliver the information in person. Or the salesperson will try to arrange for the prospect to visit a showroom, an office, or wherever the sale is normally made.

Integrated Marketing

Integrated marketing goes beyond support and lead generation. In integrated marketing, DR TV works with general image advertising, whether TV or other media, as part of an overall marketing plan. This "total" approach to marketing may also include sales promotion, public relations, package design, etc.

One of the most common examples of integrated marketing is to adapt a 30-second general image commercial so that it becomes a 60-second DR spot. This is most easily and most economically done with a wrap. In a wrap the general image commercial is used as a core with a DR opening and close.

Why would you want to wrap an existing commercial? Perhaps to offer coupons, a free sample, a premium, or to take advantage of a special event. For instance, a wrap for a soft drink might offer discounted tickets to a rock concert.

In a typical wrap, an announcer comes on for 10 seconds and says something like, "Hi! I'm Jennie, an operator here at XYZ Publishing, and I'll be right back to tell you how you can get this great clock radio—free." Then the 30-second spot runs. Afterwards, Jennie comes back and has 20 seconds to give the offer.

Sequential Marketing

Often an advertiser has a long and/or complicated story to tell. Or the marketer may have to overcome a negative image, perhaps that the product is old-fashioned or shoddy. In these cases, it may not be possible to educate people or change their perceptions with 30-second general image commercials or print ads. Sequential marketing may be necessary.

The sequential marketing technique is based on two premises:

1. Potential customers are at starting point A in their propensity to purchase and must be moved to an end point. Let's call our end point E. For a more severe marketing problem the end point might be further along the alphabet.
2. The communication must follow a strict sequence. Only when the customer understands and believes point B will he or she be ready to learn point C. And so on, until the communication is complete and the sale can be consummated.

To accomplish all this, a multimedia approach may be needed. A DR commercial might be the first step. The spot may attempt to motivate the viewer to request more information, which may be in the form of mailings, newsletters, videos, interactive disks, and/or outbound telemarketing.

Infomercials

Another way to tell a complicated story is on a 30-minute infomercial. Infomercials are primarily used to sell products, but they can also be very effective in "teaching" an audience. There probably aren't too many things that can't be explained in a half hour. Major advertisers are discovering this, and they're not the only ones. In his 1992 presidential campaign, Ross Perot used the 30-minute format to explain his positions quite effectively.

Test General Image Selling Strategies

One of the most subtle uses of DR TV is to test general image selling strategies quickly and inexpensively. Instead of having to test new creative for six months, direct response may be able to accomplish the same thing in two weeks.

Imagine that a fictitious product, "Grandma Esposito's Italian Sauce," was successfully launched with this selling strategy: "A recipe first served in Napoli in 1888." But lately Grandma Esposito's has been losing market share. A number of new strategies have been developed. In focus groups and in-depth research, the following four beat "Napoli Recipe":

1. "Slow simmered all day long, like you make it at home."
2. "Made with herbs and spices fresh from Grandma's garden."
3. "So thick you can cut it with a knife."
4. "Every jar has real imported Italian tomatoes, basil, and oregano."

The client doesn't have the budget to produce four commercials and test each for six months. Also, there's a concern that "so thick" may have production problems and that "imported" may be too expensive to implement. The field of contenders is narrowed with the help of DR. A relatively inexpensive direct response commercial is made. In order to elicit response, the commercial makes viewers an offer. To get statistically significant results, the offer is a good one: two jars free when you buy one. To eliminate executional bias, the commercials are identical except for the strategic selling message:

- Version #1 of the commercial shows a woman in her kitchen opening a shopping bag. She says, "I just bought this jar of Grandma Esposito's, the sauce that's *slow simmered all day long, like you make it at home.* And when I bought it, I got this second jar free, and I even got this third jar free. Three for the price of one, of Grandma Esposito's, the sauce that's *slow simmered all day long, like you make it at home.* How'd I get it? I just called 1-800-111-1111 and they sent me a coupon.... "
- Version #2 goes like this: "I just bought this jar of Grandma Esposito's, *the sauce that's made with herbs and spices fresh from Grandma's garden* ... ... How'd I get it? I just called 1-800-222-2222 and they sent me a coupon .... "

And so on. The four new strategies and the old one, "Napoli Recipe," are tested in five different markets. The commercials aren't meant to be creative. And the offer is merely to entice people to call. Because the only variable is the strategy, comparing the number of phone calls for each version gives the winner. Now the client is comfortable turning the winning strategy into a full-production commercial that will go into a 6-month test market.

Direct Response Television—Yes, No, or Maybe

Should you consider DR TV? You won't have enough information to know if it's right for you until you've finished the book. For now, these three examples will show you that often DR TV is the way to go, but sometimes it's not, and occasionally it's a good idea to combine it with other media.

- A new ethnic newspaper tested a combination of direct mail and direct TV. While the mail was better targeted to the audience, the TV was seen as a way to generate awareness, establish credibility, and acquire subscribers. The agency recommended an inexpensive, hard-hitting commercial that mirrored the paper's editorial policy.
- A stainless flatware company built a successful business by enclosing inserts in the billing statements that department stores send to their customers. The inserts were inexpensive, and the postage was "free."

So it would have been virtually impossible for a commercial to be as cost effective. Also, to show flatware at its best, the commercial would have had to be expensive. In this case, DR TV was not the way to go.

- A book publisher advertised its mass-market books on TV and its niche-market ones with direct mail or in specialized media. With one of its collections, certain books worked better on TV, while others worked better in print. The publisher split the media buy, capitalizing on both print and TV. Multimedia worked in this situation.

TABLE 1-1. DIRECT RESPONSE TELEVISION, COMPARED TO DIRECT MAIL

Attribute	Direct TV	Direct Mail
Channel of distribution	Comparable	Comparable
Product awareness	Better	
Flexibility	Better	
Measurability	Comparable	Comparable
Mass communication	Better	
Production cost	Comparable	Comparable
Media cost	Comparable	Comparable
Quality of response		Better
Targetability		Better

CHECKLIST: What DR TV Can Do For You

	Yes	No
Direct selling?	☐	☐
Support TV?	☐	☐
Split test?	☐	☐
"Gold Box" for premium?	☐	☐
Lead generation?	☐	☐
Integrated marketing?	☐	☐
Wrap?	☐	☐
Sequential marketing?	☐	☐
Use infomercial to teach?	☐	☐
Test general image selling strategies?	☐	☐

Research

Research will help you understand the market, the competition, and the audience. It will show you what customers are buying and why. It will give you an idea of how your product or service compares with the competition. It will help you develop a new product or service. And when you create advertising, it can be the compass that guides you to success.

Research is what you should do *before* the fact, compared to testing, which you do *after* the fact. (Testing will be covered in Chapter 13.) Research can help you develop and check the viability of creative concepts, storyboards, animatics, and commercials. These topics and research methodologies for each will be covered in Section II.

Primary vs. Secondary Research

The two categories of research are primary research and secondary research. Primary research is research you commission and pay for yourself. It is usually done by an advertising agency research department. Or the agency research department may use an outside vendor to field the actual research project. Secondary research is research that was originated, conducted, analyzed, and published by others. Free sources of secondary research include newspapers, magazines, trade journals, texts, government publications, etc. Paid sources include reports from services such as MRI, Nielsen, and Simmons. These will tell you such things as brand share of market and give you demographic, geographic, and media breakouts.

Qualitative vs. Quantitative Research

There are two basic types of primary advertising research: qualitative and quantitative. Qualitative research shows you directions or areas to pursue in your product development and in your advertising. Quantitative gives you numbers and measurements. Qualitative includes focus groups and one-on-one interviews. Quantitative includes mall intercepts and telephone surveys. In-home interviews can be either qualitative or quantitative. We will discuss these types of research in the order of how frequently they are used in direct response television.

Focus Groups

Focus groups are usually the quickest, least expensive research you can do. In a focus group, about ten people sit at a table discussing your product, product category, concept, or commercial. A trained moderator keeps the group on track and makes sure the participants answer all the questions you (and the agency) have and that they cover all the points you want discussed. The moderator keeps the group focused on the subject at hand.

Participants are recruited to fit certain criteria of your target audience, such as sex, age, household income, and product usage. Usually, two or more groups are conducted on any one subject. They should be conducted in more than one market to minimize market-specific reactions. For instance, people in Chicago and Houston may view certain products differently.

During the focus group, the direct marketer and the ad agency people sit behind a one-way mirror. They can see the group members, but the participants can't see them. This is so that the presence of observers doesn't influence the responses and so that the observers can see, firsthand, "real people reactions" to whatever is being discussed. Focus groups are usually audiotaped and sometimes videotaped.

Focus groups are qualitative, and the findings from them are directional. You cannot extrapolate statistically significant results from a sample of 10 or 20 and apply them to the target audience. You cannot say, "Nine out of ten people in the focus group believe such-and-such and that makes it 90 percent likely."

Focus groups are ideal at the early stages of a product's strategic and concept development. This is where you want freewheeling input. Comments made by real people are often the key to solving tough marketing problems, looking at things in a new way, or just hearing some good dialogue. Sometimes you want to have discussions with individual consumers. These are called one-on-one interviews.

> A direct marketer wanted to gauge consumer reaction to a premium. It was a telephone that had a built-in pen, memo pad,

and name-and-address file. Two creative executions were exposed to focus groups. The first was a straight-ahead message. It said that if you ordered the product now you would get the useful premium. It went on to explain the features. The second approach was humorous. It depicted everyday scenes where the premium would have come in handy to jot down a number or scribble a message. It even showed how it would have helped to write down the 800 number to the commercial! By illustrating an end benefit to which viewers could relate, the second execution effectively answered the question "Why do I need another phone in the house?"

Mall Intercepts

Mall intercepts are usually conducted at shopping malls. However, they also are done at other places. It is easier to screen for business people at an airport, for example. Or they may be done at tourist attractions, such as theme parks. The target audience and budget help determine location.

In this type of research, interviewers intercept passersby and find out if they fit the demographic and psychographic profiles of your potential customers. If they qualify and agree to participate, they are taken to a room and shown your strategies, concepts, storyboards, animatics, or commercials. A questionnaire is administered by the interviewer. These days, the questionnaire may be on a computer disk. The subject sits in front of an interactive television monitor and sees questions or choices pop up on the screen. He or she touches the screen to record answers or make selections. A computer processes the information instantly.

Intercepts can be expensive and time consuming. They are usually conducted with at least 100 people per commercial execution so that quantitative results can be compared and are statistically significant. The interviews are done at several locations in your market area in order to include reactions from the broadest possible base of potential consumers.

While focus groups help you decide which strategies and executions to develop, mall intercepts help you refine them so that they are more understandable and believable.

A bank had been using an illustration style in its print advertising. It wanted to find out if this style would translate into an effective DR animated commercial. Creating a complete animated commercial was not necessary. Instead, rough animation was done to illustrate the approach. One hundred people were shown the animated approach. The same number was shown the same footage shot as real-life. When the comprehension, belief, and persuasion scores proved to be comparable, the bank felt comfortable in proceeding with the animated commercial.

Telephone Surveys

Telephone surveys give you results relatively quickly. Because you can't show visuals or do in-depth probing, they do not lend themselves to the latter stages of commercial development. They can be very helpful, however, in the early stages of product development. People can be asked to rate product attributes or likes and dislikes. Telephone surveys can also be used as follow-up to people who called an 800 number. A marketer might want to know what it was about the commercial that compelled viewers to call. If they called and asked for information instead of ordering, they can be asked what they felt was lacking in the commercial.

> A direct marketer introduced a product that appealed to the entire family. The marketer was surprised to learn that while response to the commercial was good, too high a percentage of callers were not ordering the product. The ad agency had never seen anything like it. The telemarketing firm mentioned that some of the callers sounded young. A telephone survey confirmed that most of the callers were teenagers who were watching TV by themselves when the commercial aired. Because they did not have credit cards, they could not order. While they planned to ask their parents to order for them, this rarely happened. The solution was to air the commercials when families were likely to be viewing together, and to make it clear that only credit card holders were to call.

In-Home Interviews

In this research technique a researcher sets up appointments to interview people at home. The in-home setting allows the researcher to spend as much time as necessary with the subject. It also lets the researcher get a firsthand look at the lifestyle of the person being interviewed. The researcher can see how the subject uses the product, or how competing products compare. This type of research is quite expensive and is not often used in DR.

New Product Development: Product Benefit and Product Concept Research

If you're developing a new product, or deciding which of several new product ideas to pursue, product benefit research and/or product concept research may be helpful. Of the two, product concept research is done more often, usually in a focus group. Benefit research, also called promise research, is more time consuming and expensive because it is quantitative. However, if your product does many things, benefit research can help you discover which ones to include in your product concept.

Benefit Research

More than 200 years ago, Samuel Johnson said: "Promise, large promise is the soul of advertising." It's just as true today. You *must* promise your customer a benefit he or she wants and can't get elsewhere. The question is, *what* do you promise?

Benefit research finds the most important thing you can say about your product or service. It tells you what benefit is most appealing to the consumer. If your product has multiple benefits, it ranks them. It lets you know if your competition already "owns" the best benefits. And it gives you an ideal for which to aim. Benefit research starts with a laundry list of everything your product does. It might include 50 to 100 items. Each is a simple statement of one attribute.

A portion of a list for a tire manufacturer is presented in Figure 2-1. It asks the consumer to rank the importance of each attribute in one of three categories—"very," "somewhat," or "not at all" important. Note that the items overlap. Numbers 7, 10 and 11 relate to high-speed handling, while 2, 4 and 9 deal with long life. This staggering is by design and allows the researcher to see if the answers cluster together in a pattern. This research showed that consumers want a tire that lasts a long time. The consumer's ideal is a tire that never needs to be replaced. This gave the manufacturer the foundation on which to create advertising that said, in essence, "Our tires last a very long time."

Figure 2-1. Sample Benefits Checklist

TIRE BENEFITS			
How Important Is Each of These to You?	**Very**	**Somewhat**	**Not at all**
1. Gets good traction all year	☐	☐	☐
2. Lasts as long as I own my car	☐	☐	☐
3. Will never blow out	☐	☐	☐
4. Will last for 50,000 miles	☐	☐	☐
5. Self-sealing if punctured	☐	☐	☐
6. Good traction in rain	☐	☐	☐
7. Good for high speeds	☐	☐	☐
8. Puncture resistant	☐	☐	☐
9. Will last for 40,000 miles	☐	☐	☐
10. Good at cornering	☐	☐	☐
11. Good for emergency handling	☐	☐	☐
12. Good traction in mud	☐	☐	☐

Fur in a Can

At this point, we will begin to weave a thread throughout the book for an imaginary product. Our product, called "Fur in a Can," is a spray-on coating of fur that can be applied anywhere. Fur in a Can will help to illustrate methods discussed in this chapter and some of the later ones. We'll develop a strategy for Fur in a Can in Chapter 5, then a concept and a storyboard for it in later chapters. We'll continue using Fur in a Can to illustrate some other ideas. We had fun with Fur in a Can. We hope you will too.

A section of a benefit research checklist for Fur in a Can is shown in figure 2-2. We want to know which potential uses are most important to consumers. We also want to learn how important the following are to them: safe when used on the family pet, approved by animal-rights advocates, easy to use, economical, and long-lasting.

Figure 2-2. Benefit Research Checklist for Fur in a Can

FUR IN A CAN BENEFITS			
How Important Is Each of These to You?	**Very**	**Somewhat**	**Not at all**
1. Grows fur on carpet	☐	☐	☐
2. Grows fur on furniture	☐	☐	☐
3. Grows fur on draperies	☐	☐	☐
4. Grows fur on clothing	☐	☐	☐
5. Helps save lives of minks, etc.	☐	☐	☐
6. Grows fur on decks & patios	☐	☐	☐
7. Grows fur on car/boat seats	☐	☐	☐
8. Grows fur on pets	☐	☐	☐
9. Safe to use on pets	☐	☐	☐
10. It's easy to grow fur	☐	☐	☐
11. Now fur is affordable	☐	☐	☐
12. Fur lasts a long time	☐	☐	☐

Product Concept Research

Benefit research will help you create a powerful product concept that incorporates the feature or features people most want. The format of a product concept is simply a sentence or two (no more than a paragraph) that describes what your product is and what it does. For research purposes, it's important that the description be as factual as possible, without any attempt to "sell." You want unbiased opinions that have not been influenced by a skillful copywriter.

A drawing may be included in your product concept if the product is difficult to visualize. If you have an actual product, or a mockup, you might show that. The Fur in a Can product concept is presented in Figure 2-3. When you read it, notice how benefit research would have helped to create the product concept.

Figure 2-3. Product Concept for Fur in a Can

Fur "seeds" that grow thick, luxurious, and long-lasting fur on any surface. The seeds come in a can. Just pour them wherever you want fur to grow. It's easy to turn an old coat into a fur coat. Use it anywhere in the home, on rugs, curtains, drapes, chairs, pillows, and more. Fur in a Can can also grow fur on car seats, motorcycles, boats, outdoor decks, and patios. It can even safely grow fur on the family pet. Fur in a Can has been accepted by animal-rights advocates.

Researching Product Concepts

While product concepts can be created for existing products, they are most often used to gauge new product ideas. Whether in a focus group or a mall intercept, usually 5 to 10 product concepts are shown. This is done for three reasons.

1. You might be considering more than one product and want to see which is the strongest.
2. You might want to include disguised versions of competitive products, to see how yours compares.
3. You might want to include a great product that would probably be impossibly expensive to produce, and a terrible one. Reactions to these two will give you the extreme ends of the spectrum. The closer your product is to the ideal, the better.

Brand Name Perception

Knowing how your brand name affects consumer attitudes toward the new product is valuable information. You can find out by following these three steps:

1. Show generic product concepts, without revealing the name of the manufacturer.
2. Ask who would be the most likely manufacturer of the product.
3. Reveal who the manufacturer is.

The brand name perception answers can reveal your company's reputation as an innovator. It can even tell you if people will buy the product after they know it is from you. This can be particularly useful if you are launching a product that is not in your traditional line.

When to Do Research

You can spend a large amount of money on research, especially if you use it at every stage of product and commercial development. You can also spend a great deal of time on research, particularly the quantitative variety. A mall intercept may take weeks to set up, weeks to conduct, and more weeks to tabulate and analyze the results.

The answer to how much—if any—research is needed at various stages of your project can best be answered by your account executive and research expert. A good rule of thumb is that if no one has a definitive answer to key questions, or if bright people come to different conclusions, research may be in order. Some key questions to consider are shown in Figure 2-4.

Figure 2-4. Key Questions Research Helps You Answer

1. What is your market?
2. Who is your audience?
3. How loyal are they?
4. What do consumers think of your product category?
5. What do consumers think of your product?
6. Why do they buy it?
7. What would make them buy more of it?
8. If your product is new, what would make them try it?
9. How much are people willing to pay for your product?
10. Who is your competition?
11. Who buys your competitor's products?
12. Why do they buy them?
13. How do people think your product compares to the competition?
14. How does your product actually compare to the competition?

Using Research the Right Way

A sports magazine decided to introduce an exercise video based on secondary research. A listing of the top-selling videos included several exercise videos, none of which were being sold through DR TV. This popular product category was under-marketed, and the magazine saw an opportunity.

Would consumers perceive the magazine as knowledgeable in the area of exercise? Focus groups showed this was not a problem. However, the focus groups raised an interesting issue.

Who would women rather see on the video—swimsuit models, or professional female athletes? At the beginning of the discussion, about half the women wanted to see models, while the other half opted for the athletes. As the discussion went on, the pendulum swung toward the athletes. Some of the comments were: "Those models are born with perfect bodies." "I'd never have a shape like that no matter what I do." "Athletes have to work out to stay competitive." "I believe athletes know more about exercise than models."

For a while, the marketer leaned in the direction of using athletes. But eventually the marketer decided on the models, discounting some of what the focus groups said for these two reasons:

1. In a focus group, people are forced to think about a product in much greater depth than they ever do when they actually buy that same product. Thus, in a group, they tend to be more logical and less emotional, just the opposite of their behavior in the real world.
2. In a focus group, people tend to say the "politically correct" thing. Some women may not want to admit (or may not even be aware of the fact) that they would prefer to watch beautiful models instead of normal-looking athletes.

The magazine had considered doing a mall intercept. A formal one-on-one questionnaire would have given a statistically significant answer to the question of what percentage of women wanted to watch models and what percentage wanted to watch athletes. However, the consensus was that the models would be acceptable if it were made clear to the viewer that a professional trainer created the routines and that the models were following the routines. Also, time was of the essence. So the marketer moved ahead. They did the required amount of research to point them in the right direction. They interpreted the findings intelligently. And when all concerned felt comfortable, they moved forward. At a critical juncture, common sense pointed the way.

The types of research that work best at different stages of your project are shown in Table 2-1. Two types of testing are also shown in the table. As we noted earlier, we will examine testing more thoroughly in Chapter 13.

TABLE 2-1. COMPARISON OF RESEARCH AND TESTING METHODS BY PROJECT STAGE

	Research				Testing	
Project Stage	**Focus Group**	**Telephone Survey**	**Mall Intercept**	**In-Home Interview**	**Viewer Interest**	**On-Air**
Product Benefits	Y	Y	Y	Y	N	N
Product Concepts	Y	Y	Y	Y	N	N
Selling Strategies	Y	Y	Y	Y	N	N
Creative Concepts	Y	N	Y	P	N	N
Storyboards	Y	N	Y	P	N	N
Animatics	Y	N	Y	P	Y	Y
Commercials	Y	N	Y	P	Y	Y

Y = YES N = NO P = POSSIBLY

CHECKLIST: Research

	Secondary		Focus Group		Telephone Survey		Mall Intercept		In-Home Interview	
	Yes	No	Yes	No	Yes	No	Yes	No	Yes	No
Market research?	☐	☐	☐	☐	☐	☐	☐	☐	☐	☐
Product benefits?	NA		☐	☐	☐	☐	☐	☐	☐	☐
Product concepts?	NA		☐	☐	☐	☐	☐	☐	☐	☐
Selling strategies?	NA		☐	☐	☐	☐	☐	☐	☐	☐
Creative concepts?	NA		☐	☐	NA		☐	☐	☐	☐
Storyboards?	NA		☐	☐	NA		☐	☐	☐	☐
Animatics?	NA		☐	☐	NA		☐	☐	☐	☐
Commercials?	NA		☐	☐	NA		☐	☐	☐	☐

3 Is Your Product Right for Direct Response Television?

Whether your product or service is still being developed, is about to be launched, or has been advertised and distributed in other ways, there is one question you must answer: "Is it right for direct response (DR) television?"

Important Factors

A number of factors help determine whether or not a product is right for DR-TV. The breadth of market appeal, how it "shows," its availability, its life cycle, and, of course, its economics, are a few of the factors discussed next.

Mass-Market Appeal

Television is the least-expensive medium if your product has the potential to sell to a great number of people. If your product appeals to people who own cars, or who are concerned about their weight, TV is ideal. But if your product is for dentists older than 50, or farmers who grow potatoes and onions in muck, stick to direct mail or trade magazines, where you can more economically target your relatively small audience.

Easy To Explain and Demonstrate

You don't have much time to tell your story on TV. And after you're finished, there's no going back to amplify or clarify. What your product is, what it does, and why that is meaningful to the viewer must be crystal clear.

Does your product lend itself to a demonstration? Can you show it getting rid of wrinkles, shining a table, or growing a plant? From the earliest days of TV, the "demo" has been one of the most effective ways to sell. (In Chapter 5 we go into more detail about selling.) Being able to demonstrate your product on air is not essential to success, but it's a plus. Showing the results of using your product may be even stronger. And showing how your product achieves *better* results than a competitor's product may be most effective of all.

Not Available in Stores

Your product should be different than, or better than, anything available in stores. Otherwise, your viewers may already own it. Or your advertising will just convince them to buy it at a store. Also, to qualify for DR TV rates, your product should not be available in stores.

Not Already Available on Television

Does the world need another kitchen gadget or weight loss program? Apparently so, because new ones are constantly sold on DR TV. If you are in a category with heavy TV exposure, make sure you do not have a "me-too" product. Your product must be positioned as something different and better than the competition. And you must keep in mind that your potential customers may already own one or more of the products in the category. Finally, how easy would it be for someone to market an inexpensive knockoff of your product?

Short Term vs. Long Term

Consider your product's inherent life cycle. A magazine may theoretically exist forever, while the "hula hoop" was a fad. There's nothing wrong with selling a short-term product, or even a fad, if your media planner is nimble. You'll want to heavy up on spending as long as the product is doing well and quickly pull the plug when it fatigues. This may be the end, or you may be able to revive it after "resting" it for a season.

Additional Sales

If your product lends itself to repeat sales, your DR TV effort may be just the first step (and the most expensive) in a long-term relationship. Going back to the example of a magazine, after a viewer subscribes, he or she may never allow the subscription to lapse. If it does, an economical direct mail package may be all that is required for reinstatement. When you sell a subscription, the lifetime value of the customer can be huge. (We'll look into other DR offer structures in Chapter 4.)

You should think about selling additional products to your database of satisfied customers. Many direct marketers do this as a matter of course. Nevertheless, you shouldn't count on additional sales to justify a marginal product. Your initial DR effort should be profitable.

New vs. Established

If your product is new, and if the consumer perceives it as unique, you'll have traveled a long way toward success. If your product is established, you must be selling it in another medium, such as direct mail. It may seem that it should do equally well on TV, but that isn't necessarily the case. Some products do better on TV, some do worse. You won't really know until you try it.

Manufacturing/Shipping Commitment

Here are two nightmares from opposite ends of the spectrum:

1. Your cookbook did not sell. You have 10,000 copies of it occupying every square inch of your garage, basement, and attic.
2. You can't fulfill the incredible order volume for your self-sharpening knife because the only factory that makes it just burned down.

Some products are inherently good at keeping your commitment to a minimum. For instance, after the original video is produced, videos can be duplicated quickly and economically in relatively small quantities. So can audio cassettes. Compact disks (CDs) can be pressed after the calls come in. If you receive 9,269 orders, you make 9,269 CDs.

To circumvent the problem of having to commit to a product (or a premium) without knowing if it will succeed, some direct marketers resort to what is called a dry test. They advertise the product without ever having it in stock. To show it in the commercial they create a mockup or a dummy. When orders are received, they return checks and do not charge credit cards, or they offer alternate products of equal or greater value. Customers never seem to object to this. However, whether or not people complain, a dry test is illegal.

Here are some other product commitment issues to keep in mind:

- Does your product have a short shelf life? Is it perishable?
- Is your product fragile? Will it require elaborate packaging?
- Is your product too heavy, bulky, or unwieldy to ship economically?
- Are you relying on just one vendor or do you have alternate suppliers?
- Can you purchase test quantities at affordable prices?
- How quickly can you acquire rollout quantities?
- Does your offshore supplier require payment in full before shipping?
- Have you allowed enough time for shipping from overseas to the United States?
- Is your merchandise subject to U.S. Customs tariffs, duties, restrictions, etc.?

Determining Sufficient Margins

To the cost of your goods, you must add the following: telemarketing, fulfillment, credit card expense, bad debt, and media. The total is your break-even point. Can you mark your cost up enough to make a fair profit without overpricing it for TV? A rule of thumb is that for a product to be commercially viable, you should be able to mark it up from 300 to 500 percent (not counting media) when you sell it on the air.

Example 1

Let's take a look at Example 1, an exercise video marked up 300 percent with a media cost per order (CPO) of $15. (We will discuss media and the all-important concept of cost per order in more detail in Chapter 12.)

Starting with Column 1, we've estimated the cost of the video at $2.50, which is the per-unit price for duplicating VHS tapes in quantities of 500. Note that the cost does not include the one-time cost of producing the video, i.e., the product development costs. Nor does it include the cost of creating

Figure 3-1. Product Profit Worksheet at 300 Percent Markup, $15 Media Cost per Order

Exercise Video Profit—Example 1

1

	Video	$2.50
+	Packaging	.25
+	Telemarketing	2.25
+	Fulfillment	1.80
+	Returns & chargebacks	.20
=	Product cost	$7.00 →

2

	Product cost	$7.00
X	300% markup	
=	Selling price	21.00
+	Shipping & handling	2.83
=	Total sale price	23.83
X	2.9%	
=	Credit card expense	.69

3

	Product cost	$7.00
+	Credit card expense	$.69 ←
+	Media CPO (estimate)	15.00
=	Break-even (estimate)	$22.69

4

	Total sale price	$23.83
–	Break-even (estimate)	22.69
=	Gross profit (estimate)	$1.14

and producing the advertising and the packaging. If the product is successful, these costs are amortized. If the product is a failure, they become a write-off.

We added 25¢ for packaging. Telemarketing, the inbound 800 number service, adds $2.25. Fulfillment, which is packing and mailing the video is an additional $1.80. Our final cost in this column is 20¢ for returns and chargebacks. Adding all these items gives us our product cost of $7.00.

Next, we must factor in the credit card processing expense. To do this, we move to Column 2. We transfer our $7.00 product cost to Column 2 and multiply it by 300 percent. This gives us a selling price of $21.00. Next, we add $2.83 shipping and handling. This gives us our total sale price of $23.83, which is the amount callers will charge to their credit cards. MasterCard and VISA charge a fee of 2.9 percent. So we multiply the total sale price by 2.9 percent to arrive at our credit card processing expense of 69¢. (More on shipping and handling and credit card costs in Chapter 11.)

Now we move to Column 3. In Column 3, we plug in the $7 product cost and the 69¢ credit card expense. But to arrive at our break-even, we still have to add media expense. All our other outlays are fixed costs, while media is a variable cost. Thus it is the one great unknown and the riskiest element in all direct response calculations. While we can get a firm estimate on all other costs *before* the fact, we can only calculate actual media costs *after* the fact. For our example, we've arbitrarily estimated a rather low media CPO of $15. Adding our product cost, credit card expense, and estimated media cost gives us our estimated break-even of $22.69.

For our final calculations, we move down to Column 4. In Column 4, we simply subtract our estimated break-even of $22.69 from our total sale price of $23.83 to arrive at our estimated gross profit of $1.14. The reward hardly seems worth the risk.

Example 2

Assuming we can't reduce costs, to increase our margin we must increase our markup. So let's repeat the calculation in Example 2 (Figure 3-2), this time with a 500 percent markup.

A 500 percent markup gives us a $35 selling price. We've also added $1 to our shipping and handling. Now we have a much better profit margin of $15.70.

Example 3

But will people *pay* $35, when the average video costs $19.95 or even $14.95? And as we raise our price, we must also assume that fewer people will order. This will raise our CPO. In fact, under any circumstances the CPO may be higher than $15. Suppose it went up by $5? Let's look at these

Figure 3-2. Product Profit Worksheet at 500 Percent Markup, $15 Media Cost per Order

Exercise Video Profit—Example 2

1

	Video	$2.50
+	Packaging	.25
+	Telemarketing	2.25
+	Fulfillment	1.80
+	Returns & chargebacks	.20
=	Product cost	$7.00 →

2

	Product cost	$7.00
X	500% markup	
=	Selling price	35.00
+	Shipping & handling	3.83
=	Total sale price	38.83
X	2.9%	
=	Credit card expense	1.13

3

	Product cost	$7.00
+	Credit card expense	$1.13 ←
+	Media CPO (estimate)	15.00
=	Break-even (estimate)	$23.13

4

	Total sale price	$38.83
−	Break-even (estimate)	23.13
=	Gross profit (estimate)	$15.70

numbers—a 500 percent markup and a $20 cost per order—in Example 3 (Figure 3-3).

We still have a reasonable profit. But unless we come up with a way to justify our $35 price, such as a premium; or sell through another offer structure, such as a club or a continuity program, the video may not be a viable product.

Figure 3-3. Product Profit Worksheet at 500 Percent Markup, $20 Media Cost per Order

Exercise Video Profit—Example 3

1

	Video	$2.50
+	Packaging	.25
+	Telemarketing	2.25
+	Fulfillment	1.80
+	Returns & chargebacks	.20
=	Product cost	$7.00 →

2

	Product cost	$7.00
X	500% markup	
=	Selling price	35.00
+	Shipping & handling	3.83
=	Total sale price	38.83
X	2.9%	
=	Credit card expense	1.13

3

	Product cost	$7.00
+	Credit card expense	$1.13 ←
+	Media CPO (estimate)	20.00
=	Break-even (estimate)	$28.13

4

	Total sale price	$38.83
–	Break-even (estimate)	28.13
=	Gross profit (estimate)	$10.70

Example 4

Let's consider a more expensive product, an exercise machine, in Example 4 (Figure 3-4). Notice that the only cost that remained the same from Examples 1, 2 and 3 is telemarketing. All the others have gone up, including media. We're assuming that the more expensive the product, the fewer the people who will order it. Still, the exercise machine looks quite viable for DR TV. With a 300 percent markup, our media costs could increase, and

Figure 3-4. Product Profit Worksheet at 300 Percent Markup, $34 Media Cost per Order

Exercise Machine Profit—Example 4

1

	Machine	$24.00
+	Packaging	1.35
+	Telemarketing	2.25
+	Fulfillment	7.80
+	Returns & chargebacks	.60
=	Product cost	$36.00 →

2

	Product cost	$36.00
X	300% markup	
=	Selling price	108.00
+	Shipping & handling	4.56
=	Total sale price	112.56
X	2.9%	
=	Credit card expense	3.26

3

	Product cost	$36.00
+	Credit card expense	$3.26 ←
+	Media CPO (estimate)	34.00
=	Break-even (estimate)	$76.26

4

	Total sale price	$112.56
–	Break-even (estimate)	76.26
=	Gross profit (estimate)	$36.30

we'd still make a tidy profit. Alternately, we could lower our price and still make a profit.

Example 5

In Example 5, we'll go to a 500 percent markup and estimate that our media CPO will double. We'd be making big money. Obviously, our cushion in

Figure 3-5. Product Profit Worksheet at 500 Percent Markup, $68 Media Cost per Order

Exercise Machine Profit—Example 5

1

	Machine	$24.00
+	Packaging	1.35
+	Telemarketing	2.25
+	Fulfillment	7.80
+	Returns & chargebacks	.60
=	Product cost	$36.00 →

2

	Product cost	$36.00
X	500% markup	
=	Selling price	180.00
+	Shipping & handling	4.56
=	Total sale price	184.56
X	2.9%	
=	Credit card expense	5.35

3

	Product cost	$36.00
+	Credit card expense	$5.35 ←
+	Media CPO (estimate)	68.00
=	Break-even (estimate)	$109.35

4

	Total sale price	$184.56
–	Break-even (estimate)	109.35
=	Gross profit (estimate)	$75.21

these calculations derives from the fact that we are dealing with larger numbers than we were with the video. Does this mean that we should always try to sell more expensive products? Not necessarily. Our video example would have been quite different a few years back when videos were still a novelty and retailed for $49.95 or more. Also, viewers may be reluctant to order an expensive product after only seeing it on TV. Is a $180 item too much for a one-step sale? If so, follow-up literature, outbound telemarketing, or both may be required. These will increase the product cost and must be included in the profit calculations. The thing to bear in mind is that each product must be judged on its own, considering if what people are willing to pay for it will allow for a 300 to 500 percent markup.

Running Your Numbers

We've included a blank Product Profit Worksheet (Figure 3-6). You might want to copy it and try several "what ifs" based on varying costs, markups, and estimated media CPOs. Or you could run the numbers with a software program.

You want to make your worksheet estimates as comprehensive and accurate as possible. For instance, you'd want to include the expense of a premium, instructional literature, and/or a bounce-back offer flyer. Your media expert will help you fill in realistic CPO estimates, based on experience in related product categories.

Keep in mind that estimates are just that. No one can guarantee you a media CPO that will ensure profitability. If it were that predictable, everyone who sold on DR TV would get rich. That is obviously not the case. In this business, as in all others, risk cannot be eliminated.

However, we believe it can be greatly reduced by following the suggestions in this book.

New Audiences

Some products can reach more than one audience over time. This can breathe new life into an old product. Try to decide if your product can be positioned to reach an entirely new audience. Of course, if you have an ongoing relationship with your customers, you do not want to lose them in the process.

A book publisher introduced a series on the Vietnam War. The target audience was veterans and the product concept was: "These books help you remember—and show others—what it was like to be a young American soldier in Vietnam." After the veteran market was saturated, the publisher broadened the target audience to include adults who had lived through the war but had not served in the military. The product concept shifted to: "No matter what side you were on, there was much you never knew about the Vietnam War. These books give you insights and information you never had before." A few years later a third audience developed. This was people who were too young to have lived through the war but who discovered it through their parents, older siblings, or the music of the era. To this target audience, the product concept was: "These books take you back to the '60s and show you what it was like to have been an American during the Vietnam War."

Changing Your Product

Through research and/or testing, you may discover that your product is a real winner or an outright loser. In either case, your course of action will be clear. But suppose it's in a gray area between success and failure? Consider making product adjustments.

Figure 3-6. Blank Product Profit Worksheet

Product Profit Worksheet

1

	Machine	———
+	Packaging	———
+	Telemarketing	———
+	Fulfillment	———
+	Returns & chargebacks	———
=	Product cost	——— →

2

	Product cost	———
X	500% markup	
=	Selling price	———
+	Shipping & handling	———
=	Total sale price	———
X	2.9%	
=	Credit card expense	———

3

	Product cost	———
+	Credit card expense	——— ←
+	Media CPO (estimate)	———
=	Break-even (estimate)	———

4

	Total sale price	———
–	Break-even (estimate)	———
=	Gross profit (estimate)	———

One young entrepreneur had to make such adjustments. He had written a "How To Start Your Own Business Book." The book was quite good, but only 32 pages long. It would have been difficult to charge much more than $9.95 for it, which wouldn't have allowed for a 300 to 500 percent markup after media costs. The product was restructured to include a video with the book. The video added $2.50 to the cost of goods but increased the perceived value of the offer and justified a price of $24.95.

CHECKLIST: Is My Product Right for DR TV?

	Yes	No
Mass-market appeal?	☐	☐
Easy to explain & demonstrate?	☐	☐
Not available in stores?	☐	☐
Not available on TV?	☐	☐
Long-term potential?	☐	☐
Additional sales potential?	☐	☐
New product?	☐	☐
Low manufacturing/shipping commitment?	☐	☐
300%—500% margins?	☐	☐
New audience?	☐	☐
Changed product?	☐	☐
Product Profit Worksheet completed?	☐	☐

Your Offer Structure

A direct response (DR) offer can be structured in various ways. You'll want to choose the one that experience has shown works best for products like yours. In this chapter we will look at six traditional ways to sell through DR: one step, two step, subscription, catalog, club, and continuity program. There is also a relatively new approach, sequential marketing, which was mentioned in Chapter 1; it works in specialized situations.

One Step

This is the easiest to understand and the simplest for both your customer and you. Your commercial gives the viewer all the information he or she needs, and you ask for the order. The viewer calls to order the product, and that's the end of it. The sale is made in one step. Most DR products are sold this way. Examples include: car care products, kitchen gadgets, portable exercise equipment, sunglasses, and household tools.

Two Step

Here, you're not asking the viewer to order, but to get more information, which is usually free. The literature you send is a selling tool, and sometimes a salesperson will also contact the responder.

Obviously, a two step takes longer and costs more than a one step. So why would you consider a two step? Because for many products, particularly expensive ones, consumers are reluctant to order from a television commercial. They want to read about the product first. Or it may be against the law to sell the product directly.

Examples of products successfully sold as two steps include recliners, adjustable beds, insurance policies, and investments, as well as high-priced exercise equipment. A good example is a NordicTrack machine, which costs hundreds of dollars. The NordicTrack commercials do not attempt to sell products. They only offer free information. If you respond by calling their 800 number, you are sent a video, a brochure, and an order form.

Sequential Marketing

Some experts would say that sequential marketing is similar to a two step, except that it may involve three or more steps. Others would say that it is a subset of integrated marketing, because it combines various media to make a sale. We think both descriptions are accurate and helpful. Sequential marketing can be costly but may be required when there are these obstacles to the sale:

- The product is expensive and, thus, a considered purchase.
- The product is technologically complicated.
- The product is unknown or misunderstood by the potential consumer.
- The product is perceived to be inferior by the potential consumer.

Under these circumstances, no one ad, commercial, or brochure may be enough to change consumer perceptions. What may be required is a complete sequence or program of learning. Just as in a school curriculum, where the entire course is not taught in a single day, the information is communicated in easily digestible bits and pieces.

A DR commercial (as well as on-page advertisements or direct mail packages) may be the first step in the process. Like the two-step commercial, the sequence commercial promises free information. But where the two-step fulfillment piece attempts to close the sale, the sequence fulfillment piece does not. Whether it is a brochure, video, poster, interactive computer disk, or anything else, it is merely the first in series of communications.

Only when the learning is completed and the consumer is educated, does the marketer try to close the sale. At that point, DR may pass the baton to personal selling.

> An auto manufacturer used this approach to explain its new technology and change consumer perceptions. Knowing that it couldn't accomplish all that in a single commercial or even in a single brochure, it used the commercial to generate response. A series of brochures followed, each focusing on a single improvement in the car. The final step in the sequence was an invitation to take a test drive at a local dealer.

Subscription

When you think of a subscription, you probably think of newspapers and magazines. These, more than any other products, are sold as subscriptions. However, many other products can successfully be sold on a subscription basis, including nontraditional direct response products. Coffee, pantyhose and diapers have been sold as subscriptions. Subscriptions work as follows:

- The customer agrees to buy a certain amount of the product.
- The customer pays up-front.
- The product arrives periodically, i.e., weekly, monthly, or quarterly.
- The customer can cancel at any time and receives a rebate for the amount of product not yet shipped.

Catalog

The catalog is a form of direct marketing that has been around since the 1800s. Until recently, the closest that TV could come was to offer a printed or video catalog as part of a two step.

The growing number of TV shopping channels come closer to being electronic catalogs. However, the viewer cannot browse through the catalog. Interactive technology will change that. The viewer will be able to choose among catalogs, select items in a catalog, and even have specific questions answered. Perhaps minicommercials will be created for each item. And with access to the viewer's database information, catalog shopping could become extremely efficient. When Fran Future inquires about a blouse to match her print skirt, she'll not only be directed to the right place, she may also be reminded that the blue skirt she ordered 2 months ago would look good with one of the new season's jackets. If she's not interested in a jacket, she'll be asked why. If she has a jacket, she may be offered accessories for it. And so on. TV catalog shopping promises to be great fun.

Club

According to the dictionary, a club is an association of people who share a common interest or goal. Membership in this kind of club can be advertised on TV, for instance the Automobile Association of America (AAA), or American Association of Retired Persons (AARP). However, in DR terminology, a club is something entirely different.

- The customer agrees to buy a certain amount of the product.
- The customer receives the first selections of the product at a deep discount. For example, the classic "11 albums for 1¢."
- The customer must commit to buy the remaining selections at "regular club prices."
- The customer is contractually bound and may not "cancel at any time."

The delicate balancing act in a club is making the up-front offer so seemingly irresistible that the commitment is not a problem for the consumer. Offering a large selection of products is essential. Records, books, and movies have been sold through clubs for years.

Continuity Program

A continuity program combines some of the features of a subscription, one from a club, and adds a few of its own.

- The product arrives periodically.
- The customer can cancel at any time.
- The first selection is usually discounted (but not as heavily as in a club).
- If the consumer must request the product before it is sent, the continuity program is called positive option.
- If the products are shipped automatically, until the customer cancels, the continuity program is called negative option.

From the point of view of the marketer, negative option is best. From the point of view of the customer, any continuity program offers one advantage over a club—no commitment to buying additional product and the opportunity to cancel at any time. Due to human inertia, many people stay in a continuity program longer than they intend to. Products sold in a continuity program include tableware, videos, collectibles, gourmet coffee, and toys.

> A typical negative option continuity program was for the CBS Videos "Vietnam War History," a collection of 14 videos. The commercial offered the first video, "The Tet Offensive," for only $4.95, a bargain price. Then it explained the standard continuity deal: "Other videos will follow, about one a month. Keep only the ones you want, cancel anytime. There's no club to join, no minimum purchase, no obligation."

The product continues to arrive until the consumer says: "Stop." Even if the consumer rejects a particular product, the sequence will continue. This often happens. A consumer may accept product #1, #2, and #3, send back #4, keep #5 and #6, send back #7, and so on.

Continuity marketers know from experience that a small minority of customers will cancel after the first shipment, a larger minority will order the entire collection, and the majority will quit the program somewhere in the middle. To keep people in as long as possible, a premium is sometimes offered after the midway point. For instance, an extra video, or a case to display collectibles.

CHECKLIST: Offer Structure

	Yes	No
One step?	☐	☐
Two step?	☐	☐
Sequential marketing?	☐	☐
Subscription?	☐	☐
Catalog?	☐	☐
Club?	☐	☐
Continuity program?	☐	☐
Positive option?	☐	☐
Negative option?	☐	☐

How to Sell on Television

We can only devote a chapter to a subject that has been the subject of many books. Whether you are a large or small advertiser, it is imperative to take the time to develop a strategy that will sell your product.

The first step in selling on television is to generate a selling strategy. (Some ad agencies use the terms "creative strategy" or "communication strategy.") The offer structure is not the selling strategy. The offer structure is the framework upon which the selling strategy is overlaid. The offer tells the viewer *what* is for sale and *how* to buy it, the strategy tells them *why* they should buy it.

If your product is truly unique, or offers the viewer a legitimately great benefit, the offer and the strategy can be the same. If you have the cure for baldness, your commercial almost writes itself. All you have to do is say, "Baldness cured!" and show proof of your claim. Then just tell men how to order. They'll pay any price you ask. You don't have to have a strategy that tells them they'll look younger, be more successful, or get more dates. They know that. All you have to say is, "Baldness cured!" If your product fits into this category, your life will be easy, at least until the competition catches up.

The Strategy Statement

Because the strategy is so important and because everyone must understand it and agree to it, it's essential to get it down on paper. Most agency strategy documents are similar to the one shown in Figure 5-1. We show it filled out for Fur in a Can.

Properly completing a strategy statement is difficult. If the form is going to be helpful, it can't be dashed off. The answers demand hard thinking. They may require research. We will go through the form, line by line, to give you an idea of how to make it effective.

Figure 5-1. Selling Strategy Statement for Fur in a Can

WHO IS OUR AUDIENCE?
People who like the look and feel of fur.

WHAT DO THEY THINK AND DO NOW?
They won't buy real fur because of moral concerns. They rarely buy fake fur because it doesn't look and feel like the real thing.

WHAT DO WE WANT THEM TO THINK AND DO?
Use Fur in a Can because it's the only way to create a furry coating on anything.

WHAT PRODUCT PROMISE WILL MAKE THEM DO SO?
Fur in a Can is the easy way to create a coating of thick, luxurious fur on any surface. It can even be used to grow fur on pets. It's safe, long-lasting and 100 percent acceptable to environmental and animal-rights experts.

WHAT IS THE PROOF OF OUR PRODUCT PROMISE?
Testimonials supported by clinical tests. These can be used as before-and-after product demonstrations.

HOW IS IT BETTER THAN THE COMPETITION?
No direct competition. The indirect competition is apparel made from animal fur and synthetic fur.

WHAT IS THE BRAND IMAGE?
Attractive, interesting, entertaining, and socially aware.

DO WE HAVE ANY SPECIAL WINDOWS OF OPPORTUNITY?
While we have a patent on Fur in a Can, we must assume that other companies are developing alternate formulas. We must quickly get on TV with preemptive advertising while we continue to develop and market other types of fur.

DO WE HAVE BUDGET/LEGAL/MANDATORY RESTRAINTS?
New company with small ad budget. New product concept will appeal at first to trendsetters and innovators. So the creative must sparkle.

Who Is Our Audience?

The answer should be as specific as possible, both demographically and psychographically. Demographics include: age, sex, income level, education level, ethnic background, marital status, and profession. Psychographics include: beliefs, values, and lifestyle.

It's important to know who your audience is, so you can target your message to it. It's obvious that a product named Fur in a Can would appeal to people who like the look and feel of fur. But we'd like to know more about them. Are they mostly women, the traditional target audience for fur? Are they younger, a group that tends to be more aware of ecology and the environment? These and other questions can easily be answered with research.

What Do They Think and Do Now?

What product do they buy now? Why do they buy it? Do they know your product exists? How do they compare it to the competition?

In the case of Fur in a Can, we have two important pieces of information about our potential audience. We know why they won't buy real fur and why they won't buy fake fur.

What Do We Want Them to Think and Do?

The answer is not: "Like our product and buy it." That's too simplistic. This question is really the continuation of the one above and should be a way to solve the problem raised above. There *must* be a problem, or even more than one. Otherwise, everyone would already be using your product, and you wouldn't have to advertise.

Fur in a Can solves both customer problems. However, it is a new product, so it has a problem of its own: No one has ever heard of it. So we must be sure to introduce it with excitement and explain it with clarity. Ambiguity or confusion can be fatal when we are attempting to convince people that our product is the answer to their problem.

What Product Promise Will Make Them Do So?

The answer to this question is fundamental to the success of the project. What does your product offer that will motivate the consumer to buy it? To help us find out, we'll take another look at the Fur in a Can product concept we developed in Chapter 2, and then we'll break it down into the actual product promise, how it works, and applications (Figure 5-2).

Figure 5-2. Product Concept and Product Promise for Fur in a Can

Product Concept

Fur "seeds" that grow thick, luxurious, and long-lasting fur on any surface. The seeds come in a can. Just pour them wherever you want fur to grow. It's easy to turn an old coat into a fur coat. Use it anywhere in the home, on rugs, curtains, drapes, chairs, pillows, and more. Fur in a Can can also grow fur on car seats, motorcycles, boats, outdoor decks, and patios. It can even safely grow fur on the family pet. It's accepted by animal-rights advocates.

Product Promise

Fur "seeds" that grow thick, luxurious and long-lasting fur on any surface. It's accepted by animal-rights advocates.

How it Works

The seeds come in a can. Just pour them wherever you want fur to grow.

Applications

It's easy to turn an old coat into a fur coat. Use it anywhere in the home, on rugs, curtains, drapes, chairs, pillows, and more. Fur in a Can can also grow fur on car seats, motorcycles, boats, outdoor decks and patios. It can even safely grow fur on the family pet.

Will It Sell?

As you can see, our product promise comes out of our product concept, while how it works and its applications will be subordinate points in our commercial. This is as it should be. The product is the hero. Now that we have our product promise, we should be certain that if we communicate it to consumers, they will buy our product. If we're less than comfortable, we may want to do some research or explore other product promises.

The Benefit beyond the Benefit

We should always express product attributes as consumer benefits. We might try to go even deeper and tap into the benefit beyond the benefit. Let's do it for Fur in a Can. When we first think about it, the benefit seems to be that we can have beautiful fur anywhere. But when we think further, we realize that Fur in a Can appeals to various human aspirations. It shows others that we are creative, because we apply it ourselves. It says we are cultured, because fur is a prestige possession. At the same time, it tells the world that we are socially responsible, because the product is synthetic.

We can add to the list of benefits beyond the benefit for Fur in a Can. We should do so for any product and try to communicate the most powerful ones in our commercial. Examples of benefits beyond the benefit are shown in Table 5-1.

TABLE 5-1. EXAMPLES OF BENEFITS BEYOND THE BENEFIT

Product Attribute	Consumer Benefit	Beyond the Benefit
Soap with two deodorants	No body odor	Social comfort Sex appeal
Book series on home woodworking	Save money by doing it yourself	Creativity Masculinity Pride of possession
News magazine	Read about U.S. and world developments	Be intelligent Be knowledgeable Curiosity
Movie club	Save money over store prices	Pride of possession Pride of collection Appreciation of art
Exercise bike	Get in shape	Health Strength Appearance Sex appeal Self-confidence
Fur in a Can	Beautiful fur anywhere	Creativity Pride of possession Cultured Trendsetter Socially aware

Unique Selling Proposition

Can we distill all of this thinking into one memorable phrase that is a unique selling proposition (USP)? The USP was developed in the 1950s by Rosser Reeves for Ted Bates & Company and explained in the book *Reality in Advertising*.

"Unique" means something your competition can't say, something exclusive to your product. If it is not exclusive, by saying it first, you preempt your competition from saying it. "Selling proposition" is not some esoteric point of difference, but a real advantage that will compel people to buy your product.

Classic Ted Bates USPs include: "Wonder Bread helps build strong bodies 12 ways," "Rolaids absorbs 47 times its weight in excess stomach acid," and "Certs is two mints in one." Notice that the USPs are catchy, short, and memorable, and include the product name. While the USP concept was developed to sell packaged goods, its logic can be applied to selling through direct response.

Positioning

Some product and service categories do not lend themselves to a USP. For instance, where the government has disallowed superiority claims or decreed parity. This includes insurance, banking, brokerage, attorneys, physicians, and so on. It would also be difficult to develop a USP for an association, a charity, a commodity product, or a political/social advocacy. If your product or service falls into one of these categories, positioning may help you succeed.

Positioning was conceived by Al Ries and Jack Trout and explained in their book of the same name. Ries and Trout maintain that consumers have a certain amount of "room" in their minds for information on any product category. It's as if each category were a pie chart with each brand representing a slice. But in a "positioning pie," there can only be three or four big "slices." Otherwise things get muddy, and the customer becomes confused.

The products with the clearest, easiest-to-remember positions are the ones that do the best. For instance, Coke and Pepsi dominate the cola positions. It would be extremely difficult for a third soft drink to occupy a position as a cola. So Seven-Up was positioned as "The Un-Cola."

But notice that "The Un-Cola" does not explain what Seven-Up is. It also does not give you a reason to buy it. A good positioning statement should be more than a slogan. Just as much as a packaged goods USP, it should give a consumer a solid reason to choose one product or service over another.

Positioning the Product

U.S. News & World Report has a solid positioning that comes out of its editorial policy. Instead of reporting on arts and entertainment, as do *TIME* and *Newsweek*, *U.S. News* gives practical advice on taxes, health, education, and so on. Its advertising positions it as the magazine with "news you can use." *Sports Illustrated* dominates the "sports magazine" position. If *Inside Sports* or *Sport Magazine* wanted to seriously challenge this franchise, it might help them to stake out a clearly differentiated position.

Positioning the Consumer

For years, Pepsi has been positioned as the soft drink for young people. Dr. Pepper has been positioned for people who don't follow the crowd, i.e., they don't drink colas. The National Rifle Association positions itself as the defender of Americans who support the Second Amendment to the Constitution.

A Test of Positioning

Your *product* positioning statement should allow consumers to purchase a product *without* having to say the brand name. If you went into a hardware store to buy the tools that "help you do it right," you'd choose Stanley. If you had a package that "absolutely, positively has to be there overnight," you'd use Federal Express.

Your *consumer* positioning statement should allow you to complete this sentence: "This product or service is the ideal one for you if you're a person who meets these criteria: … …"

Proving the Product Promise

Assuming you have a good promise, you must be able to substantiate it. Otherwise people won't believe you. And many people are leery of advertising claims to begin with. Do you have research, testimonials, or laboratory data that prove your point?

For Fur in a Can, we will demonstrate the product in action and show the beautiful results. We will also include testimonials from satisfied users as well as professional endorsements.

How Is It Better Than the Competition?

If you have a "me-too" product, you can't expect people to be interested in it. Especially if your competition is entrenched. Even if you have an advantage, you must make sure customers know about it. They may think their current brand offers them the same thing.

Most products aren't better than the competition, only different. If this is true of yours, make sure you say so on your strategy document. Don't use words like: "best," "first," and "only."

But you can still do a lot to differentiate yourself from the competition. One technique is the parity claim. A parity claim may sound something like this: "Nothing is better than XYZ brand." Does this seem to say that XYZ brand is the best? Then why not say, "XYZ brand is the best"? Because it's not. XYZ brand is at parity with the other brands. So the more accurate statement (but not a way to sell it) would be: "No brand in this category is better than any other, including XYZ brand."

Fur in a Can is a new and unique product. So we should capitalize on this and build a product franchise, before the inevitable competition appears.

What Is the Brand Image?

All products should have an image, and many general image products are sold on the basis of their image. If your brand is supported by general image advertising, you want all your direct response (DR) efforts to be consistent. Never do anything in direct that negatively affects the brand image.

This includes maintaining a certain level of commercial production values. If viewers see a shoddy commercial, they may think the product is inferior.

"Image" is an interesting word. Its synonyms aren't "truth" or "reality." They're such things as: "illusion," "semblance," and "symbol." In other words, product attributes that don't exist in reality, but only in our imaginations. Still, to the believers, they *are* true.

They accept the notion that very stylish people wear a certain brand of jeans. They believe that intelligent people drive a particular kind of car. They agree that beautiful women use a certain type of lipstick. Brand image taps into the deepest human emotions. It is extremely powerful.

Brand image promises that if someone wants to be perceived as stylish, intelligent, or beautiful, the brand in question will help. Communicating such a message is a subtle, delicate job. It could never be expressed as a USP. It would be an overstatement to say: "Women in perfect shape wear our jeans," especially when the jeans are made in sizes up to 18. It's just as effective to hint to consumers. Let them draw their own conclusions. Why do people believe that inanimate objects have personalities? Because they *want* to believe. They want products to help them communicate *their image of themselves* to the world.

A way to identify your brand image is to anthropomorphize your product. Imagine it's a human being. If so, what would it be like? How old would it be? Would it be a man or a woman? What would it do for a living? What would it do for fun? Who would it be friends with? And so on.

This is always a fascinating exercise. It can turn out that you are describing exactly whom you sell to—your target audience. But it can reveal that your brand image is not what you want it to be.

A good way to learn how to anthropomorphize your brand is to practice on famous ones. Start with a classic, like Marlboro cigarettes:

> I'm a man, but I could be a woman who shares my values and beliefs. I'm a cowboy, but I could work at just about anything. The important thing is, I believe in good, honest, hard work, self-reliance and simple pleasures. I'm a part of America we don't see much any more, and that's a shame. But I'll keep fighting for my beliefs. I'm the Marlboro man.

Now try a newer one, Nike footwear:

> I could be a man or a woman, young or old. That doesn't matter. What does is that I never sit on the sidelines of life. I believe in

> action, getting on with it, getting into it. I push beyond my own limits every day. And the right equipment helps me get there. Then, no excuses! Put on your shoes, go out and "Just do it."

Here's what we could do for Fur in a Can:

> I'm a woman, but I could be a man with a sense of taste and style. I appreciate beauty wherever I see it. I consider myself an artist. I like to create a lovely environment for my family and me. I think that creating should be interesting and that art can be fun. On a larger scale, I believe all of us must help to preserve and protect the environment we call Earth, as well as the animals with whom we share the planet.

Windows of Opportunity and Other Considerations

Are there seasons, special events, or other things that may affect our timing? With Fur in a Can, we want to get it to market as soon as possible. If your product is positioned as a Christmas gift, it should be on air a few weeks before Thanksgiving. Your selling season is short and ends abruptly on December 26. If your product appeals to self-improvement, whether physical, psychological, or educational, you want to be on air starting January 1. This is when people are determined to keep their New Year's resolutions. They also have money to spend because their holiday shopping bills have not arrived yet. And don't forget the DR rule of thumb: the first and third quarters of the year seem to work the best.

Budgetary/Legal/Mandatory Restraints?

If they are of the legal kind, we want to find out sooner than later. For Fur in a Can, we must be sensitive to the budget and, at the same time, create advertising that breaks through the clutter.

Signing Off on the Strategy

In most agencies, the account management team writes the strategy. In a few, the creative team does it. We think the best strategies are joint efforts.

But no matter who writes it, account, creative, and the client must sign off on it before going any further. The strategy is the blueprint for everything else that follows so it's essential that everyone involved agree on it.

Changing Strategies

If your strategy is working, don't change it, unless you can come up with a better one. The Fur in a Can strategy is generic to the product category. It defines the category and is appropriate for now, while Fur in a Can "owns" the category. If a competitor emerges, a generic strategy will help sell the newcomer. We might have to develop a more competitive strategy, one that shows why Fur in a Can is the best "canned fur" product.

Even without competition, down the road, we may want to expand the category. We would probably only have to modify the strategy to do so. We could show new uses for the existing product or introduce new Fur in a Can variations. Arm & Hammer Baking Soda did this by showing new places to use the product. The Buns of Steel exercise video did it as well, by introducing Buns of Steel 2, Buns of Steel 3, and Abs of Steel.

Turning a Strategy Upside Down

For years, a popular magazine offered a videocassette as a subscription premium. The selling strategy was, "Here are all the features of this magazine. And when you subscribe, you'll get this free video." The video came in at the halfway mark in the commercial and less than 13 percent of the total running time of the spot was devoted to the video.

This was not a very good strategy. It belonged to the nonfocused "tell everything about the product" school of thought. In-depth research showed that consumers already knew the features of the magazine. But they had no idea that they got a free video with their subscription. On-air testing indicated that commercials that best communicated the free video generated the most offers and the lowest cost per order. Clearly, a new strategy was needed, one that turned the old one upside down.

The new selling message was, "Here's a great new video. You get it free when you subscribe to this magazine." Now, the commercial opened with the video and got to the magazine at about the halfway point. Almost half of the running time was spent on the video. This strategy sold more magazines at more profit than ever before. It also changed the way the client advertised on TV. While premiums and creative executions have changed, the strategy of making the premium the star has stayed the same.

The Hardest Thing in Advertising

Coming up with a good, solid selling strategy is the most difficult thing in this business. But it's also the most important thing. If you have a great creative execution based on the wrong strategy, you'll surely fail. In fact, this will *hasten* your brand's failure because it will more effectively call attention to it. But if you have just a mediocre creative execution based on a great strategy, you'll be successful. And with great creative based on a great strategy, your product or service will enjoy phenomenal success.

CHECKLIST: Selling on TV

	Yes	No
Do we know our audience?	☐	☐
Do we know what they think and do now?	☐	☐
Do we know what we want them to think and do?	☐	☐
Do we have a product promise that will make them do so?	☐	☐
Do we have proof of our product promise?	☐	☐
Is it better than the competiton?	☐	☐
Do we have a USP?	☐	☐
If no USP, can we use positioning?	☐	☐
Product positioning statement?	☐	☐
Consumer positioning statement?	☐	☐
If no USP, should we use a parity claim?	☐	☐
Do we know our brand image?	☐	☐
Do we have any special windows of opportunity?	☐	☐
Should we be on the first and third quarters of the year?	☐	☐
Do we have budget/legal/mandatory restraints?	☐	☐

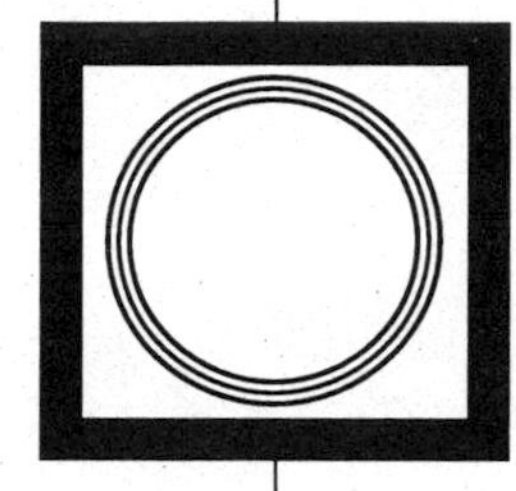

SECTION TWO

Creating Your Commercial

6 Who Should Help You Do It?

If you don't already have someone doing direct response (DR) television for you, you can proceed in various ways. In this chapter, we'll look at them all, including: free-lancers, general image ad agencies, full-service DR agencies, limited-service DR agencies, production companies, and TV stations. We'll also get to know the functions and titles of the personnel likely to work on your project. Finally, we'll discuss legal issues and compensation options.

Free-lancers

Success in using free-lancers depends on the caliber of the individuals. Sometimes even the largest general image and DR advertising agencies will bring in free-lancers for certain projects. But they usually know the professionals they're dealing with, and have worked with them before. If you know good free-lancers, fine. If not, rely on the recommendations of people whose judgment you trust.

General Image Agency

If you already have a general image agency, it might seem logical for them to handle your DR TV, especially if they do a lot of TV. What's more, they're probably most eager to help you in this area. You know them. You trust them. What can go wrong?

Everything! Many general image experts are duffers at direct. Even large, experienced ones may have no idea of the complexity of DR creative, production, and media, and how different they are from general image advertising. The easy solution is to make sure they *have* done it before. Ask to see their DR reel and case histories.

Do not accept a special DR free-lance team that has been brought into a general image agency, unless all you require is creative. But if that's all you need, why would you go to the general image agency in the first place?

Full-Service Direct Response Agency

This route makes a lot of sense. A full-service direct response agency can make your life easy. They have the resources and the experience to handle every aspect of your project. If you don't know which one to choose, you can do a number of things. Look at trade publications and the *Standard Directory of Advertising Agencies* (see Appendix A, "Recommended Reading"). You can also contact the American Association of Advertising Agencies, the Direct Marketing Association, or the National Infomercial Marketing Association (see Appendix B, "Associations and Organizations"). Do some homework and you'll find out which agencies did work you've seen and admired. Invite them to present their credentials to you. Most will welcome the opportunity.

Even if you decide to go ahead with a full-service DR agency, there are a few things to be aware of:

1. Is the agency really familiar with TV, or is its background in direct mail and print? Many old-line direct agencies (and their employees) are not experienced in TV. A direct agency that doesn't understand TV can be just as much a problem for you as a general agency that doesn't understand DR.
2. What does the agency reel look like? Is the work current? Was it successful? What did the productions cost? Are they in the range of what you'll be spending? Who at the agency did the commercials on the reel? Are they still there? Will they work on your business?
3. Is the size of the agency compatible with the size of your business? If the agency is a giant and your business is small or a start-up, will you get the attention you need? If your business is large, can a small shop handle it?
4. Can you afford to pay for a full-service agency if you don't need all its services all the time?

Limited-Service Direct Response Agency

Limited-service agencies specialize in one area, such as creative or media. Using them may make sense for smaller advertisers who cannot afford full-service agencies. It also may make sense to larger advertisers but not as an alternative to full-service agencies. Larger advertisers often use limited-service agencies in conjunction with their full-service "agency of record."

For large and small advertisers, using limited-service DR agencies represents extra legwork in finding them and negotiating separate arrangements. Extra paperwork and telephone time are involved in dealing with multiple suppliers. Finally, there's the problem of constantly coordinating between them, so that the right hand knows what the left hand is doing.

Still, for some advertisers, this is the way to go. Being able to choose services on an ad hoc basis can be efficient and economical. It can also result in acquiring top specialists in each area. Finally, for many large advertisers, the diligent use of outsiders (including free-lancers) keeps their agencies of record (or their in-house staffs) on their toes.

Production Company

Whether you employ free-lancers or an advertising agency, they will subcontract a production company. So you may wonder, why not go directly to a production company yourself and eliminate the middleman?

This could be a cost-effective way to proceed, if you already know what you're doing and know exactly what you want. But you can't expect production companies to provide you with research, marketing, or media. Their expertise is in making movies. However, to expand their services, some production companies have been offering creative, with either on-staff or free-lance writers and art directors.

Again, it's a good idea to make sure that everyone involved has DR experience.

Television Station

Many larger cities have fully equipped TV studios. Because the primary business of these studios is producing shows, they often have a great deal of downtime. So you may be able to rent their studios, equipment and technicians for very reasonable rates. And if you can work during odd hours—when the studio would typically be closed—you may really catch a bargain. However, TV stations are only set up for video, not film. You'll find out whether this matters to you in Chapter 15. And remember that the production company caveats apply here as well.

Ad Agency Personnel

When all is said and done, most direct marketers turn to a full-service DR advertising agency to be their marketing partner. A typical roster of personnel who will be involved in your DR TV project is presented here.

Account Executive

Handles all the business ends of the project, including development of the marketing plan and liaison between you and all other personnel.

Research Director

Recommends and oversees research and testing projects and analyzes the results.

Media Planner

Plans the media buy, analyzes the results, and adjusts the buy to achieve maximum efficiencies.

Media Buyer

Negotiates with the various TV stations and cable networks for the best rates. In smaller agencies, the buyer may also be the planner.

Copywriter

Together with the account executive and the art director, does the selling strategy. Together with the art director, generates creative concepts and the storyboard. Works with the art director and the TV producer on all phases of production.

Art Director

Together with the account executive and the copywriter, does the selling strategy. Together with the writer, generates creative concepts and the storyboard. Most likely draws the storyboard frames. Works with the writer and the TV producer on all phases of production.

Creative Director

May be a copywriter or an art director by trade and may still work at it. Supervises the copywriter and art director and often, the producer.

TV Producer

Responsible for transforming the *idea* of a commercial on paper into the *reality* of a commercial on film or tape. Commissions a production company and oversees all aspects of production. Responsible for the production budget.

Legalities

If you enter into a relationship with a full-service agency, you'll probably want to have a contract drawn up. If your organization does not have a standard contract, the agency will probably have one. The contract should be reviewed by your attorney and should include:

1. Term of the contract;
2. Agency responsibilities;

3. Client responsibilities;
4. Ownership of the finished work;
5. Confidentiality and nondisclosure;
6. Indemnification of the agency;
7. Indemnification of the client;
8. Remuneration for the agency; and
9. Method and timing of termination.

A typical agency-client contract is in Appendix C. It runs several pages because it takes great pains to protect both parties. Section 8.11 of the contract illustrates alternative compensation options. You may want to use this pro forma contract as the basis for your contract, filling in the blanks and changing the specifics to fit your requirements, and of course, checking it with your attorneys.

Confidentiality and Ownership Agreement

If you are working with free-lancers or a limited-service agency, or if your project is short term, you may not require a full contract. However, you should always require that these outside people sign a confidentiality and ownership agreement. An example of such an agreement is shown in Figure 6-1.

Agency Compensation

You'll find quite a range in what various agencies and free-lancers will charge you for the same job. You'll also find various ways to structure the payment. The time to learn the options is at the beginning, before you decide who is going to be your marketing partner.

Traditional Commission

For generations, advertising agencies made their money by placing media for their advertisers. Whether print or broadcast, they received a 15 percent rebate on the cost. If the media budget was large enough, the marketing,

Figure 6-1. Confidentiality and Ownership Agreement

In consideration of the Corporation retaining the undersigned to perform Advertising Works, the undersigned agrees to the following:

1. The Advertising Works will be the property of the Corporation.

2. Any research, data, reports, documents, databases, mailing lists, and other learning and information shall likewise be the property of the Corporation.

3. The Corporation agrees to allow the undersigned to exhibit the Advertising Works in the pursuit of new business and to enter and exhibit them in advertising awards competitions.

4. Confidential Information that may be disclosed by the Corporation to the undersigned in the course of the Agreement shall remain the property of the Corporation.

5. Confidential Information shall be held and maintained in utmost confidence and trust. The undersigned agrees that it, its employees, and agents shall not, directly or indirectly, use, disclose, or exploit the Confidential Information of the Corporation. The undersigned agrees to allow access to Confidential Information on a "need to know" basis only.

6. The undersigned shall take all measures necessary, and as may be reasonably required, to carry out its obligations under Paragraph 5.

____

(DATE)

____

(SIGNATURE)

____

(NAME & TITLE)

____

(ORGANIZATION)

research, and creative services were free. Actual production costs were always billed to the client, and marked up 17.65 percent. We'll get into this at the end of this chapter.

New Commission and Fee Structures

In recent years, many advertisers have demanded that ad agencies share the rebate with them, resulting in a commission of 12 percent, 10 percent, or even less for the agency. If the client uses a media buying service, the agency that does the marketing and creative will be compensated with a fee.

The financial arrangement you work out with your marketing partner(s) will depend on whom you employ. Does your agency have a media department? Smaller DR agencies may not have the staff to handle your media buy. The same is true if you employ limited-service agencies and/or free-lancers.

Will you use a media buying service? If so, they should receive less than a full-service agency if you're going to have to pay someone else for marketing and creative work.

If your creative agency will not be getting the media rebate, their fee can be either a certain amount you mutually agree on, or an hourly rate. We have done both and, interestingly enough, they usually come out to about the same.

Tiered Compensation

Sometimes direct marketers will ask for speculative creative work. Agencies should resist this like the plague. It's one thing to pitch a $10,000,000 media account. Most agencies would turn cartwheels for that opportunity. But it's simply bad business to burn up too many hours pursuing an inherently smaller DR TV budget.

On the other hand, many direct marketers are reluctant to pay for creative work they may not be able to use. This is a particular concern if the business relationship is new or if the marketer is just starting out in DR TV.

A good way out of the impasse is tiered compensation. With this win-win arrangement, the agency is paid in three stages.

Tier One

The first tier is for coming up with 3 to 5 ideas, usually in the form of concept boards. (We discuss concept boards in Chapter 7.) If the marketer doesn't like any of them, the outlay has been relatively small, and the agency has at least been compensated for its work.

Tier Two

If the marketer wants to continue, the agency is paid for developing one or two of the concepts into full 2-minute storyboards, including all testing variations. One-minute boards are usually done after the 2-minute ones have final approval. (We discuss storyboards in Chapter 8.)

Tier Three

The third tier is the actual production of the commercial. Marketers who are new to the game sometimes wonder why agencies charge so much for involvement at this stage. Aren't they just picking up the phone and letting a production company do the work? No, they're not! Whether you're working with an agency or with free-lancers, professionals will want to be—demand to be—involved at every step of the way. There is a tremendous amount of work to do *after* the storyboard is approved, perhaps half the hours that go into the total job. What's more, these hours are concentrated into a few long days, not spread over weeks or months as in the earlier stages of the project.

Traditional Production Compensation

Whether an agency was compensated with a percentage of the media buy, a flat creative fee, or an hourly rate, when it came to production, traditional agency compensation was 17.65 percent of the production cost.

This works out well for general image commercials, which usually cost 3 to 10 times more than DR ones. So to compensate a DR agency fairly, a different arrangement may be called for. Just as with the earlier creative work, it could be a flat fee or an hourly rate.

TABLE 6-1. AGENCY COMPENSATION OPTIONS

	Traditional	Flat Fee	Hourly Rate
Tier 1 Concept Boards	15% rebate on media	As agreed to	As agreed to
Tier 2 Storyboards	15% rebate on media	As agreed to	As agreed to
Tier 3 Production	17.65% of production	As agreed to or 17.65%	As agreed to or 17.65%

Flexible Compensation

It's a creative business. Many people are open to new ways of being paid. Free-lancers and even some large agencies may be willing to forego some or all of their fee in exchange for a piece of the back end. Of course, fixed costs still have to be covered. But if your product or service looks like a winner, you may be able to entice people to work for less in exchange for a share of the profits.

Another interesting option to consider is working out a production-media deal with a TV station. This can be ideal if you want to get your product on air in the least-expensive way possible. Just remember that a TV station will probably know very little about DR. And again, this need not be a problem if your other partners—free-lancers or staff—are experienced.

Getting Your Money's Worth

When you sit down to negotiate fees and rates, please keep two thoughts in mind. The first is that even if you're presented with an "official" rate card or fee structure, everything is negotiable. It can't hurt to ask the people sitting across from you to "sharpen their pencils."

Having said that, we hasten to add this thought: There's a world of difference between getting a rock-bottom price and getting a bargain. The ideal is to pay the lowest price commensurate with quality. That's true value. Say someone wants a dollar to do a job. If you talk them down to 75¢, you'll still get a dollar's worth of work, and you'll have gained 25¢ in value. But if you keep pressing and force the person to do the job for half a dollar, you'll get 50¢ worth of work, not a penny more. You'll have saved money but lost value. Your commercial will absolutely be affected by the attitudes of the people working on it. You'll give your product its best shot when you give the other party a fair profit.

CHECKLIST: Selecting a DR TV Partner

	Free-Lancers		General Image Agency		Full-Service DR Agency		Limited-Service DR Agency		Production Company		TV Station	
	Yes	No	Yes	No	Yes	No	Yes	No	Yes	No	Yes	No
Know DR TV?	☐	☐	☐	☐	☐	☐	☐	☐	☐	☐	☐	☐
Current reel?	☐	☐	☐	☐	☐	☐	☐	☐	☐	☐	☐	☐
Good reel?	☐	☐	☐	☐	☐	☐	☐	☐	☐	☐	☐	☐
Did TV work?	☐	☐	☐	☐	☐	☐	☐	☐	☐	☐	☐	☐
Affordable TV budgets?	☐	☐	☐	☐	☐	☐	☐	☐	☐	☐	☐	☐
Are people who did TV still there?	☐	☐	☐	☐	☐	☐	☐	☐	☐	☐	☐	☐
Will they work on your spot?	☐	☐	☐	☐	☐	☐	☐	☐	☐	☐	☐	☐
Right size company?	☐	☐	☐	☐	☐	☐	☐	☐	☐	☐	☐	☐
Fair pricing?	☐	☐	☐	☐	☐	☐	☐	☐	☐	☐	☐	☐
Traditional compensation?	☐	☐	☐	☐	☐	☐	☐	☐	☐	☐	☐	☐
Flexible compensation?	☐	☐	☐	☐	☐	☐	☐	☐	☐	☐	☐	☐
Contract or confidentiality agreement?	☐	☐	☐	☐	☐	☐	☐	☐	☐	☐	☐	☐

7 Concepts

This chapter will show you how to develop the concept—or idea—that will be the foundation of your commercial. We'll see what concepts look like and how to choose the best ones. We'll also look at a number of commercial techniques and explore the difference between these techniques and concepts.

Strategy vs. Concept

If a strategy is *what* you say, a creative concept is *how* you say it. (Note that a *creative* concept is different from a *product* concept, which we discussed in Chapter 3.)

The commercials for Energizer batteries are a good example of the difference between strategy and concept. The concept was a battery-powered bunny that kept interrupting fake commercials. The strategy was that the batteries last a long time. Given the strategy, any number of concepts could have been used. For example: A little boy is lost in the woods and has been using his flashlight to try to signal for help. When the last search plane flies overhead it sees his light because there's still enough power left in his batteries. Same strategy, different creative concept.

What a Creative Concept Should Look Like

It should be a key visual or two and a short description of what happens in the commercial, usually no more than a paragraph or two. If you can't show your concept in a few frames, it's probably too complicated. A creative concept for our imaginary product, Fur in a Can, is shown in Figure 7-1.

Figure 7-1. Fur in a Can Concept Board

FUR IS BACK!

We see 1950s-type people who are excited and enthusiastic about what they've done with Fur in a Can. Then the announcer explains what it is and how it works. He reassures us that it's safe and acceptable to environmentalists and animal-rights advocates. We see more surface areas that can now be covered with fur and the free brush premium being used on them. We close on a strong call to action. The '50s feeling sets the tone because they were "Happy Days" and Fur in a Can is fun.

A creative team, consisting of a writer and an art director creates a concept. A creative team gives you someone who knows how to communicate with words and someone who knows how to communicate with visuals. A top-notch creative team gives you more: a writer who can visualize and an art director who can write. Now you have a synergistic effect: 1 + 1 = 3.

Commercial Techniques

The chances are that your concepts will fall into one or more of the following categories. They've all worked in the past. They'll all work in the future. However, techniques are *not* concepts. That is, they are not ideas, merely ways of executing ideas. A good analogy may be feature film genres. Whether you're watching comedy, drama, melodrama, fantasy, musical, sci-fi, film noir, or any other genre, a good movie is based on a big idea.

Tabletop

As the name implies, this refers to shooting that can be done on top of a table. There are no actors on screen, only the product and/or props. Even if you are shooting a different type of commercial, the product will most likely be shot on a tabletop. Composition, lighting, camera angle, and movement can be carefully controlled. The product beauty shot will be edited into the body of the commercial.

Talking Head

This is one step up in degree of difficulty. Here you have an actor, or a celebrity, who talks to the audience about the product. Also, most commercials where the client is on camera are talking heads. A talking head can be leaden if the speaker is insipid and has nothing interesting to say. But a talking head can also be intimate and personal, a powerful one-on-one that touches the viewer. When the president of the Hair Club For Men reveals that he is balding and says, "I'm also a customer," he hits a responsive chord.

Sometimes a talking head can be more visually interesting if the spokesperson has a visual aid, as if he or she were a public speaker. A creative director enjoyed success by invariably having a talking head write, underline, or check off something on a blackboard. He believed that our years spent in classrooms conditioned us to pay attention.

Slice of Life

This is the most popular technique in general image commercials, because it's so effective. A typical slice has two people, let's call them Midge and Madge, in a real-life setting, such as a kitchen. Midge is the "doubter" and Madge is the "convincer." Midge has a problem. Her boyfriend hates her hair or her kids hate her fried chicken. Madge says that her brand of shampoo or frozen fried chicken will solve the problem. But Midge isn't sure. At this point, there's usually a product demonstration to convince her—and the viewers—that the product really is the best. The final scene is Midge's boyfriend saying how great her hair is, or her kids gobbling up her fried chicken.

Keep the following thoughts in mind if you consider a "slice."

- Casting is critical. Good actors will be required to make the dialogue sound believable. It helps if they have memorable faces, voices, and mannerisms, as well.
- An announcer may be required because the protagonists can't be expected to know ordering and mandatory information, without losing credibility and becoming shills.
- The situation should not be contrived. On the other hand, it should not be mundane. Strive for interesting and relevant.
- Dialogue should be as believable as possible, not a contrived conversation that would never occur in real life.
- A dramatic opening should visualize the problem the product solves. An effective opening scene for a pediatric analgesic was a sad-faced toddler who trudged into her parents' bedroom in the middle of the night and exclaimed, "Mommy, I don't feel good."

Hidden Camera

An adaptation of the old "Candid Camera" television show, this technique features someone who doesn't know he or she is being filmed and who says positive things about the product. A hidden camera commercial can be very effective. People who don't know they're on camera are extremely believable and say things no copywriter would think of in a million years. But the logistics are tricky. Where will the camera be hidden? How will the people be found? Also, it takes a lot of shooting to get a few good people. A hidden camera commercial can take a long time and be very expensive.

Testimonial

When a real person endorses a product, it's a testimonial. That allows you to superimpose on the screen the person's name, occupation, and the city and state where he or she lives. If you use a professional actor to simulate a testimonial, you can't super any of these things.

Testimonials are as effective as the person giving them. If you use real people in your advertising, no matter how much you pay them, you *must* have them sign a release. We'll talk more about "real people" testimonials in Chapter 19.

Celebrity Presenter

More and more celebrities are selling more and more products. However, before, during and after you throw your lot in with a celebrity, many things should be considered. This is particularly true in DR. We'll discuss the pros and cons of using celebrities in advertising in Chapter 19.

Continuing Central Character

A celebrity spokesperson who appears in a number of commercials can be thought of as a continuing central character (CCC). However, the CCC is usually considered to be a non-celebrity. It can be an actor playing a character, such as Ronald McDonald, Juan Valdez, or the Jolly Green Giant. It can be an animal, such as Morris the Cat, the Dreyfus lion, or the Merrill Lynch bull. Or it can be imaginary, such as the Pillsbury Doughboy, Tony the Tiger, Charlie the Tuna, or the Peanuts cartoon characters for Metropolitan Life.

Demonstration

The demo makes the maximum use of the power of TV. It is as close as you can get to a live salesperson who proves how your product works or, in a side-by-side demo, how it is better than the competition. The best demos are clear, interesting and irrefutable.

> A classic demo was for a heat-resistant cardboard. A box was made of the material. A baby chicken was placed inside the box, which was then immersed in boiling water. When the box was removed, the chick had suffered no ill effects.

Sometimes demos must be symbolic, but these, too, can be effective. For instance, when Rolaids shows water changing color to signify neutralizing excess stomach acid.

The demo you should avoid is one that doesn't really prove anything or proves a minor product point. If your product doesn't lend itself to a compelling demonstration, perhaps you should seek a different way to promote it.

Problem-Solution

With this technique, a problem is shown as dramatically as possibly. Then the product solves the problem. The problem should be one with which the audience can identify, and the product should be the best way to solve it. It can be argued that many other commercial techniques may use a problem-solution structure. For instance, a CCC or a celebrity presenter could say, "If you've always had such-and-such a problem, I want to tell you about the way I solved it."

Comedy

Can comedy work in DR? Yes, but just as in general image advertising, it's extremely difficult to do. Not everyone can write comedy, and the worst thing in the world is a joke that doesn't work. Even if your commercial is funny, make sure you're not falling into one of these traps.

- Comedy may be inappropriate to the product category. Alka Seltzer learned this the hard way when their wonderfully funny commercials of the 60s lost them market share. People in pain don't want to laugh. They want relief.
- Don't make fun of your product. You're on much safer ground if you poke fun at what can happen if people don't use it, or if they use the competition's product.
- Don't make fun of your customers. If you absolutely must, do it in the

beginning of your spot, and let your product make him or her a hero at the end.

- People will laugh at burlesque, which is an exaggeration of reality. They won't accept unreality.
- Parody goes over most people's heads. You're compounding the error if you parody something "esoteric," such as the latest TV show or blockbuster movie. *Jurassic Park*, the most popular movie of all time, grossed about $350 million. At about $6 per ticket, we can estimate that 60 million people saw it. That is less than 25 percent of the population. Do you want to pay for advertising that 75 percent of your audience won't recognize?
- Don't let the jokes get in the way of the sale. Funny commercials can be so entertaining that people forget who the advertiser is and what they're supposed to buy.

With all these pitfalls, why take a chance with comedy? Because if it works, it can cut through commercial clutter with less airings than a bland slice of life or demo. "Alex the Dog" for Stroh's beer, "Bo Knows" for Nike, "Great Taste, Less Filling" for Miller Lite, "Absolutely, Positively Overnight" for Federal Express, and "Where's the Beef?" for Wendy's were much easier to remember than a talking head or a slice of life. Try to think of a commercial you saw last night. Chances are the one you remember was funny.

Nevertheless, if you're tempted to try it, our recommendation is to *always* test a comedy commercial against a noncomedy one. Never put all your eggs in the funny basket.

Vignettes

Vignettes are very short, usually humorous, anecdotes. They're often used to illustrate, in a lighthearted way, what can happen when people don't use the product or service in question.

The pacing of a vignette commercial should be deft. Typically, a 30-second general image spot will have two vignettes, a product demo or usage shot, and a final vignette "capper." A two-minute DR spot might open with three vignettes, include one or two interspersed in the middle of the commercial, and end with a vignette "button." If there is a concern that the final vignette complicates the ending, perhaps it can be mortised into a corner of the screen.

Music

Can music work in DR? *TIME* magazine sold a lot of magazines for many years with its evocative "Time Flies" jingle. Music can reach your pocketbook by touching your heart. Even if they don't use music to sell, 2-minute commercials can seem *verrry* long unless they have a musical "rug." But music can be expensive. We'll deal more with music in Chapter 21.

Animation

Animation is very effective if you're selling to children. It also is expensive. If you're combining live action with animation it's even more expensive. Before you get into the expense of animation, make sure your idea warrants it. This goes for computer animation as well. And particularly in computer animation, don't let technology become a substitute for a strong idea.

Stop Motion

With this technique, an inanimate object can seem to move on its own. It works like this: A frame or two are shot of an inaminate object, say a chair. Then the chair is moved slightly. Another few frames are shot. The chair is moved again. Another few frames are shot. And so on. The result is film that shows the chair seeming to move on its own.

Anything that can be moved can be animated with stop motion, including multiple objects. For instance, an empty room can magically be filled with furniture. Also, people and animals can be "moved" with stop motion. They travel without their legs moving. People and animals can also be made to instantly jump from place to place. A "jump cut" is considered a mistake in normal shooting, but in stop motion, it may be done by design to create a desired effect.

Claymation

In this type of stop motion, flexible clay puppets are moved slightly after the camera shoots a frame or two. When the film is run, the puppets appear to be moving by themselves. Pillsbury's "Poppin' Fresh" and the California Raisins are examples of claymation. This is also expensive to do. So make sure you have a big idea built around it.

Morphing

This commercial technique digitally transforms one object into another. Morphing was introduced to the public in the movie *Terminator* 2. It's been used in rock videos and a number of commercials. The effect can be quite dramatic; however, it is expensive.

Concept Execution: No Easy Answers

A slice of life is not a concept. A celebrity presenter is not a concept. Music is not a concept. None of these techniques are concepts. Creative people should *never* start an assignment by saying, "Let's do animation," or "Let's make a funny commercial." They should start by coming up with creative concepts that translate the strategy into executions.

None of these techniques, by themselves, are concepts. The concept may turn out to be an innovative way to execute one of the techniques. Or bits and pieces of two, three, or more techniques may find their way into the concept. For instance, the Energizer bunny may be thought of as a humorous demo.

Whether the execution of the concept turns out to be a slice, vignettes, claymation, or some combination is not nearly as important as how well it answers a number of questions.

Is It on Strategy?

If a concept isn't 100 percent on strategy, no matter how good it is, it must be rejected. Having said this, you should be open to a phenomenon that occurs from time to time. The concept is off strategy but such a big idea that a new strategy should be developed to accommodate it. It's the cart leading the horse, but it's happened, and it's been successful.

Is It Clear?

Sometime a concept isn't as sharp as it could be. It may be that the idea is inherently muddy and will never work. Or it just may need further development. Many concepts start out shaky. Resist the impulse to kill them. See if the creative team can develop them.

Is It Believable?

This is particularly important if you're doing comedy. You want to make sure your humor hasn't gone over the edge into silliness. But it's also important if you're doing a very straight commercial. Too many spots revolve around situations that would never occur and conversations that would never happen. These hackneyed solutions send this message to the viewer: "Here comes another phony commercial. Now is the time to get a snack—you won't miss anything."

Is It Producible?

Anything can be done on film. But everything has its price. If there's any doubt whether a concept is technically or economically feasible, check with your producer. The sooner the better.

Is It Tasteful?

There's a famous scene in *The Hucksters*, one of the classic films about the advertising business. Sidney Greenstreet, the client, asks Clark Gable, the account executive, if he knows how to get a consumer's attention. Greenstreet doesn't think much of Gable's pat answers, so he decides to show him how. Whereupon Greenstreet spits on the table. Gable is horrified, and you should be too. "Shock-the-viewer" tactics only indicate the lack of a big idea. Any product can be advertised boldly, bravely, *and* with taste.

Is It Appropriate?

You wouldn't use the same tone and manner to advertise a bank and a record club. And you wouldn't advertise a classical record club the same way as a hard rock club. Choose a style that is in harmony with your product or service.

Is It Creative?

Creativity is subjective. Ask any ten advertising people to define it and you'll probably get ten different answers. We think creativity means "unique, different, and new." Simple, no? But difficult to do. And a paradox, in that in a creative business, unique, different, and new ideas are often resisted. Yet, it's essential to stand out from the crowd.

Why should advertisers care about creativity? Creativity increases *efficiency.* That's why advertisers should not only nurture it, but insist on it. Some advertisers subscribe to the "beat the consumer over the head until they surrender" theory. Repeating the same boring advertising message will work—eventually. But it's not very efficient. The more innovative your communication, the more easily it will cut through the clutter of other advertising and attract more people at a lower cost.

One test of a concept is simply to see if it's *possible* to illustrate the idea in a few frames. Television is a visual medium. A concept built around a big visual idea will have a good chance of catching the eye of TV viewers.

The pie chart (Figure 7-2) shows the rule-of-thumb breakdown of factors that affect success in DR TV. Most people give about equal importance to: 1. product; 2. pricing/premium/offer; and 3. creativity, including, of

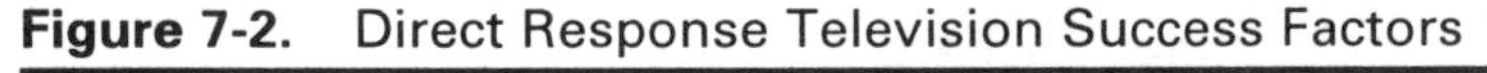

Figure 7-2. Direct Response Television Success Factors

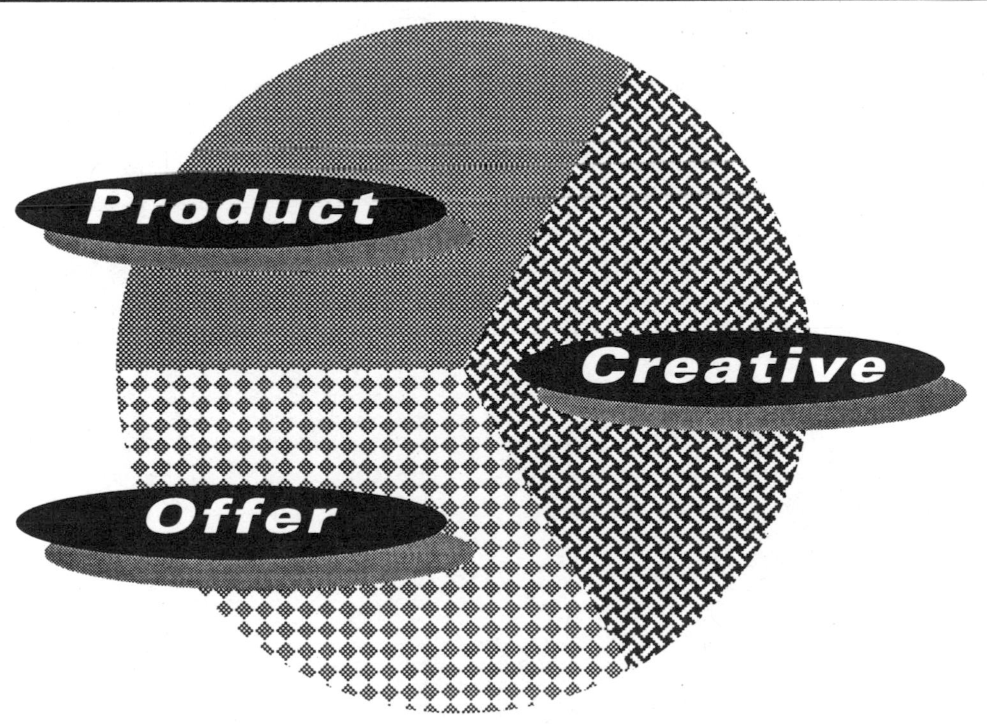

course, the strategy. Doesn't it make sound business sense to strive for maximum efficiency in an area that represents one third of your chance for success?

Good creative directors constantly exhort copywriters and art directors to hit home runs. In the real game of advertising, as in the real game of baseball, a single is often as good as it gets. Still, in an environment where creative people aren't afraid to step up to the plate and take a good healthy whack at the ball, they'll play their hearts out for you. And once in a while, they'll knock one out of the stadium.

CHECKLIST: Concepts

	Yes	No
Tabletop?	☐	☐
Talking head?	☐	☐
Slice of life?	☐	☐
Hidden camera?	☐	☐
Testimonial?	☐	☐
Celebrity presenter?	☐	☐
Continuing central character?	☐	☐
Demonstration?	☐	☐
Problem-solution?	☐	☐
Comedy?	☐	☐
Vignettes?	☐	☐
Music?	☐	☐
Animation?	☐	☐
Stop motion?	☐	☐
Claymation?	☐	☐
Morphing?	☐	☐
On strategy?	☐	☐
Clear?	☐	☐
Believable?	☐	☐
Producible?	☐	☐
Tasteful?	☐	☐
Appropriate?	☐	☐
Creative?	☐	☐

8 Storyboards

After you narrow down your concepts, flesh out the best ones as full storyboards. This chapter will show you what a storyboard looks like, why you should do them in the first place, and how to judge them.

What Is a Storyboard?

A storyboard is a frame-by-frame blueprint of the commercial, somewhat like a comic book. Each frame *shows* what is happening on screen, *explains* what is happening, and includes all dialogue, music, sound effects, etc. A storyboard should time out to no more than 2 minutes. About 5 to 10 seconds less is safer, to allow for visual time and camera moves.

Why go to the expense of creating storyboards in the first place? Aren't most full-length movies made from nothing but scripts? Actually, some directors work with storyboards, especially for complicated or special effects scenes. Alfred Hitchcock used them for every scene in every movie he made.

Commercial storyboards are a good idea for at least three reasons. First, they visualize the idea. This is important because television is a visual medium. You want to do more than create a radio commercial with pictures. Second, storyboards let you see how successfully the concept translates into a full commercial. Not all do. Many are played out after 20 seconds or so. Third, they help the production company plan the shots.

The AIDA Formula

Claude Hopkins, one of the first great copywriters, wrote a book called *Scientific Advertising*. In it, he said advertising is "salesmanship in print." Of course, today he would have added "and electronic media." With that in mind, a storyboard will also let you evaluate how well your commercial follows the four traditional steps to a sale. (Other books on advertising or selling may list five steps or have different names for them. But the idea is pretty much the same.) The four steps create the familiar acronym AIDA.

Attention—Does the commercial break through and get noticed?
Interest—Does the commercial arouse the viewer's curiosity about the product?
Desire—Does the commercial make the viewer want to own the product?
Action—Does the commercial make the viewer call to order right now?

What a Storyboard Looks Like

Many different formats are used for storyboards. Some are vertical, some horizontal. Some have four frames on a page, others have two. Some are large, others are small. It's not the format that matters, but the *idea.* The Fur in a Can storyboard, shown in Figure 8-1, has 26 frames.

Eight-Frame Storyboards

An intermediate step between a concept board and a full storyboard is the eight-frame storyboard. This is simply the beginning of a commercial, about the first 15 to 20 seconds. It may not be a bad idea to do this, to make sure everyone agrees the commercial is starting off the right way. Also, the beginning of any commercial is the all-important "hook" that attracts the viewer's attention. After all concerned are comfortable with the opening eight frames, the rest of the commercial can be boarded.

Flaws the Storyboard Will Identify

Another reason to do a storyboard is that problems with the commercial will be easy to spot. At this stage, they're also easy to fix. Here are 11 things a good storyboard should illustrate.

Figure 8-1. Fur in a Can Storyboard

FURRY ENTERPRISES - "FUR IS BACK" - :120 - 9/2/94 - PG. 1

-1-

VIDEO Open on wife #1 showing her husband her new fur coat. Husband reacts.

AUDIO Husband: You look stunning, but how can we afford it on our budget?

MUSIC [50s "Happy Homemakers" type of music throughout]

-2-

VIDEO Cut to another couple admiring their new fur living-room carpet.

AUDIO Wife #2: Frank, it's beautiful. Do you think we're the first people in the neighborhood to have a plush fur carpet?

Frank: I bet!

-3-

VIDEO Cut to a close-up of a dog with a heavy coat of fur.

AUDIO Wife #3: (Voiceover VO) Oh look, Ralph! Buster is gorgeous with his new fur coat.

Buster: [BARKS HAPPILY]

-4-

VIDEO Cut back to wife #1 with fur coat.

AUDIO Announcer: (VO) Turn that old wool overcoat into a fur coat.

FURRY ENTERPRISES - "FUR IS BACK" - :120 - 9/2/94 - PG. 2

-5-

VIDEO Cut back to couple #2 admiring their fur carpet.

AUDIO Fur carpet? Why not!

-6-

VIDEO Quick dissolve to the announcer holding Buster.

AUDIO (on camera [OC]) And Buster, a whole new breed of Chihuahua!

-7-

VIDEO Slowly move in on announcer as Buster leaves and announcer picks up the product.

AUDIO It's true and it's here.

-8-

VIDEO Cut to close-up of Fur in a Can.

AUDIO (VO) It's called Fur in a Can.

FURRY ENTERPRISES - "FUR IS BACK" - :120 - 9/2/94 - PG. 3

-9-

VIDEO Close-up of announcer.

AUDIO (OC) How? Simple. It comes

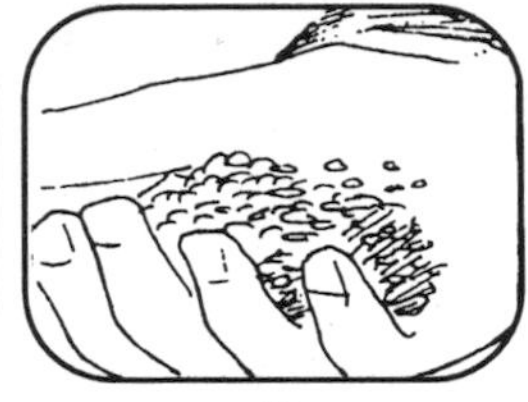

-10-

VIDEO Cut to announcer's hand holding seeds.

AUDIO (VO) in seeds.

-11-

VIDEO Back to close-up of announcer holding Fur in a Can.

AUDIO (OC) That's right. Seeds! But unlike conventional seeds, you do not, I repeat, do not plant them. All you do is sprinkle these fur seeds on any surface

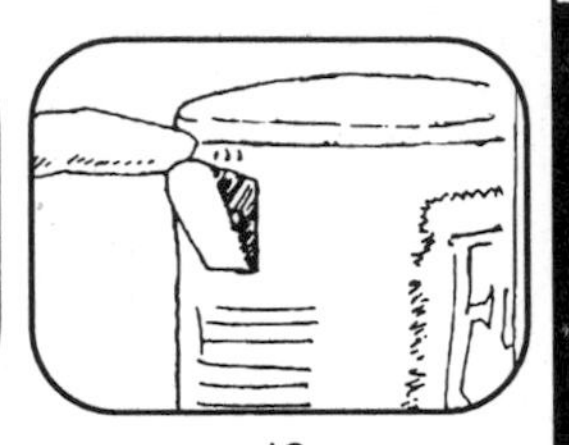

-12-

VIDEO Announcer demonstrates the pull-out spout.

AUDIO with the handy, pull-out spout.

FURRY ENTERPRISES - "FUR IS BACK" - :120 - 9/2/94 - PG. 4

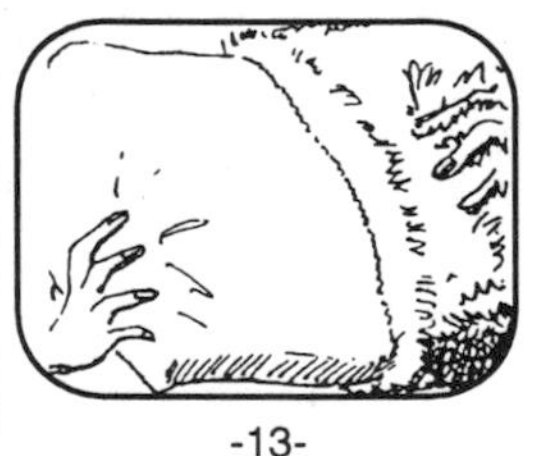

-13-

VIDEO Quick dissolve to close-up of woman's hands holding a pillow half covered with fur.

AUDIO (VO) For example, one-half of this beat-up old pillow was covered with Fur in a Can a week ago ... genuine fur.

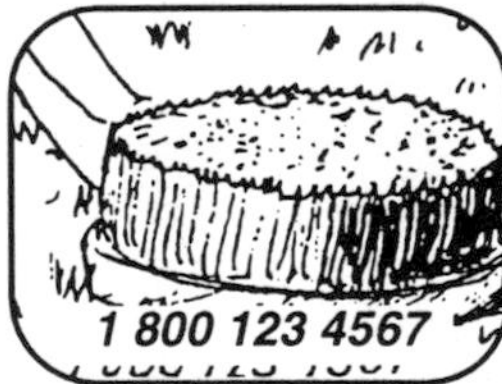

-14-

VIDEO Dissolve to beauty shot of Fur in a Can brush.

SUPERS 800 NUMBER FREE

AUDIO Call now and you'll receive this Fur in a Can brush — FREE!

-15-

VIDEO Cut to woman's hands demonstrating the brush.

AUDIO This beautifully handcrafted wood brush is designed for the easy care of your sofa ...

-16-

VIDEO Cut to curtains, already treated with Fur in a Can, being brushed.

AUDIO curtains ...

FURRY ENTERPRISES - "FUR IS BACK" - :120 - 9/2/94 - PG. 5

-17-

VIDEO Cut to car seats just brushed.

AUDIO or car seats.

-18-

VIDEO Cut to animal activist about to throw paint on person wearing Fur in a Can fur coat. Freeze frame.

AUDIO And because it's ecologically smart, you can step out in your new Fur in a Can overcoat without any worry.

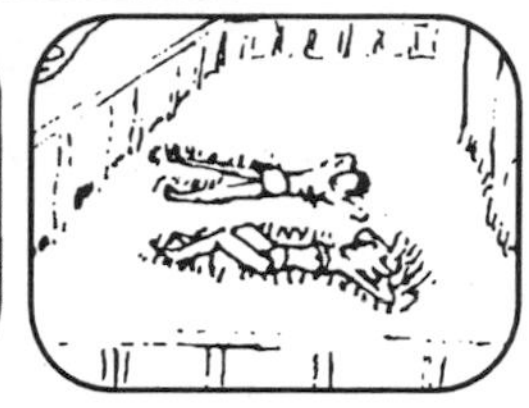

-19-

VIDEO Cut to couple spread out on their sun deck, covered with fur.

AUDIO Or get a suntan in the lap of luxury.

-20-

VIDEO Cut to a very hairy man.
SUPER WARNING

AUDIO But remember, it's called Fur in a Can, not "Hair in a Can." It's irreversible. Please do not do this to yourself.

FURRY ENTERPRISES - "FUR IS BACK" - :120 - 9/2/94 - PG. 6

-21-

VIDEO Cut back to announcer as he makes more of the offer.
SUPER 800 NUMBER [TO END]
AUDIO (OC) Call to take advantage of this introductory offer and you'll receive

MUSIC [UP TO END]

-22-

VIDEO Close-up of brush.
SUPERS FREE 800 NUMBER [TO END]
AUDIO (VO) this beautiful, wood, thick bristled Fur in a Can brush. Free only if you take advantage of this offer right now.

-23-

VIDEO Camera pans across closeup of fur.
SUPER CREDIT CARDS

AUDIO Think of it. Soft, plush, luxurious fur. Only possible through

-24-

VIDEO Close-up of Fur in a Can.
SUPERS ONLY $29.95 PLUS POSTAGE.

AUDIO Fur in a Can. Real fur on your back ... living room ... car seats ... wherever.

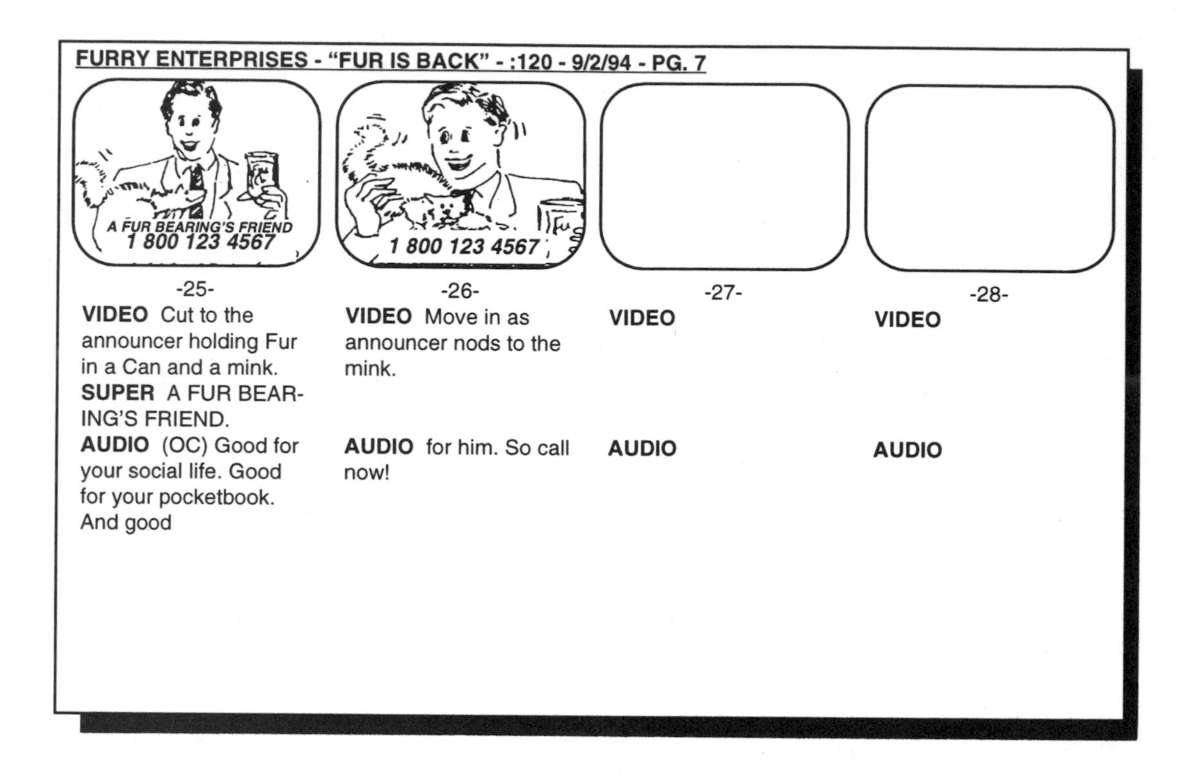

1. The commercial should open with a big idea that entices the viewer. You have just 10 to 15 seconds to keep him or her from flicking to another channel or going to the refrigerator.
2. Your spot should be built around a big visual idea. Remember, TV is a visual medium.
3. The promise should be clear and easy to understand. Sometimes advertisers get caught up in executional fluff called "vampire video." Viewers remember the commercial but don't know who the advertiser was.
4. It's a good idea to repeat the offer, even in abbreviated form, near the end of the spot.
5. It's also a good idea to have a beauty shot with the complete offer in it. It can help the sale to show the viewer everything he or she gets.
6. In a 2-minute spot, the phone number should be shown for 45 seconds. This will give the viewer a chance to find a pen and paper and write it down, or better yet, call while the commercial is still on.
7. If you're using union talent, whether on camera or voiceover, only say the 800 number within the last 15 seconds of the spot, never sooner. If

you roll out with numerous 800 numbers, you'll save a fortune on union announcer talent payments.

8. If you're using union talent, don't have an actor say the 800 number or the price while he or she is facing the camera. If you want to change anything later, you'll have trouble synchronizing the words with the lip movements. Instead, say anything subject to change as a voiceover, or "cheat" the scene with the person who is saying the price looking away from the camera.
9. Show the credit cards you accept. The credit card companies will supply you with art of their logos.
10. Make sure the commercial feels right. Does it flow? Is it interesting? Does it sell? If you were a consumer, would you pay attention to it? Believe it? Respond to it?
11. Finally, see if it still works when you cut it down to 60 seconds. It's important that it does. Two-minute commercials are becoming harder to clear, especially on cable. The 60-second storyboard is probably the last thing you will do, after the 2-minute version has final approval.

CHECKLIST: Storyboards

	Yes	No
Not radio commercial with pictures?	☐	☐
Attract attention?	☐	☐
Build interest?	☐	☐
Create desire?	☐	☐
Call to action?	☐	☐
Big opening?	☐	☐
Big visual idea?	☐	☐
Promise easy to understand?	☐	☐
Offer repeated?	☐	☐
Beauty shot?	☐	☐
800 number on for 45 seconds?	☐	☐
800 number said only during last 15 seconds?	☐	☐
800 number/price not said on camera?	☐	☐
Credit cards shown?	☐	☐
Does commercial "feel" right?	☐	☐
Can commercial work in 60 seconds?	☐	☐

Animatics and Other Test Commercials

Although you can use a storyboard to go directly to shooting a fully produced commercial, you can take another step first. You can create animatics or other test commercials. Most smaller direct marketers do not have the budget to do either. Still, this chapter teaches you techniques you may implement if your business grows. And if you are a larger marketer, this chapter should be important to you.

Animatics

Animatics are research tools. They are storyboards shot on film (or videotape). While an animatic can be animated to some extent, usually the only movement comes from the camera panning or zooming and dissolving between scenes. An animatic costs between 10 percent and 25 percent of a fully produced spot.

Why spend *any* money on a commercial you'll eventually discard? Because an animatic, not a fully produced commercial, is the ideal place to find out if you have a winner, a loser, or a problem that can be fixed.

Animatics can be particularly helpful with a new product, or one that's new to television. Animatics can test different strategies (although a winning strategy should be agreed upon before the animatic stage), but animatics are best at testing different creative concepts and different offers.

Animatics can be used in various research formats. They can be shown at focus groups, in-depth mall intercept interviews, and viewer interest groups. They can even be run on air.

But animatics can be a trap. Some ideas are inherently easy to execute as animatics, while others are not. Say your concept calls for people to dance with your product. It's difficult to show movement in an animatic. Or suppose your concept is a conversation among four college roommates. It'll be very hard to find four voices that sound different enough for the viewer to know who's talking to whom. On the other hand, some ideas seem wonderful as animatics but fail when fully produced.

Animatics are not a panacea. They are a research tool to help you make a more informed decision.

Photomatics

Photomatics are essentially the same as animatics, except that instead of drawings, photos are used. Photomatics are more realistic than animatics, but because they require a photo shoot, they cost more. Unless there's a need for the extra realism, there's not much point in spending the extra money.

Stealomatics

Stealomatics are sometimes called "ripomatics." Both names mean just what you think they do. Footage is "borrowed" from a movie or a TV show, or scenes from other commercials are edited into yours. The obvious advantage of a stealomatic is that it costs next to nothing. But there are a number of disadvantages, the biggest being the legality and ethics of what you're doing.

The legal issue is simple. You are not allowed to use someone else's intellectual property without their permission. Not even one frame of it.

The ethics are more complicated. Are you doing harm by using a few seconds out of a 2-hour movie to help get your idea across to ten people in a focus group? Or is asking the question this way avoiding the point that wrong is wrong, no matter what the situation?

You may never have to wrestle with your conscience over a stealomatic. Because of a limitation in what they can accomplish, you may not want to do one. The problem is you can never get *exactly* the scene you want. You're always compromising. And you can exacerbate the problem if you allow the creative idea to be dictated by the footage that's available.

Another problem is that your final commercial may not look as good as the stealomatic. A $60,000 DR production budget isn't going to get you the same cinematic quality as the stealomatic footage that was lifted from a $60,000,000 Hollywood production. This happened to a DR agency. It created an exquisite stealomatic that helped land a piece of business. But then the agency was put in the embarrassing position of not being able to produce an on-air commercial that looked as good and stayed within the client's budget.

We think you're much better off not appropriating someone else's work. Hire a good storyboard artist to render your animatic frames in the detail required and you won't have any trouble communicating *your* idea for test purposes.

Test Commercials

Sometimes major DR advertisers create inexpensive commercials exclusively for test purposes. The first eight frames of a test commercial for Fur in a Can are shown in Figure 9-1. (Notice that no actors are on camera and that the announcer is voiceover. This makes for a cheaper production and lower talent payments. Also, a different price could easily be tested by changing frame 6, and an alternate premium could just as simply be tested by changing frame 8.

A test commercial should be flexible and versatile enough to test anything you can foresee today and years from now. Because you'll have to bring back the same actor to record new voiceover copy, make sure the financial deal you work out doesn't let you get held up later on.

Don't look for the lowest possible cost per order from a test commercial. Its only purpose is to give you a clear reading on your strongest offers, pricing, premiums, terms and conditions, and so on. Combine the best elements and you will have the foundation of a powerful commercial.

If you're going to be doing a great deal of testing during the next 3 to 5 years, you may amortize the cost of a test commercial. But if you only have the budget to produce one commercial, that one will have to be your test vehicle. It will have to be somewhat modular, so that editing alternate test versions does not become cost prohibitive. At the same time, it will have to be good enough to sell your product profitably.

CHECKLIST: Animatics/Test Commercials

	Yes	No
Animatic?	☐	☐
Photomatic?	☐	☐
Stealomatic?	☐	☐
Test commercial?	☐	☐

Figure 9-1. Fur in a Can Test Commercial Storyboard

FURRY ENTERPRISES - "TEST SPOT" - :120 - 7/28/94 - PG. 1

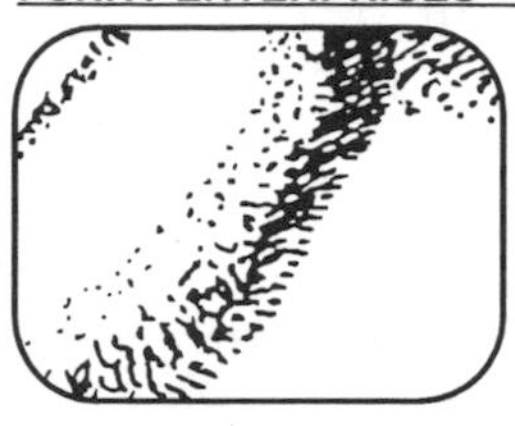

-1-

VIDEO Open on close-up of fur coat.

AUDIO Announcer: (VO) Now you can turn any coat into a fur coat.

MUSIC [50s "Happy Homemakers" type of music throughout]

-2-

VIDEO Cut to a new fur living room carpet.

AUDIO Sink your feet into a plush, furry carpet.

-3-

VIDEO Cut to a close-up of car seats covered with fur.

AUDIO Drive on luxurious, fur-coated car seats.

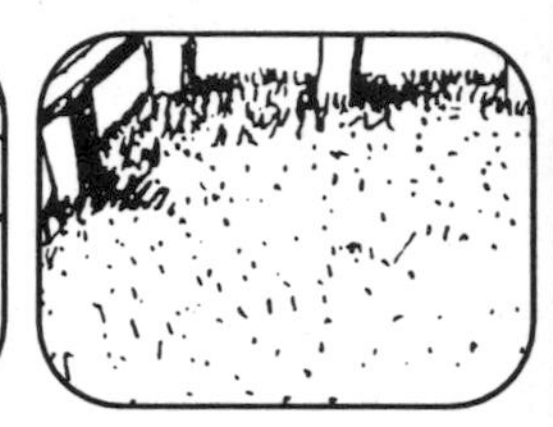

-4-

VIDEO Cut to a close-up of a sun deck covered with fur.

AUDIO Soak up the sun on a comfortable, furry deck.

FURRY ENTERPRISES - "TEST SPOT" - :120 - 7/28/94 - PG. 2

-5-

VIDEO Cut to a close-up of a dog with a heavy coat of fur.

AUDIO Even grow a coat of beautiful, thick fur on the family dog.

-6-

VIDEO Cut to a close-up of Fur in a Can.

AUDIO It's new Fur in a Can, and it's only $29.95, plus postage.

-7-

VIDEO Cut to a close-up of seeds.

AUDIO Yes! Now you can have fur anywhere you sprinkle these amazing new fur seeds.

-8-

VIDEO Dissolve to beauty shot of Fur in a Can brush.

AUDIO Call now and you'll receive this Fur in a Can brush — FREE!

Infomercials

Infomercials have been popular for a long time. The term was coined by Warner-Amex in 1977, as part of the now-defunct QUBE service. Ross Perot's homespun infomercials, along with those of celebrities such as Cher, Jill St. John, Joanna Kearns, Sally Struthers, and Vanna White have even made them trendy. Everyone seems to be jumping on the infomercial bandwagon. This chapter will help you decide if you should jump on, too.

What Are Infomercials?

Infomercials are 30-minute commercials, nothing more and nothing less. They are not a guarantee of success. You only see the ones that work. Somewhere between 85 and 90 percent of infomercials do *not* work. These are the ones you never see. Add the fact that infomercials cost 3 to 4 times as much as 2-minute commercials to produce and 5 to 10 times as much to air. Multiplying your production budget by 3 to 4 and your media budget by 5 to 10 will result in a rather large number.

Keep these numbers in mind and think of infomercials dispassionately. Forget the hype and other marketers' success stories. The only thing that matters is whether infomercials are the best communications and media vehicle for your product or service.

Having said that, we must add that an infomercial may be the *only* way to sell your wares. The less people know about your product or service, and the more complicated it is to explain, the more time it's going to take you to sell it to a viewer. Also, the more expensive your product, the more time it may take to convince people to order. We have seen products fail in 2 minutes and succeed in 30. And because you can generally sell a higher-ticket item on an infomercial, you may want to create a product specifically for this length, with little or no thought of attempting to sell it in 2 minutes.

The creation of an infomercial should reflect everything we have talked about in this book. The chapter on strategy applies. The chapter on research holds true. So do the chapters on product development, the offer structure, and so on. The chapters to come—on such topics as media, testing, telemarketing and production—will apply as well.

Can an Infomercial "Fix" a 2-Minute Spot?

If your 2-minute commercial is not doing well, can an infomercial save the day? Perhaps the extra time may help you get your message across. But don't fall into the trap of using the extra time to relate every esoteric nuance of your product. And don't assume the extra time will let you widen your appeal and be all things to all people. It's important to stay focused and single-minded.

> A 2-minute commercial was created for a new product that showed great promise. But when the commercial was tested, more people called for information than to buy. Follow-up telephone surveys confirmed the problem. It would take longer than 2 minutes to explain the product and its benefits. So the decision was made to create an infomercial.
>
> However, the 30 minutes were not used effectively. Instead of focusing on the key product benefits, the infomercial had everything in it but the kitchen sink. Telling viewers more than they needed to know about the product did not solve the original problem. It exacerbated it. The infomercial had fewer callers than the original 2-minute commercial.

Infomercials: Television Shows

Infomercials are paid programming and should be identified as such at the beginning and the end. But to those watching, infomercials are real half-hour TV shows. (Both shows and infomercials actually run closer to 28 minutes to allow for station breaks.) Many infomercials copy these television program formats.

1. The Variety Show. This features a high-energy host on a stage, an enthusiastic studio audience, and one or more guests who represent the product.
2. The Talk Show. Here the host (there may be co-hosts) is seated, as are the guests. There may or may not be a studio audience. The late-night talk shows are prototypes.
3. The Interview Show. This isn't too different from a talk show. It's usually more intimate, such as the "Barbara Walters Interviews." Other things that differentiate it from a talk show are that there isn't an audience, and it's usually not done in a studio, but on location or in a home.
4. The "Patchwork" Show. In this format, we never see the host and/or hostess in the same place and time as the guests. The host may be in an office, a home, a school, or wherever is appropriate to the product. The host introduces the guests, who are wherever they happen to be. This format is relatively economical to produce because the guest segments only have to be patched together with the host's.

Much mixing and matching can be done within these four. And there are many other models to follow. Be creative. Try new approaches. Two that struck our eye were a pseudo sitcom family for a phone company, and a comedian incorporating his "stand-up routine" into the infomercial.

You want infomercials to be entertaining, but you never want to trick people into thinking they're watching an actual program. The worst thing you can do is to clone a news show. If you attempt to deceive viewers into thinking they're watching the news, stations will reject your infomercial. They will reject any commercial that tries this.

Which Products Work for Infomercials?

Traditionally, infomercials fell into two categories: get rich and self-improvement. Today, approximately three-quarters of infomercial sales come from five product categories: exercise equipment, diet products and programs, health and beauty aids, general self-improvement, and financial success (see Table 10-1). But today, infomercials also sell nontraditional products and services. Recently, they have been used to generate leads for high-ticket products, such as automobiles. Infomercials are excellent for this type of communication because their length allows them to tell a complicated story. Nevertheless, the majority of infomercials still sell products that promise self-improvement, whether physical, psychological, or both.

Audience Flow

Viewers tend to begin watching shows when they start, that is, on the hour and the half hour. If they lose interest, they will search for alternatives. So for any show, viewership is highest at the opening and declines as the show continues. However, the dissatisfied viewers of show "A" will tune in to show "B," which is already in progress. So some of the decline in original viewership is made up with new viewers. The phenomenon of audience flow is important to infomercial direct marketers for a number of reasons.

Because viewership is strongest at the beginning of the infomercial, you want to present your complete story and ask for the order long before 30 minutes have expired. Does this violate the idea of the infomercial being 30 minutes long? Not at all. Viewers are accustomed to commercial breaks. If they call to order before the end of the infomercial, fine. This is what usually happens. After they've called, these viewers are likely to switch to another program. When infomercials try to sell more than one product, say as two 15-minute infomercials, the product on first does the best.

TABLE 10-1. PRODUCTS AND BENEFITS: INFOMERCIAL BEST-SELLERS

Product	Benefits
Men's hair weaving	Youth, appearance, opposite sex
Women's hair products	Youth, beauty, style, fashion
Cosmetics	Youth, beauty, style, fashion
Juicers	Health, vitality, fitness
Exercisers	Health, strength, appearance
Teeth whiteners	Appearance, opposite sex
Weight reduction programs	Appearance, youth, health
Small kitchen appliances	Health, nutrition, family approval
Better grades seminar	Self-confidence, success in life

Prototype Infomercial

With this basic information in hand, let's examine a prototype infomercial. We'll try to find out if there is an ideal structure and timing of an infomercial and its internal "commercials."

Opening

Infomercials begin on the hour and the half hour, when most shows begin. Viewers are likely to be scanning the channels with their remote controls, searching for something that catches their eye. It's critical that the infomercial opening hook them. The first minute or two must entice them to stay tuned. This is a formidable challenge for your creative team. They're competing against the offerings of every other channel.

First 15 Minutes

After the opening, the show should establish itself. Host and guests should be introduced. The topic should be stated. Product demonstrations and advantages should be communicated. The show should start with energy and enthusiasm, but not frenetically, so that it can't build and has nowhere to go. Pacing is a different animal when you move from 2 minutes to 30.

The first time to ask for the order is *after* you've conveyed enough information to make the sale and *before* viewers start switching to other channels. For most successful infomercials, this happens at around the 15-minute mark. Other experts believe the first commercial should appear around 10 minutes into the infomercial. In any case, the first show segment should be long enough to fully explain the product, build interest, answer any questions the viewer is likely to have, and allay any fears about non-performance.

Commercial Within the Infomercial

Compared to creating a true direct response (DR) commercial, an infomercial commercial is relatively easy. It doesn't have to be particularly creative because it doesn't have to attract viewers. The infomercial has already done that. Instead, the commercial should clearly show the complete offer, the price, and the 800 number. It should give the key benefits. It should be hard-hitting, straight-ahead, and impassive. It doesn't matter if it's a particular length; however, around 2 minutes seems to work for most products.

Second 15 Minutes

What do you do for the second half of your infomercial? Your audience consists of viewers from the first half who are still not sold, plus new viewers who have no idea what's going on. So you want to reiterate the first half, covering the basic product features and advantages, but with new demonstrations, new testimonials, and so on. Add a little twist to keep the show fresh. It may also help to add a benefit to persuade those who haven't called yet. Play devil's advocate and think of what might inhibit someone from buying your product after you've told your story for 15 minutes. Try to answer this objection in the second 15 minutes.

This is something you may want to test in a focus group. Show the group the first half of your infomercial, stop the tape and find out who is ready to buy, who isn't, and why not. Then show the second half of the infomercial and see if it persuades the undecided viewers.

Ending

The final minute or so of your infomercial is where you pull out all the stops. This is your last chance to make the sale, so go for it. Quickly convey the key product benefits, the urgency to call now, and any guarantee you offer. Remember to show the 800 number. An impassioned tone and manner may help. Remember, right now you have nothing to lose.

Structure and Timing

We've been talking about a prototypical infomercial. Of course, there is no one formula for structuring infomercials. The approximate timings, in minutes, of ten successful ones, is shown in Table 10-2. Notice how the structure and timings vary quite a bit among infomercials A through K.

Infomercials A through D stick closely to what we've been discussing. E gives up an ending for a longer second half of the program. F divides the

TABLE 10-2. STRUCTURES AND TIMINGS OF TEN INFOMERCIALS

Structure	A	B	C	D	E	F	G	H	J	K
Show	16	14	5	14	13	7	7	6	7	20
Commercial	3	2	2	3	2	2	2	4	2	8
Show	5	8	5	6	11	9	6	6	7	
Commercial	2	2	3	3	2	2	6	4	2	
Show	2	2	3	2		8	5	4	7	
Commercial							2	2	2	
Show								2	1	
Total Time (in minutes)	28	28	28	28	28	28	28	28	28	28

show into three modules and gets to the first commercial sooner. G through J also get to the first commercial rather quickly and break the infomercial into even more components. Just to show that the exception makes the rule, notice that K is all show for the first 20 minutes and then all commercial to the end. And remember, from A to K, these timings are all from successful infomercials.

Producing Infomercials

When infomercials were new, it seemed that virtually anything could be sold on them. Now, viewers are more selective and the failure-to-success ratio has gotten worse. While products must be carefully selected, the shows themselves must be better.

Their production values must be professional. They don't have to be big budget extravaganzas, but they shouldn't be tacky or shoddy. They must be interesting and entertaining. The key is to hold the viewer's attention long enough to make the sale. Some things that may help: interesting locations, upbeat music, not staying on any one shot too long, and the right host or hostess.

To keep costs down, infomercials are shot on videotape. If they take place in a studio, they'll be shot with multiple studio cameras, just like a TV show. The entire show is run through once or twice. The director, who's in the control room, edits the show in real time by switching between the cameras. By working this way, an infomercial can be completed in a day or two, compared to weeks to shoot multiple takes and edit them in postproduction. Beta SP (a high-quality version of Beta) is most often used for location shots that are edited into a studio setup and for infomercials shot entirely on location. Even on location, as much editing-in-the-camera as possible is done.

Celebrities for Credibility

Just as in other kinds of advertising, celebrities are no guarantee of success. However, if your product is unknown, a believable, relevant celebrity can give you instant recognition and credibility. You can almost picture people in front of their TV sets, saying, "If so-and-so is associated with this product, it must be a good one." As we saw at the beginning of this chapter, more and more celebrities are doing infomercials. In many cases, they share in the profits. If you have a product or service that's a natural for a particular celebrity to endorse, you might want to consider contacting his or her agent. We'll talk more about celebrities in Chapter 19.

Infomercial Production Companies

In Chapter 6, we saw that there are various ways to get the professional help you need for DR TV. When it comes to infomercials, you have another option. You can use one of the companies that specialize in creating and running infomercials. Typically, these organizations will create an infomercial for you, pay for producing it, choose the media, and even pay for that. You risk nothing. In exchange, they typically want 80 to 90 percent of the profits. Is that a good deal? Only you can decide.

A woman had a small but successful cosmetic business. She sold her products directly to beauty salons. An infomercial production company wanted to work with her, mostly because she was attractive and articulate and would have made a good spokesperson. But the woman could never come to terms. She didn't want to give away 90 percent. The company explained that she had 100 percent of a tiny pie, whereas they were offering—at no risk to her—10 percent of a potentially huge pie. In the end, she said no. The company found another woman with a small cosmetic business and made a successful infomercial.

In this case, the infomercial company was actively looking for a partner. Even if *you* seek *them* out, there's no guarantee they'll want to handle your product. If they don't believe in it, they won't invest their money. But if you'd like to work with one of them, we suggest you become an infomercial fan for a while. Watch cable channels late at night and early in the morning on Saturday and Sunday. The names of the production companies will come on at the end of the infomercials. Contact them or call the 800 number for more information. You may also get names from the National Infomercial Marketing Association (see Appendix B).

Some major DR agencies have set up infomercial production departments, divisions or subsidiaries. They may be more flexible in working out an arrangement where you keep the profits. However, you will want to see their infomercial reel, learn about their media expertise, and find out about their track record in this arena.

CHECKLIST: Infomercials

	Yes	No
Does product improve your life?	☐	☐
Are benefits demonstrated?	☐	☐
Is format entertaining?	☐	☐
Is opening a grabber?	☐	☐
Does first segment tell full story?	☐	☐
Is "commercial" effective?	☐	☐
Does second segment recap and add?	☐	☐
Does end go for broke?	☐	☐
Celebrity spokesperson?	☐	☐
Infomercial production company?	☐	☐

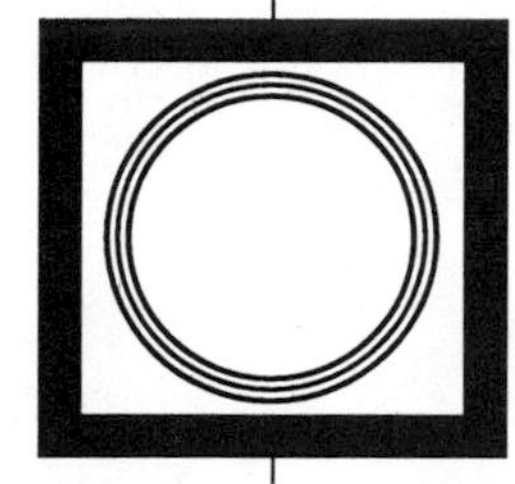

SECTION THREE

The Economics of Direct Response Television

Pricing, Payment and Premiums

Any salesperson will tell you that the trickiest part of the job is the close, where he or she must ask for the order. At some point in a direct response (DR) commercial, you also must close. What might help? A good deal? A sale? A guarantee? Something for free? In this chapter we'll consider a number of options to keep in mind.

Pricing

Price Perceptions

We all have some strange perceptions about prices. Round numbers seem higher than they are. To many people, $15.00 appears to be much more than $14.95, even when shipping and handling are added to the $14.95. Also, there are price thresholds. Anything above $20 may not be an impulse purchase. Anything above $50 may be a considered purchase.

Legal Prices

If the product is on sale, or even just at a very low price, that may become part of the strategy. Don't play games with imaginary sales. You'll have the Post Office and the Federal Trade Commission (FTC) after you. Federal Trade Commission guidelines are shown in Figure 11-1.

Figure 11-1. Federal Trade Commission Guidelines for a Sale or a "Special" Price

- The product must have a normal, everyday price.
- The sale or special price must be at least 10% less.
- The sale must last long enough to allow consumers to take advantage of it, but not so long that it becomes the normal, everyday price.
- After the sale, the price must revert to the normal, everyday figure.

Price Testing

Test prices that are higher and lower than what you think your actual price should be. If you believe a fair price is $19.95, you should also test $14.95 and $24.95. Chances are, you'll sell more units at the lower price and fewer at the higher one. Simply multiplying units sold by selling price will show you your most profitable price point. If the higher price works, test an even higher one. There's a point of diminishing returns. But you'll never find out "how high is up" if you don't price test.

Price Structure

A subtlety of pricing is how to structure your price. Say your actual price is $59.95. Should you ask for that amount? Or, "3 easy payments of $19.99 each"? Or, "4 easy payments of $14.99 each"? Smaller numbers usually work better. Testing will show you the right way to express your price.

Selling Too Soon

Being eager to sell, advertisers sometimes make the mistake of getting to the price too soon. No matter how good the price, the consumer must first want the product. Then, a good deal can close the sale.

One of the most successful 2-minute commercials spent the first 45 seconds charming the viewer into wanting the *premium.* The price wasn't mentioned until the 90-second mark.

Shipping and Handling

Consumers expect to pay extra for shipping and handling. Shipping and handling (S&H) can make you a little extra money, because you can usually charge more than your actual fulfillment costs. A rule of thumb is that viewers will not balk if S&H does not exceed 10 percent of the purchase price. The actual S&H should be a number that seems to reflect postage rates. So choose odd amounts like $3.77, $2.53, $4.37, and so on. Make sure that the S&H is shown as a super for at least 3 seconds at the same time as the price. The S&H can be much smaller than the price, as long as it's legible. It should read: "Plus $0.00 S&H."

Method of Payment

An important consideration for any direct marketer is how to get paid. The possibilities are: credit cards, check or money order, COD, and "bill me." Most direct marketers prefer accepting only credit cards. But if you have an ongoing customer relationship, say through direct mail or catalog sales, you may want to be more liberal when these people call to order. However, television customers tend to be more impulsive and less loyal than direct mail customers.

Credit Cards

The best way to get paid is with a credit card. Show three or four major credit card logos in your commercial while your announcer says, "Have your credit card ready when you call." It's a clean deal. The money is instantly yours, minus the percentage the credit card company charges. If you haven't established an account with the credit card companies, your telemarketing firm will take orders into its account. Always have a credit card ordering option.

Check or Money Order

This is not nearly as good as a credit card order. Viewers may never get around to mailing their checks or money orders. Even if they do, you have to wait for payment. You have to deal with paperwork. And you have to be prepared for a certain percentage of bounced checks.

COD

At first this seems like a good option. After all, the product is not delivered unless payment is made. But it's expensive. Some people will have moved. And, again, some checks will bounce. Most direct marketers don't accept CODs.

"Bill Me"

This can drown you in paperwork and correspondence unless you already have a large billing department. Or unless your product is something like a magazine, where you can suspend delivery after a few issues and not sustain a major loss.

Premiums

Should you include a premium? The right premium will usually give you a lower cost per order. But after you give away premiums, you'll condition your audience to expect them and you may never be able to get off the premium treadmill.

Should you have more than one premium? We've seen cases that would let us argue both sides. Be careful of appearing to give away the store. This can create confusion and cheapen your product image.

Should your offer build, that is, keep getting better and better? It's easy to do this if you have more than one premium. But again, having too many premiums may confuse the communication and cheapen your image. It will also add to your costs.

Should you offer a choice of premiums? We've never seen this work. Choice depresses response. Some people can't decide which premium they want and never get around to making up their minds.

Should your premium be related to the product? Ideally, yes. However, the perceived value of the premium is more important than its affinity with the product.

As a free premium with purchase, an advertiser tested a pen and a 35mm camera. Both premiums cost the advertiser the same, about $5. Can you guess which won? The camera, very easily. Why? Because while you can pay hundreds or even thousands of dollars for a pen, you can also pick one up for 19¢. But you can't get a 35mm camera for much less than $50. So the perceived value of a camera is higher than that of a pen. The truth is, the pen was better quality than the camera. You can't get a decent camera for $5, even in quantity, but $5 will buy you a good pen. Still, it's *perceived value* you want to remember.

Guarantee

Should you offer a money-back guarantee? The newer and more expensive your product, the more a guarantee may help it gain acceptance. A very small percentage of people bother to return a product that works, even if they're not totally satisfied with it. But consider the nature of your product. Is it mechanical or electronic and not top quality? A 5 to 10 percent return rate can destroy your profit margin. And remember, after you offer a guarantee, you *must* live up to it. A guarantee is a testable proposition. Does your offer with a guarantee (and some returns) pay out better than the offer without a guarantee?

800 and 900 Numbers

Which to Use

Most DR orders are made with an 800 number, but that costs you money. A 900 number is charged to the caller and appears on the caller's phone bill. It's the fastest, cleanest way to make a sale. But there's been a great deal of controversy with 900 numbers. Some people have them blocked out of their phone service. And stations are taking a closer look at all 900 offers. Still, there's no reason why legitimate 900 offers can't do quite well. If you go the 900 number route, you must make it perfectly clear to the viewer that there will be a charge and how much the charge will be. Also, there are limits to how much people will charge to their phone bill.

Getting a Number

The major advertisers can afford to have mnemonic numbers—ones that spell a word or phrase. Don't be concerned if you can't. Sometimes those words are hard to pick out on the phone. And if you're doing any degree of testing, you'll need many numbers. If you're really successful and roll out nationally, you might require as many as 80 to 100!

How do you obtain these numbers? Your telemarketing service assigns you as many as you need for as long as you need. It's as simple as that.

CHECKLIST: Pricing, Payment, and Premiums

	Yes	No
Round number?	☐	☐
Legal price?	☐	☐
Impulse price?	☐	☐
Considered purchase price?	☐	☐
Test prices?	☐	☐
Price structure worked out?	☐	☐
Shipping & handling decided?	☐	☐
Credit card ordering?	☐	☐
Check or money order accepted?	☐	☐
COD?	☐	☐
"Bill me"?	☐	☐
Test premium?	☐	☐
High perceived value?	☐	☐
Affinity to product?	☐	☐
Test guarantee?	☐	☐
800 number?	☐	☐

12 Media

Don't assume a general image media person or agency can handle direct response (DR) media. They're very different disciplines. This chapter will explain the differences and show you how DR television media is planned, bought, and analyzed. It will also underscore the importance of establishing a relationship with a good DR media person, buying service, or the media department of a DR ad agency.

General Image vs. Direct Response Television

General image advertising tries to influence *attitude.* Direct tries to influence *behavior.* Also, general assumes the viewer will be exposed to the advertising message a number of times and can *gradually* change his or her attitude toward the product. In direct, you can't assume any cumulative effect. Each commercial must be a totally self-contained selling message that influences the viewer's behavior *immediately.*

The goal of general TV is to build product image; air time is bought with the objective of achieving a certain reach, frequency, and number of gross rating points (GRPs) against a given audience. To accomplish this, programs or dayparts are bought based on the viewing habits of the audience. General advertisers pay a premium for guaranteed programming and dayparts.

The goal of DR TV is to generate leads or make sales; reach, frequency, and GRPs are not factors, only a high response rate at a low cost per order (CPO). We touched on the idea of cost per order in Chapter 3.

Cost per Order

Direct response media time may cost as little as 25 percent of general image time. This is because DR media is bought by dayparts and is preemptible.

Figure 12-1.

Cost per Order Calculated for Two Stations

Station	Media Cost	÷	# of Orders	=	Cost per Order
WAAA	$100		5		$20.00
WBBB	$200		12		$16.67

It's not the cost of media, per se, that you care about, but the CPO. Consider two fictitious TV stations with about the same size audience, WAAA and WBBB. WAAA charges you $100 each time it runs your spot, whereas WBBB charges you $200. So at first sight, WAAA might seem to be the better media buy. Every time your commercial runs on WAAA, you average five orders. So your CPO is $20 ($100 ÷ 5). But every time your commercial runs on WBBB, you average 12 orders. So your CPO is only $16.67 ($200 ÷ 12), and WBBB is the better station for you.

We've seen CPOs for the same product range from $5 to $100. The break-even for this product was around $20. So at a $5 CPO the marketer would have gotten rich and at $100 would have gone broke. An experienced media person might have some idea of the CPO range into which your product or service might fall. But don't expect them to predict numbers. No one can. For that, you're going to have do an on-air test, which we will discuss in the next chapter.

Buying Television Time

Dayparts

Broadcasters charge general image advertisers according to how many people are tuned in at a particular time of day. For instance, prime time is from 8 p.m. to 11 p.m. It is when most people watch TV, so it costs the most to advertise then. Other time slots include daytime, fringe, late night, etc.

The DR media planner determines which dayparts fit the product's target audience and finds out the availability of these dayparts at different stations. The buyer constantly negotiates daypart rates with TV stations.

A DR media plan might include buying certain dayparts. For instance, the audience for a sports magazine is predominantly male. So it would make sense to run the commercials when men are home from work. So the media buy might include early fringe—from 6 p.m. to 8 p.m.—and late fringe—from 11 p.m. to 1 a.m.

Run of Station

If your product has universal appeal, it doesn't matter *when* your DR spot runs, as long as a large enough *percentage* of viewers respond to make it profitable. So you may consider buying time according to what is generally referred to as run of station (ROS).

As the name implies, ROS means that the station can air your commercial any time of the day or night, according to its schedule. Compared to buying dayparts, ROS is a buckshot approach to media. However, if you have a very tight budget, keep in mind that it is the most economical, except for "free" air time, which we'll discuss next.

ROS may seem to be the bargain basement approach to media. However, an experienced media buyer, and/or a large media department will request and negotiate for your commercial to air on certain days and at certain *approximate* times of day.

Per Inquiry

With a per inquiry (PI) deal, you pay nothing for media time. The station runs your commercial at its discretion, usually where it has unsold air time. You only pay the station for orders it receives. But this no-risk option for advertisers is not as easy to obtain as it once was. Many stations found that the reward wasn't worth the risk. They weren't generating enough revenue to make up for not selling the same time slots, even at deeply discounted rates.

Today, if stations will even consider PI deals, they'll probably first want good test results as proof that your commercial works. Even so, they may only give you a partial PI arrangement. You may get a discount on the media, while they get a smaller percentage of the sales. Your media expert will advise you on how and where to attempt PI deals.

Commercial Clearance

When you run a general image commercial on a particular show or a certain time slot, you pay a premium rate because you're guaranteed your spot will run at that time. But these premium rates are too high for DR advertisers to make a profit. So DR time can be preempted.

Suppose a station that had daypart availabilities gets a last-minute media buy that uses them up. Or suppose another DR media buyer is willing to pay a bit more for time. Your spot may not run at all that day. In DR terminology, it did not "clear." You won't be charged for air time, but you won't make any money either.

Finding a 2-minute time slot is obviously more difficult than finding a 1-minute slot. That's why it is advantageous to have a :60 with a :120.

Getting your commercial to clear is difficult when the new TV season starts in September. This is because many major advertisers have been off the air for the summer. Now they are back sponsoring the new season's shows.

Clearance is usually worst during the Christmas season when many seasonal advertisers and retailers are on TV. However, during a recession many advertisers, particularly local retailers, may not have the money to advertise on TV. So you'll be more likely to clear your spots. But viewers may not be able to afford your product!

The problem of clearance underscores the need for having good DR media buyers who can strike a balance between getting a low rate and getting your commercial to air.

Spot vs. Cable

Direct response commercials run on both spot and cable. By definition, the cable viewer is a more qualified customer because it costs money to subscribe to cable.

We've seen commercials succeed in cable and fail on spot. We've *never* seen the reverse. The axiom is that if your commercial works on spot, it'll work on cable. However, there is one large caveat. It's very difficult to get a 2-minute commercial to clear on cable. You may be limited to 1 minute. If so, you may have to rely on good telemarketing to help close the sale. We get into telemarketing in Chapter 14.

But if your offer is too complicated, or legal mandatories eat up too much time, a :60 may not work at all. Some direct marketers have to make the difficult decision to run only 2-minute commercials on spot television. You won't know this until after you air your commercial. That's why a 2-minute commercial should always be constructed so that a :60 can easily be "lifted" out of it.

A :60 tends to work about half as well as a :120; it's logical that it should. Whether on spot or cable, a station might try to charge you 60 percent or 70 percent of the price of a :120 for a :60. It's up to your media buyer to try to negotiate a 50-percent rate.

Media Strategy and Analysis

The DR media expert has a number of reference tools at his or her disposal. These include the "television" edition of *Standard Rate and Data* (SRDS), the *Television, Radio and Cable Factbooks,* and the Nielsen and Arbitron Rating Services.

In addition to these tools, the media pro knows through experience which areas of the country, which cities, and which stations seem to work for different types of products. Sometimes there's no logic to it, but it works. It's this intuition—acquired over years—that elevates top media people above their colleagues.

Your media strategy will include:

1. Determining daypart availabilities;
2. Negotiating for the best daypart rates;
3. Estimating commercial clearance based on historical performance, station availabilities, and seasonality;
4. Buying dayparts at expected clearance levels; and
5. Adjusting media buying during the campaign according to results.

The initial media plan is only the beginning. One of the most important roles of your media expert is to constantly analyze the results. To do this, media needs two things. First, timely and accurate information from the telemarketing center on the number of calls each 800 number received. Second, timely and accurate reporting on which stations cleared your spots. Now the media department has the numbers to calculate CPO *per station and per daypart.* The media analyst will constantly refine the buy by heavying up spending on good stations and cutting back on less-efficient ones.

The astute media analyst may find other keys to success in the numbers. Do stations in the Midwest have lower CPOs than the rest of the country? Are you attracting people who watch TV at a certain time of day? Does an analysis of station viewer profiles tell you what type of person you're appealing to? The more information you media expert has, the more insights he or she will be able to provide you.

Qualifying for Direct Response Television Rates

Because DR air time is bought by dayparts, and because it can be preempted, it can cost as little as one quarter of the fixed spot rate charged to general image advertisers.

Paying 25 cents on the dollar not only makes DR TV economically viable, it makes it attractive to general advertisers. However, it takes more than an 800 number at the end of a general image spot to qualify for DR rates. Here are some guidelines:

- An offer must be made to the viewer. For instance, a product for sale, a free sample, or free information.
- If the offer is a product for sale, it should not be available at retail stores.
- If the offer is for free information, there should be a perceived value to it, and it should be an integral part of the commercial.
- An 800 or 900 number must be provided. (Some stations charge more for 900 number commercials.)
- A good rule of thumb is the more the offer seems like DR, the better the chances of qualifying for DR rates.

CHECKLIST: Media

	Yes	No
DR TV media buyer?	☐	☐
Media strategy?	☐	☐
Buy by dayparts?	☐	☐
Run of station?	☐	☐
Per inquiry (PI)?	☐	☐
Spot?	☐	☐
Cable?	☐	☐
Qualify for DR TV rates?	☐	☐
Offer to viewer?	☐	☐
Not available at retail?	☐	☐
Perceived value to free information?	☐	☐
800 or 900 number in spot?	☐	☐
Ongoing media analysis?	☐	☐

Testing

In Chapter 2, we saw how focus groups and mall intercepts can be used for research. In this chapter, we'll find out how they can also be used to test animatics and finished commercials. We'll also explore other testing options for animatics and finished spots, including viewer interest tests and pre-post tests. We'll find out the differences among on-air tests: market tests, matched market tests, fixed spot tests, and back tests. Finally, we'll learn when and how to roll out with a successful commercial.

Viewer Interest Tests

Viewer interest tests can be combined with focus groups. All you need is a focus group facility set up with the necessary equipment.

In viewer interest tests, a group of people watches an animatic or a commercial. Each viewer holds a little rheostat-like device. Depending on how much they like what they are seeing at the moment, they turn the dial up or down. The result is a real-time graph of viewer interest, somewhat like a barometer.

The most interesting part of this research is when the graph is overlaid on the commercial. Then you can watch a video that shows you, at any given moment in the spot, the degree of audience interest. On the minus side, this research tends to confirm what you already suspect. Interest goes up during the funny or emotional parts and down when you ask for the sale. Figures 13-1 and 13-2 show viewer interest graphs for two test commercials.

Commercial A

In Figure 13-1, the vertical axis shows how much viewers like Commercial A, starting at the neutral point. The horizontal axis shows changes over

Figure 13-1. Viewer Interest Test—Commercial A

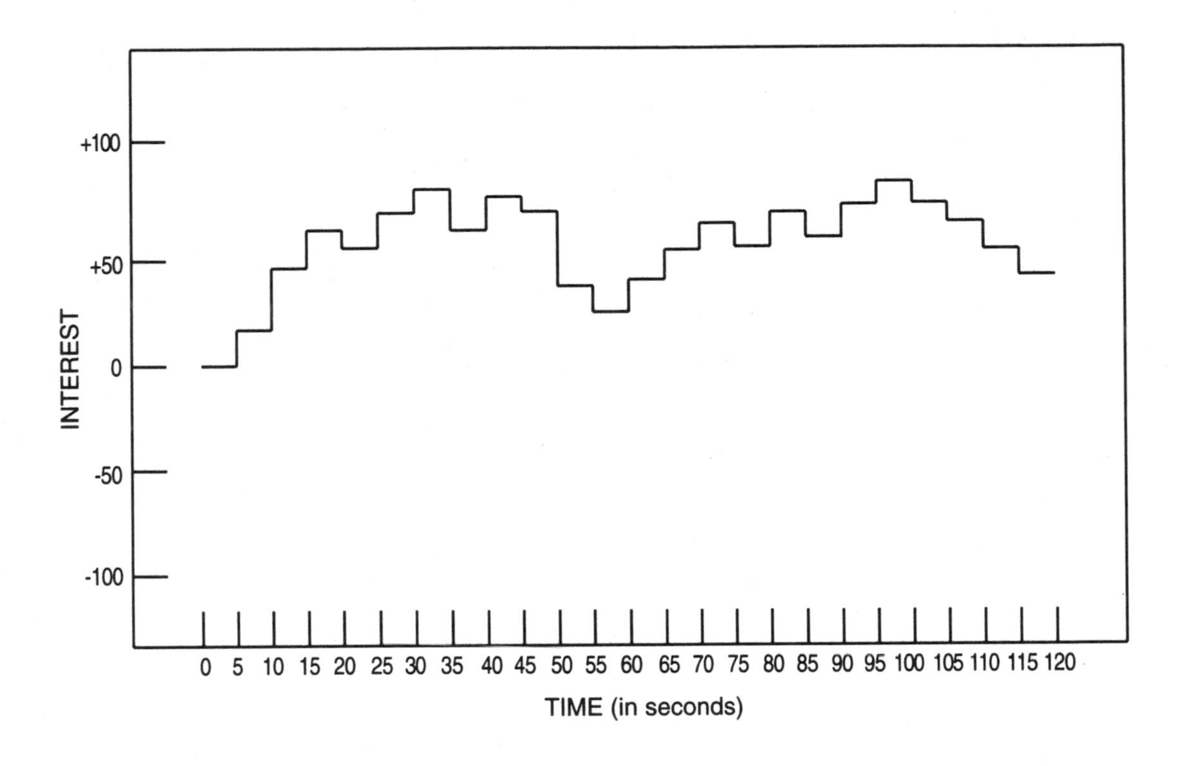

time, from 0 to 120 seconds in 5-second increments. The graph clearly shows that viewers like this spot and can be expected to watch it at home.

Commercial A starts off strong and keeps building. It only trails off at the very end, but this is to be expected, because this is where the commercial asks for the order. Notice that at about 50 seconds into the commercial, there is a sharp, ten-second drop in interest. This may be a matter of concern, depending on what is happening in the spot at that point.

Commercial B

Figure 13-2 shows how viewers like Commercial B. Like Commercial A, this spot also starts off in the neutral zone, but goes the wrong way. It

Figure 13-2. Viewer Interest Test—Commercial B

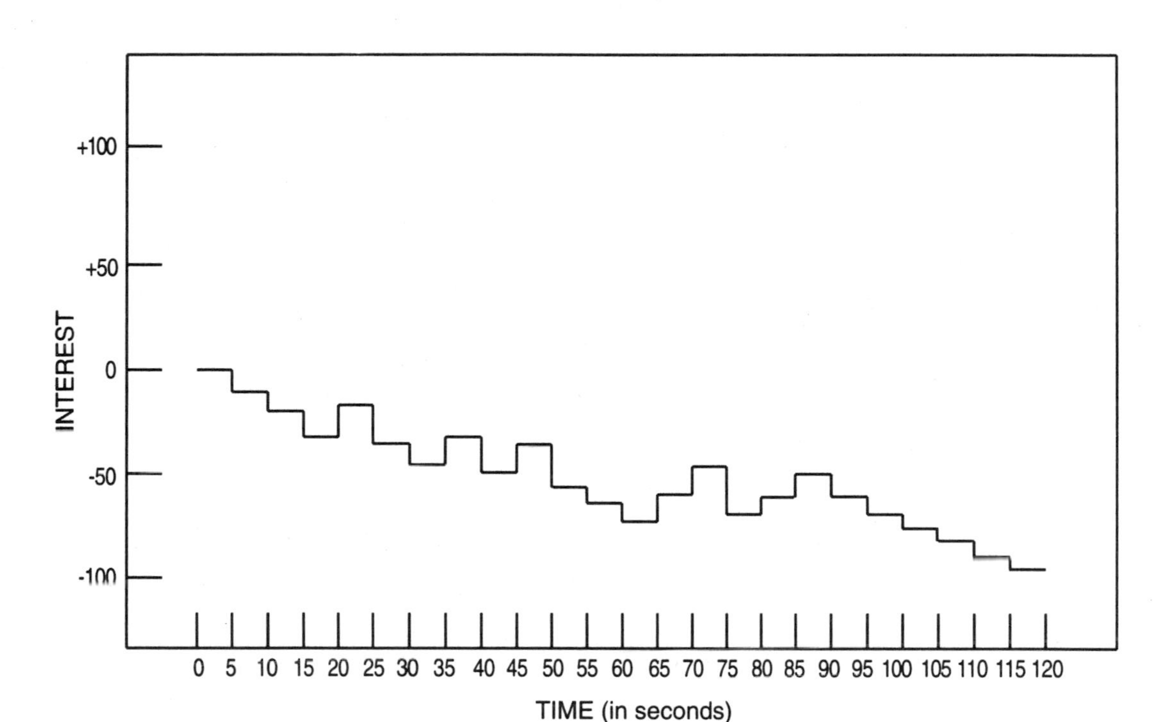

achieves below-average interest throughout. The differences between the two spots is more evident when the two graphs are overlaid, as shown in Figure 13-3.

Commercials A and B

When the charts are overlaid, it becomes very clear that Commercial B never achieves the level of interest of Commercial A. It is this clarity of comparison that makes viewer interest testing so valuable. However, the test is only measuring interest, not purchase intent. To gauge that, viewer interest tests sometimes include a pre-post test (discussed on pages 120–21).

Figure 13-3. Viewer Interest Test—Commercials A and B

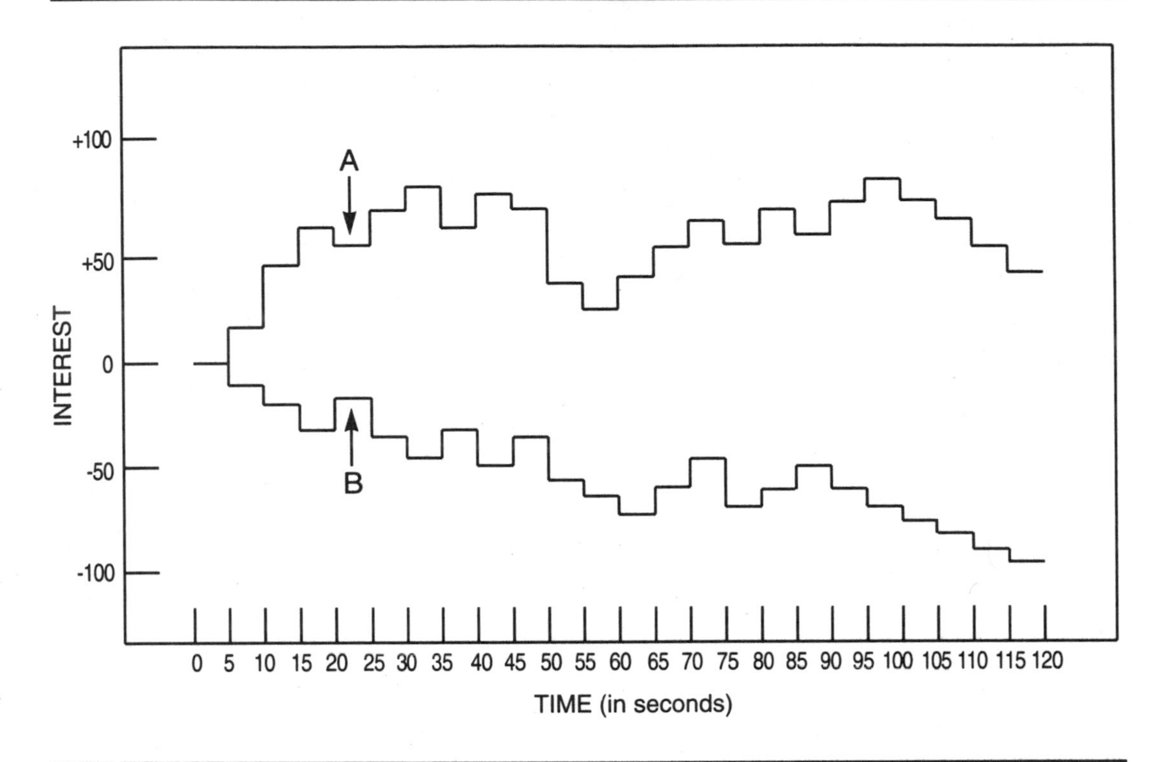

Other Tests

Pre-post tests and on-air tests, the most commonly used kinds of tests, are discussed next.

Pre-Post Test

Packaged goods advertisers are the biggest users of pre-post tests. Typically, an audience is asked to select which free product sample they'd like to receive. They choose from a list of ten products that cost about the same. The product in the commercial they're about to see is on the list, along with others that are there to establish base scores. After they see the commercial, the audience is again given the list and asked if anyone would like to change their choice. The difference between the number of people who wanted the product before and after seeing the commercial is the pre-post score.

The more people who want the product after seeing the commercial, the better the score. If *fewer* people want the product, the commercial is working negatively.

It may be difficult to do a pre-post test in direct response (DR), unless all the products or premiums in question can be received at the same time. Products or premiums that arrive immediately may have a built-in positive bias over those that arrive at a later date. However, if all the products or premiums arrive later, the playing field will still be level.

If your product or premium does not lend itself to a pre-post test, the next stage in testing after viewer interest may be to run your commercial on the air.

On-Air Testing

Not just commercials, but animatics (storyboards on film) can be tested on air. You can run an animatic on television and people will actually call to order. But an on-air test is expensive. You have to buy spot time, as opposed to dayparts. And you have to run your test for at least a week or two. You also have to produce more polished animatics, which cost more.

Test Matrix

Imagine you produced three commercials, each as a :120 and a :60. Suppose you wanted to test three different premiums and two price points. To determine which variables are causing which effects, you can test only one variable per execution. But if you finished and tested each variation, you'd have 36 commercials (3 x 2 x 3 x 2) and an impossibly expensive matrix to test. The complete matrix is shown in Table 13-1.

Fortunately, there's a way to learn everything about the 36 versions that were shot without having to test them all. The secret is testing each variable and then combining the winning variables. You do this by arbitrarily picking one commercial as your "tester." Now your test matrix is cut down from 36 to nine cells, as shown in Table 13-2.

TABLE 13-1. COMPLETE MATRIX FOR THREE COMMERCIALS, TESTING THREE PREMIUMS AND TWO PRICE POINTS

Length	Commercial A	Commercial B	Commercial C
:120	Premium A Price A	Premium A Price A	Premium A Price A
:120	Premium A Price B	Premium A Price B	Premium A Price B
:120	Premium B Price A	Premium B Price A	Premium B Price A
:120	Premium B Price B	Premium B Price B	Premium B Price B
:120	Premium C Price A	Premium C Price A	Premium C Price A
:120	Premium C Price B	Premium C Price B	Premium C Price B
:60	Premium A Price A	Premium A Price A	Premium A Price A
:60	Premium A Price B	Premium A Price B	Premium A Price B
:60	Premium B Price A	Premium B Price A	Premium B Price A
:60	Premium B Price B	Premium B Price B	Premium B Price B
:60	Premium C Price A	Premium C Price A	Premium C Price A
:60	Premium C Price B	Premium C Price B	Premium C Price B

Test Matrix 1 will tell you the four things you're trying to learn:

1. What is the best :120 commercial?
2. What is the best :60 commercial?
3. What is the best price point?
4. What is the best premium?

TABLE 13-2. TEST MATRIX 1

Length	Commercial A	Commercial B	Commercial C
:120	Premium A Price A	Premium A Price A	Premium A Price A
:120	Premium A Price B		
:120	Premium B Price A		
:120	Premium C Price A		
:60	Premium A Price A	Premium A Price A	Premium A Price A

The Best :120 Commercial

Look at the top row of cells in Table 13-2, from left to right. You're comparing three different commercials, each with the same length, premium, and price. It doesn't matter what the premium and price are, as long as they're the same. The only variable is the commercial itself. This is how you'll find out which commercial is best.

The Best :60 Commercial

Look at the bottom row of cells in Table 13-2, from left to right. The same logic applies to the 60-second commercials.

Some advertisers wouldn't even bother finding out which :60 is the best. They'd just use the :60 from the winning :120. This would further simplify the test by cutting it down to just six cells. This is often safe to do. However, there have been cases where one commercial was the best :120, but another was the best :60.

The Best Price Point

Look at the left-hand column in Table 13-2. The two top cells have the same commercial in the same length, and the same premium. The only variable is the price. So this will tell you which price is most effective.

The Best Premium

Look again at the left-hand column in Table 13-2. The top cell, the cell two below it, and the cell just below that give you a constant commercial length and price. The only variable is the premium.

Putting It All Together

Commercial A with price A and premium A is your control. If it's the winner, fine. But more often than not, the test won't work out so cleanly. Say the winning commercial is B, the winning price is B and the winning premium is C. You haven't tested this combination of variables. But the logic of your test tells you it *should* work.

Predicting Results

At this point, you can actually make a ballpark prediction of your rollout CPO. To do so, while keeping our example simple, let's plug some CPO numbers into just the :120 columns of our previous test matrix, as shown in Figure 13.3.

We can see that Commercial B with Premium A and Price A had a CPO of $24.00. We can also see that Price B had a $6.00 lower CPO than Price A. (If Price B is lower than Price A, we are assuming that the better CPO more

TABLE 13-3. TEST MATRIX 1 WITH CPO NUMBERS INCLUDED

Length	Commercial A	CPO	Commercial B	CPO	Commercial C	CPO
:120	Premium A Price A	$32.00	Premium A Price A	$24.00	Premium A Price A	$28.00
:120	Premium A Price B	$26.00				
:120	Premium B Price A	$33.00				
:120	Premium A Price A	$30.00				

than makes up for it.) We can also see that Premium C had a $2.00 better CPO than Premium A.

So we can predict that the CPO of Commercial B will be $8.00 less when is has price B and Premium C (6 + 2 = 8). This will bring the CPO down to $16.00. Will it work out this neatly and this well? Probably not. But there will certainly be improvement and now you will know the maximum theoretical improvement.

If Nothing Works

What do you do if combining the best elements gives you a theoretical CPO that is still not acceptable? It may be time to take a hard look at the offer, the creative strategy and execution, and the product itself. Obviously something must be changed if you are to have any chance of success. Now is the time to do what is necessary.

Statistically Significant at the 95 Percent Confidence Level?

Test results usually indicate a clear winner. Our example of Commercial A with a CPO of $32.00, and Commercial B with a CPO of $24.00 would leave no doubt. But if the CPO numbers were closer, would you be able to tell the winner? Say that Commercial A had a much better CPO of $24.41, while Commercial B still had a CPO of $24.00. Would Commercial B continue to be the winner? Or would it be a toss-up?

To put it in direct marketing terms, you want to know if 41¢, which is the difference between $24.41 and $24.00, is statistically significant or just a standard deviation due to random factors. Also, you want your answer to be at the 95 percent confidence level. This means that you will be 95 percent certain that the 41¢ difference either is, or is not, statistically significant.

Arriving at the answer requires knowing the sample size, which is the number of orders for each commercial. A higher level of confidence usually requires too large a sample size. Thus, working at the 95 percent confidence level is more-or-less standard in the industry.

With the sample size and CPO numbers in hand, your market research professional will perform a statistical analysis that will give you the answer. You will know if the 41¢ difference in CPO is statistically significant at the 95 percent confidence level.

The thing to do now is to get the takes that were "in the can" and re-edit Commercial B to include price B and premium C. Roll out with it or at least do a mini rollout. If you're unsure about the validity of all this mixing, matching, and analysis, do a "back test."

Back Test

To do a back test, test the winner against the second-best combination. If this were Commercial B, premium B and, of course, price A, the matrix might look like Table 13-4.

At first glance, the back test seems to violate the basic principle of testing one variable at a time. It may seem that you are comparing apples and oranges. However, the back test results can be compared to the *first* test results. Now you're back to apples and apples.

Double-Checking

Advertisers don't usually do an elaborate back test. Most often, the CPOs make the winner unambiguous. If a back test is done at all, it's to double check just one thing. For instance, if there were still some concern about

TABLE 13-4. TEST MATRIX 2

Length	Commercial B	Commercial C
:120	Premium B Price A	Premium C Price B
:120		Premium B Price A
:60	Premium B Price A	Premium C Price B

TABLE 13-5. TEST MATRIX 3

Length	Commercial B	Commercial C
:120	Premium C Price B	Premium C Price B

which commercial is really the best, the back test would simply be as shown in Table 13-5.

Another Back Test Scenario

On the other hand, if Commercial C had a CPO of $62 and Commercial B still came in at $24, there would be no point in spending any more money testing Commercial C. It would be impossible for it to improve enough to become an alternative to Commercial B. But suppose premium B did almost as well as premium C? Then the back test would be as shown in Table 13-6.

Market Testing

If you're only testing one commercial, you can simply choose a cable network or a smaller market or two, buy air time, and see what happens after a week or so.

Matched Market Test

If you're comparing commercials against each other, you might do a matched market test. Here, commercial #1 runs only in market #1. Commercial #2 runs only in market #2, which is chosen to match market #1 as closely as possible.

Fixed Spot Test

A more accurate way to compare commercials is with a fixed spot test. Here, all the commercials run in the same market or markets, but their posi-

TABLE 13-6. TEST MATRIX 4

Length	Commercial C	Commercial C
:120	Premium B Price B	Premium C Price B

tions on the same shows are rotated during the course of a week or two. A fixed spot test is generally considered to be the most accurate predictor of commercial success. Sometimes both a matched market test and a fixed spot test will be used, for an even greater degree of accuracy.

A matrix for a two-week, three-commercial fixed spot test might look like the one in Table 13-7. The commercials are coded A, B, and C.

Notice these points about a fixed spot test.

1. The commercials are in A-B-C sequence on both the horizontal and vertical axes of the matrix.
2. The spots are fixed because air time is bought on specific shows, just as in general image media.
3. Each commercial runs the same number of times on each show.
4. Each commercial has the same amount of media money spent on it.

TABLE 13-7. FIXED SPOT TEST MATRIX

	Week 1					Week 2			
Market	**M**	**T**	**W**	**T**	**F**	**M**	**T**	**W**	**T**
Denver 6 p.m. news	A	B	C	A	B	C	A	B	C
Denver 3-3:30 p.m. Cosby	B	C	A	B	C	A	B	C	A
San Jose 5-5:30 p.m. Brady Bunch	C	A	B	C	A	B	C	A	B
San Jose 5-5:30 p.m. Cheers	A	B	C	A	B	C	A	B	C
Tampa 5-6 p.m. Live at Five	B	C	A	B	C	A	B	C	A
Tampa 5:30-6 p.m. MASH	C	A	B	C	A	B	C	A	B

All this ensures that each commercial gets a fair and equal opportunity. When you look at the results of a fixed spot test, it's usually quite apparent which commercial is the winner. There are two more things you should know about a fixed spot test.

1. Because you're not buying dayparts, you're paying normal media rates. So fixed spot tests are rather expensive.
2. The raw CPO numbers must be divided by four to arrive at true direct response (DR) CPOs. Say it cost $400 to run a commercial on "Cheers" in San Jose. If Commercial A generated five orders when it ran on the first Monday of the test, its *raw* CPO would be $80 (400 ÷ 5), which is extremely high. But because DR media rates are about 25 percent of general media rates, you simply divide the $80 CPO by 4 to arrive at a much more acceptable CPO of $20 (80 ÷ 4).

Mini Rollout and National Rollout

Once you're sure you have a winning commercial, you might try a mini rollout. In a mini rollout you just buy time in, say, six markets for a week or so. And you can continue rolling out this way, safely and slowly evolving into a national rollout.

Your media analyst will constantly adjust your spending, refining the buy for efficiency. Some stations will get more dollars, others will get fewer. But sooner or later, you will see a definite downward trend in orders. This will show up as an increase in your CPO. Remember, a CPO is like a golf score; the lower the better. Your CPO may go up for several reasons. The commercial may have fatigued and require a fresh approach. The product may need to be revitalized. Or it may simply have run its course. Some products can come back after being off the air for a while. Others cannot. Look to your marketing team for guidance. One last thing to keep in mind is that success on DR TV may open the door to in-store distribution.

CHECKLIST: Testing

	Yes	No
Viewer interest test?	☐	☐
Pre-post test?	☐	☐
On-air test?	☐	☐
Test matrix done?	☐	☐
More than one commercial?	☐	☐
More than one price?	☐	☐
More than one premium?	☐	☐
Back test?	☐	☐
Market test?	☐	☐
Matched market test?	☐	☐
Fixed spot test?	☐	☐
Statistically significant results?	☐	☐
95% confidence level?	☐	☐
Mini rollout?	☐	☐
National rollout?	☐	☐

14 Telemarketing and Fulfillment

Is the job over when someone calls your 800 number? Not necessarily. Imagine that you had a store. Even if someone came in determined to buy, any number of things could turn him or her off. It's the same with telemarketing. This chapter will help you learn how to close the sale, capture information for your database, and complete the sale through fulfillment.

Roles of Telemarketing

If you've watched a commercial that begins with, "Hi, I'm Jennie, an operator here . . . ," you have an idea of what a telemarketing center looks like. When a viewer responds to a direct response (DR) commercial by calling an 800 number, the call goes to one of the operators at the center. Each operator responds to different 800 numbers. For instance, if someone calls 1-800-123-4567, they'll reach Jennie. If they call 1-800-765-4321, they'll reach Johnny. Each 800 number is like a coupon code that corresponds to a different television station or cable network. So when Jennie's 1-800-123-4567 number rings, she knows that the person ordering was watching station WAAA.

In Chapter 12, we said that providing information for media analysis was one of the most crucial roles of telemarketing. It's worth repeating that, along with information from the broadcasters, your media analysis relies on accurate and timely telemarketing information. Other important telemarketing functions include closing the sale, up-selling, testing, and capturing information for your database.

Closing the Sale

Nothing is more frustrating than losing a sale at the telemarketing stage. But many people who call an 800 number aren't quite ready to order. They may need more information. Or some reassurance. These days, telemarketers must be more than order takers. They must be trained in sales techniques so that they can close a sale.

The need for telemarketers who can provide information and close the sale will only increase with the increase in 60-second commercials. In a sense, the telemarketer becomes the other half of the commercial, filling in the blanks by communicating sales information to the caller.

Up-Selling

A telemarketer should also be able to convert an order into a more profitable one by increasing the number of units sold, selling other products, or more expensive ones.

Testing

Telemarketing can be an inexpensive way to test. An association had been giving a hat as a premium to new members. When people called to join, they were asked if they'd prefer a penknife. In this way, the association quickly and inexpensively found out the penknife was a better premium.

Capturing Information

As a direct marketer, you don't just want to sell. You also want to know who your customers are so you'll be able to sell them again later on. You can also rent your list to other direct marketers. A good telemarketer should be able to ask a number of demographic and/or psychographic questions before the caller gets annoyed.

Work with Telemarketers

Don't lose sight of the fact that the most important thing a telemarketer can do is sell your product. Make sure your telemarketers understand your product. Let them see your commercial. If possible, let them have a sample of your product and your premium. If you can afford it, let them keep both! Make sure they understand the script. Go over possible consumer questions and objections.

After your commercial has aired a few days, call your 800 numbers and pretend you're ordering. You'll learn firsthand how the telemarketers are doing. Then tell them you're conducting a test and they should purge the information from their computer screens. Ask if they're experiencing any difficulties with their real callers.

The Telemarketing Script

This should not be left to chance. Work closely with the telemarketing company to make sure it's easy for your callers to order, and also easy to up-sell, test, and capture information. The priority is making the sale. A neophyte direct marketer put so many research questions at the top of the script that callers became annoyed and many hung up. *After* you've captured the caller's name, address, and credit card number, is the time to ask a reasonable number of questions.

It's a shame to lose potential customers who've gone so far as to call your 800 number. But not everyone who calls is ready to order. Put on your consumer hat and try to have a good answer for every possible question or objection.

Figure 14-1 is a simplified and abridged version of a telemarketing script for Fur in a Can. Notice how questions 1 to 6 attempt to immediately close the sale. Question 7 has two branches, which separate callers who are ready to order and those who are not. Questions 8 and 9 try to up-sell the ready-to-order group. Then they go to question 11, a database question; an actual script may have several of these.

Meanwhile, the people who were not ready to order after question 7 have been jumped to question 10, which attempts to convert them by reiterating the product benefits. If the caller decided to order after question 10, they go back to question 8 and 9 for a try at up-selling. If they have still not decided after number 10, they jump down to number 12, where specific obstacles to the sale can be addressed.

Automated Telemarketing

The more you ask telemarketers to do, the more it's going to cost you. Suppose you are giving away a free sample? Callers don't have to be sold or up-sold. All you need to capture is their names and addresses, and perhaps a marketing question or two. In situations like this, where your offer does not require human involvement, you may want to consider automated telemarketing.

Figure 14-1. Telemarketing Script for Fur in a Can

Q1. Thank you for calling to order Fur in a Can. May I have your full name please?

Q2. May I have your address and zip code please?

Q3. Which credit card will you be using?

Q4. What is the name on the card?

Q5. May I have your account number?

Q6. What is the expiration date on the card?

Q7. Thank you. How many cans of Fur in a Can would you like to order today?
Customer ready to order. Go to Q8.
Customer not ready to order. Go to Q10.

Q8. Have you considered the convenience of ordering additional cans now? Many people enjoy Fur in a Can so much, they wish they didn't have to wait to order more.
Go to Q9.

Q9. Would you like to order additional cans as gifts? Fur in a Can is a great surprise for family and friends.
Go to Q11.

Q10. Can I answer any questions about Fur in a Can? It's the new, easy way to grow thick, luxurious, long-lasting fur on any surface. Just pour the little seeds anywhere you'd like fur to grow. Sounds like fun, doesn't it? Would you like one can, or more?
Customer ready to order. Go to Q8.
Customer not ready to order. Go to Q12.

Q11. To help us serve you better, I'd like to ask you a few questions. Where do you plan to use Fur in a Can?
A. In your home B. In your car C. On a person D. On a pet E. Other (specify)

Q12. Please tell me what else you'd like to know about Fur in a Can before you decide to order.
Safety. Go to Q13.
Price. Go to Q14.
Long-lasting. Go to Q15.
Beauty. Go to Q16.
Difficult to use. Go to Q17.
Might make a mess. Go to Q18.
No artistic talent. Go to Q19.

This technology won't intimidate or confuse your callers. We've all experienced it before. We've called an 800 number and heard: "If you want information on such-and-such, press 1. If you want information on this-and-that, press 2." And so on. If your product or service lends itself to automated telemarketing, you will probably save money.

Fulfillment

Your media person will also arrange for a fulfillment house. Sometimes telemarketing and fulfillment are under one roof, sometimes not. There's no right or wrong way to do it. It comes down to order volume, cost, and the services you require. You will have to make a number of decisions about fulfillment. All of these should be done as early on as possible. All have economic implications.

Packaging

- How will your product be contained?
- Does it require a box, an envelope, or a bag?
- Can packaging be off-the-shelf or does it have to be customized for your product?
- Is there a visual? If so, of what?
- Who will draw it?
- Will there be a graphic treatment or logo design?
- And what about typography?

Extras

- Do you have to include instructions or a guarantee?
- Should there be a questionnaire so you can learn more about your customers? You may want to re-use your mailing list or rent it to other direct marketers.
- Do you want to include a catalog or a bounce-back offer to buy additional products? While your focus should be on making your first sale, you should plan for future business.

Shipping

- How will your product be delivered?
- UPS?

- Overnight, at extra cost? This can be a good idea at Christmas.
- Through the mail? Check with the Post Office to make sure your mailing costs are as low as possible.

Remember the Federal Trade Commission guidelines that you have about 4 to 6 weeks for your product to arrive in your customers' homes. "Allow 4 to 6 weeks for delivery" should be supered in your commercial.

Multiple Products

If you're sending more than one product, or product-and-premium, they'll probably come from different vendors. You can use one fulfillment house or do multiple fulfillment. Check costs and keep these things in mind:

1. Inserting more than one item may complicate your packaging.
2. Shipping from multiple sources increases the possibility of loss.
3. Will your customers mind not receiving everything at once?

CHECKLIST: Telemarketing and Fulfillment

	Yes	No
Telemarketing strategy?	☐	☐
Timely information for media?	☐	☐
Closing the sale worked out?	☐	☐
Up-selling?	☐	☐
Testing?	☐	☐
Capturing database information?	☐	☐
Work with telemarketers?	☐	☐
Telemarketing script prepared?	☐	☐
Test order?	☐	☐
Automated telemarketing?	☐	☐
Packaging completed?	☐	☐
Extras considered?	☐	☐
Shipping arranged?	☐	☐
Multiple products?	☐	☐

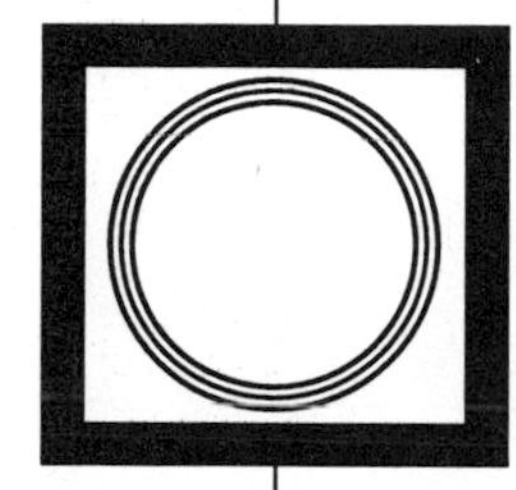

SECTION FOUR

Producing Your Commercial

Production Basics

If you've been testing your way and everything is positive, you can safely do a full-up commercial. You've increased your odds of success, because you've refined and improved your communication along the way. Still, this is where you'll be spending a great deal of money, so this is where you want to be particularly careful. Minute for minute, commercials often cost more than feature films. This chapter will give you the basics.

The Three Stages of Production

Whether you're making a Hollywood extravaganza, a television show, a documentary, or a commercial, your project will break down into three discrete stages:

1. Preproduction, everything that happens before the shoot;
2. Production, the actual shoot; and
3. Postproduction, everything that happens after the shoot.

Shooting Formats

The producer will recommend whether to shoot on film or videotape, and *which* film or tape format. Not too many years ago, the choice would have been easier. There was no such thing as videotape. If you were shooting on a medium to high budget, you'd opt for 35mm. If you were shooting on a medium to low budget, you'd use 16mm. Now, in addition to film, there are various videotape formats. To further complicate matters, the format you shoot on will not be the one you edit on. So you should know the plusses and minuses of each. We'll learn more about these formats in Chapters 20 and 21. Shooting formats are compared in Figure 15-2.

35mm Film

When you go to the movies, you're watching 35mm film. When you shoot a commercial on 35mm, you're doing what they do in Hollywood. Today, and for many years, 35mm will be the highest-quality way to take pictures. Many commercial directors will only shoot 35mm.

Any original picture is reproduced more faithfully on film than on tape. Film has a wider range and more gradations. Blacks are black, not dark gray. Whites are white, not light gray. Film captures more shades of color, as well as more nuances of brightness, darkness, and intensity. Technically speaking, the three color dimensions of hue, value, and chroma are greater for film than for tape. When producers and directors talk about the look of film, these are the qualities they are referring to.

The only disadvantage of 35mm film is its cost. The film stock is expensive. After it's been exposed, it can't be reused, like videotape. Film requires extra sound people and additional camera operators. Finally, it must be transferred to videotape for release to television stations. When you add all the extra costs, a commercial shot on 35mm can cost 30 to 50 percent more than the same one on videotape.

16mm

A way to achieve the look of film at a savings is to shoot on 16mm. Its emulsion quality has been greatly improved in recent years. It gives you the same gradations and ranges of color as 35mm, and a better picture than 1-inch videotape. However, it is more expensive than tape. But if you don't have to shoot sound, you will save enough money so that 16mm will cost about the same as 1-inch videotape. One potential disadvantage of 16mm to keep in mind is that its surface area is only 25 percent of 35mm (see Figure 15-1). If 16mm is enlarged too much, it appears grainy.

Super 8

Super 8mm film is not capable of rendering the detail necessary for commercial filming. It is only used in rare circumstances where that particular look is desired. For instance, if a scene in the storyboard called for showing home movies, 35mm could be doctored, but it might be more realistic to shoot the scene in Super 8.

Figure 15-1.

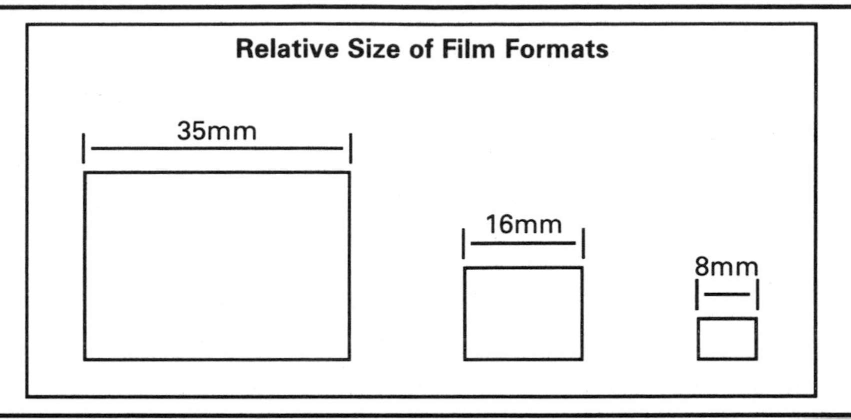

One-Inch Videotape

This is the broadcast industry standard. Television programming is on 1-inch. While it does not match the quality of 35mm, a scene shot on 1-inch can be beautiful, as are many TV shows.

However, those beautiful shows are shot in studios, with large, heavy cameras and massive lights. If your commercial can be shot in a studio, you can achieve the same quality. But if it requires traveling to a location, it's very difficult to match the results of studio-quality 1-inch.

If you shoot a feature film on 35mm, it will be projected in movie theaters in 35mm. But if you shoot a commercial on 35mm, or any other format, it will be transferred to 1-inch videotape before being sent to TV stations for broadcast.

It's a fair question to ask if transferring from film to tape doesn't negate all the advantages of shooting on 35. If the commercial is going to wind up on 1-inch, why not shoot it on that to begin with? The answer is that the commercial will still look better if it is shot in 35mm. The superior gray scale, hue, value, and chroma will not be diminished. The reason is that the equipment that transfers film to tape is better at maintaining fidelity to the original than a videotape camera is at capturing it in the first place.

Editing Formats

Some of the formats discussed below can be used for both shooting and editing. Editing formats are compared in Figure 15-3.

Digital

As this is being written, 1-inch is being replaced by digital as the broadcast standard. Digital was first used in editing and is now also used for shooting. There are two great advantages to digital. It opens up a new world of special effects. And every generation is a perfect copy of the original. The analog tape formats, including 1-inch, are inferior in these areas.

Beta SP

This is the format used by TV news crews. It is versatile, inexpensive, and generally considered to be the minimum quality acceptable for commercial production. Beta SP is extremely popular for shooting and editing commercials. Many editing facilities now even use this format for on-line editing and then transfer to 1-inch for duplication.

Other Video Formats

These include Beta, S-VHS, and VHS, which are ½-inch formats, and HI-8, which is 8mm. These low-budget formats are suitable for off-line editing, the rough editing done before the final on-line editing. However, they can't begin to match the quality of Beta SP for shooting. For this reason, they are used primarily for industrials and training films.

Three-Quarter-Inch Videotape

This format is used almost exclusively for off-line editing. For years, ¾-inch was the most popular off-line format for the off-line rough cut. Because of this, ¾-inch players are the familiar ones seen in most advertising agencies and client offices. They are used to screen rough cuts and finished commercials.

Nonlinear, Random Access

As of this writing, editing on disk has virtually replaced editing on tape. One advantage is how quickly material can be found. Just as on a home CD player, the access is instantaneous. There's no need to wait for tape to rewind. This makes assembly of the commercial very rapid. Another advantage is the ability to "open up" the program and add or delete material without having to rebuild it from the beginning. Finally, as we saw before, the system is digital, so special effects are easier to create and multiple-generation copies are perfect. The only disadvantage of editing on disk is the up-front cost of transferring the original material onto a computer hard drive or software. The finished edit will probably be transferred to a 3/4-inch cassette for viewing because the 3/4-inch machines still predominate.

Future Formats and Technologies

As this was being written, the electronic highway seemed just around the corner and high-definition TV was a few years down the road. These developments—and ones that are still dreams—are good news to the direct marketer. High definition means your wares will look better to the viewer. More channels means more media options. Narrowcasting means that niche products may become economically feasible to advertise on TV. And interactive television means it will be easier for viewers to order. The future looks bright for direct response TV.

Figure 15-2. Shooting Formats Compared

35mm Film—Best quality, most expensive

16mm Film—The "look" of film at a reduced cost

8mm Film—Amateur format, only used for "home movie" look

Digital Video—Best-quality video, replacing 1-inch

1-inch Video—Long-time broadcast and studio standard

Beta SP—Very popular format, inexpensive, acceptable quality

Hi-8—Amateur format, marginally acceptable for commercials

S-VHS—Amateur format, marginally acceptable for commercials

VHS—Amateur format, not acceptable for commercials

Figure 15-3. Editing Formats Compared

Non-Linear—Becoming the industry standard for off-line and on-line

1-inch Video Tape—Long-time broadcast standard and on-line format

3/4-inch Video Tape—Still popular for off-line editing

Beta SP—Becoming more popular for off-line editing

Hi-8—Amateur format, marginally acceptable for commercials

S-VHS—Amateur format, acceptable for off-line editing

VHS—Amateur format, not acceptable for editing

CHECKLIST: Production Basics

	Yes	No
Shooting format chosen?	☐	☐
35mm?	☐	☐
16mm?	☐	☐
1-inch?	☐	☐
Beta SP?	☐	☐
Editing format chosen?	☐	☐
Digital?	☐	☐
1-inch?	☐	☐
3/4-inch?	☐	☐
Beta SP?	☐	☐
Hi-8?	☐	☐
Super-VHS?	☐	☐

16 Preproduction

A successful commercial requires a great deal of planning before the shooting begins. This chapter will go over everything you need to know, starting with how to choose a producer, a director, and a production company. We'll discuss union rules, right-to-work states, travel, stock footage, and other budgetary considerations. We'll also find out why you need a shooting board and when you need a shooting matrix. And we'll see how everything comes together in the all-important preproduction meeting.

While bidding and casting are part of the pre-production process, they are somewhat complicated. So we have devoted the next chapter to bidding and chapters 18 and 19 to casting.

The Producer

The first step in preproduction is deciding on a producer. Your agency may have one or more on staff. These days, producers are often free-lancers. Try to find one with direct response (DR) experience. Like a movie producer, the commercial producer must take an idea on paper and transform it into film or videotape. The producer is responsible for all elements of production and manages the budget.

After the producer has seen the storyboard and discussed it with the creative team, he or she may make suggestions. A good producer will have thoughts on how to make the board work better as film. After the final storyboard is agreed upon, the producer will recommend directors and call in their reels. The agency/producer team will show you the three they'd like to have bid on the job. Or, in cases of a fixed budget, the one director they recommend.

The Commercial Director

Unlike the feature film director, the commercial director usually does not follow through with the project to the end. After the shoot, the commercial director will move on to his or her next project.

Evaluating the Reel

When you look at a director's reel, try to separate the commercial from what the director did with it. This is difficult and one reason why we like to screen reels at least twice. The first time we just look at the commercials. The second time we analyze the director's contribution and experience. Does the director "paint" pretty pictures with good lighting and interesting camera angles? Does the camera move in innovative ways? Is there any DR on the reel? Has the director shot products or services similar to yours? If the commercial needs special effects or technical requirements, is he or she the person for the job?

If your commercial will use people, the most important criterion is how well the director directs talent. There should be a consistent level from commercial to commercial on the reel. Do the people reach out to you? Do you like them? Do you believe them? Are they funny without being ridiculous? Are they warm without being saccharine? Does the director have a knack for capturing different types of people? Your commercial may depend on children, teenagers, adults, the elderly, men, women, celebrities, athletes, and so on.

Can the director quickly establish a relationship and create a special moment, one that you haven't seen many times before? How is *this* kiss more romantic? What makes *this* farewell more poignant? A good director will touch you in a very human way. You will know it when you experience it.

Don't be afraid to express your opinion now and at any stage of production. We've all seen enough movies, TV shows, and commercials to have an idea of what's good and what's not.

You'll probably find that the recommended directors are at the same level of talent and experience. This is as it should be because they will probably be in the same price range. Make sure you'd be comfortable with any of them because you may want to triple bid the job. If you do, the low bidder will have an advantage.

Occasionally you'll see a reel that will be head and shoulders above the average. *Every* commercial on it will be a gem. The lighting will be superb. The acting will be magnificent. The funny spots will make you laugh. The warm ones will bring a tear to your eye. You'll know you're watching a real talent.

You may not be able to afford that director. Top directors make $15,000 and more a day! However, in DR, you don't need to spend nearly that much to get a very good director who will film a spot you'll be proud of.

Two Money-Saving Strategies

We've had success in getting good directors by following two strategies. The first is having our producer look for young, hungry directors who are on the verge of making it, but not quite there yet. Their reels won't have many spots (and maybe no DR) but their talent will show through. Use these directors if you can because in a year or two you won't be able to afford them.

The second strategy that's worked for us on a number of our commercials is using a producer/director. Your producer may have done some directing and want to add your spot to his or her reel. If so, you may be able to save money and get an excellent end product. Some top commercial directors started this way.

Production Companies

The director will be affiliated with a production company. Make sure the production company is comfortable with shooting DR. We've seen very good ones decline the assignment when they realized the complexity of the shoot. A typical 30-second image spot is a breeze compared to a DR shoot with two commercial lengths, perhaps three price tests, and a few premium tests thrown in. It's easy to get confused.

A good producer, director, and production company will find ways to economize on shooting, bring quality production values to the storyboard, and take the original idea to a higher level of creativity. If they're doing their jobs, you'll be saying, "What a great idea, they've really made the commercial come alive."

Major Cost Issues in Preproduction

The major issues relating to how to shoot the commercial are: number of versions, film or tape format, union or nonunion cast and crew, size of cast, travel, set or location, and possible use of stock footage. You should know the cost implications of each.

Number of Versions

You'll most likely want various price, premium, and offer versions of your commercial. But even a simple change of dialogue may require an extra 10 to 15 minutes of shooting. This may not seem like much, but as the versions add up, the shooting day gets longer and more expensive. Also, as we will discuss below, union actors are paid for *each* version.

Advertisers sometimes want to add versions to the original commercial *after* the job has been awarded. But if the production company can't accommodate them all at the bid price, they must ask for more money. If there is no more money in the budget, the advertiser may ask the production company to find other ways to cut back the bid to the original number. As a result, the original commercial may be compromised. The result can be multiple versions of a commercial that doesn't work.

Signatories to Union Contracts

Many corporations with strong unions are signatories to the various union contracts that relate to film production. Most large advertising agencies and production companies are signatories. Being a signatory means that the company in question will only employ a union cast and crew. Also, the production must be 100 percent union. You are not allowed to use a union actor for the lead and nonunion actors for the smaller, less demanding parts.

Union vs. Nonunion Crews

The International Alliance (IA) is the governing union for all crew members except for vehicle drivers, whose union is the Teamsters. The vast majority of feature films use union crews. So do most commercials. Major production centers, Los Angeles in particular, have a film tradition that spans generations. Many crew members on an LA shoot had their fathers and grandfathers in the same craft. Using a union crew guarantees you the highest level of professionalism.

On the other hand, we have worked with industrious, knowledgeable, and friendly nonunion crews in various cities, including Baltimore, Philadelphia, Miami and Orlando. Even much smaller cities have the people, facilities, and equipment to do a professional job for you. The bottom line is, an actor or director may make or break your commercial. A crew member probably won't.

"Right-to-Work" States

As of this writing, there are 20 states where a worker need not be a member of a particular union to be hired. This means that if you shoot in one of these "right-to-work" states, listed in Table 16-1, both your cast and crew can be nonunion. If you use union talent, they can perform in one of these states without having to follow union rules or be paid according to union schedules.

The cost savings can be significant if you shoot in a right-to-work state. However, there may be a need to shoot in a union-shop state, such as California or New York. Or the cost of travel may outweigh the savings.

Table 16-1. Right-to-Work States

Alabama	Nevada
Arizona	North Carolina
Arkansas	North Dakota
Florida	South Carolina
Georgia	South Dakota
Iowa	Tennessee
Kansas	Texas
Louisiana	Utah
Mississippi	Virginia
Nebraska	Wyoming

Size of Cast

The creative concept may determine the number of actors in your commercial. For instance, a slice of life may only require two players. But suppose you are using quick-cut testimonials at a shopping mall. How many actors should you have? If you use union talent, you will have to pay them session fees and residuals, subjects we discuss in Chapter 18. How many extras will you need as passersby? And, don't forget, you'll need a voiceover announcer. Your creative team will help you achieve a balance between too thin a cast and excessive talent payments.

Travel

Even if you're not thinking of going to a right-to-work state, you may have to travel for a different reason, usually the weather. It's simply too difficult to shoot in northern climates in the middle of winter. The days are short, the skies are gray, the equipment freezes, and so do the humans.

That's one reason why the film industry moved from New York City to Los Angeles in the early part of the century. LA weather is generally sunny and mild. The days are long, so you can shoot longer. A director of photography once told us that there's even a fringe benefit from the smog and pollution. The air filters the sun and shifts it toward the red end of the color spectrum. Everything is modeled with soft, beautiful light. Flowers look prettier. People look healthier. Depending on your product category, that may be something to consider.

Set or Location

Your producer will advise you on the best way to achieve the sense of reality so essential to your production, whether you shoot on a set or go on location. A set has the advantages of privacy, quiet, and complete control of lighting. It also has everything you need right there. For tabletop, talking head and limbo shooting, it's clearly the way to go. However, if your concept calls for an elaborate set, going on location may be more economical. For instance, it's usually cheaper to rent an entire home for a day than to construct a realistic kitchen set. Also, if your concept calls for shooting out of doors, say at a park or on a city street, a location is more realistic. A location scout will find suitable places and arrange for permits and so forth.

Stock Footage

A commercial for a news magazine called for a crowd scene celebrating the end of World War II. In cases like this, it's usually much more economical to use stock footage than to create a historical scene. Stock footage is also the most economical way—and the easiest—to acquire a travel scene such as the Eiffel Tower, or an exotic one such as the interior of an active volcano.

Stock footage is often used for more mundane scenes, even in feature films. Imagine that we see a woman in her office in Manhattan. She says she's going to a meeting in San Francisco. We cut to stock footage of a jetliner, a stock footage establishing shot of the San Francisco skyline, and stock footage of a San Francisco cable car passing by a building. When we see the woman in her meeting, we believe she's meeting in that San Francisco building.

Your product itself may dictate the use of stock footage. If you are selling videos, or offering them as premiums, scenes from the videos will most likely become the core of your commercial. This, of course, is an ideal situation. (You will still want to shoot a beauty shot of the product.)

There are companies that specialize in stock footage. They work in much the same way as stock photo houses. They charge you for a search of your category and send you a cassette of the footage they have. You pay an additional charge for the scenes you select, depending on what you chose and how you plan to use it. Finally, you receive a broadcast-quality copy that can be edited into your commercial.

Another source for stock footage is the National Archives in Washington, D.C. Much of its material is in the public domain. If you have the time to do the research, this could be a valuable resource. Also, you can hire D.C.-based researchers to do the searching for you.

Preproduction Meeting

The final preproduction step is the preproduction meeting. This is very important. The ad agency and production company present a detailed description of how they're going to shoot the commercial. They discuss the coverage they'll give each scene, how long they plan to stay on each setup, and their overall interpretation of the storyboard. It's critical that everyone agree to these things at the preproduction meeting. Now is the time to voice any concerns and make any mandatory changes. It's very difficult and costly to make changes in the middle of filming.

The prepro is the place to make final decisions on casting (which we'll cover in Chapters 18 and 19) and any other remaining issues. If you're shooting on location, the location scout will have photos of alternate locales. If a set is being constructed, the set designer will have a sketch. If a certain style or design of props is integral to the production, the prop master may have samples. The agency and production company will make recommendations to you. Unless you have a very good reason to disagree, you should not.

In the rush to accomplish things before the shoot, sometimes the preproduction meeting is postponed until the day before the shoot. This doesn't allow you any time to resolve issues that may surface during the meeting. Ideally, the prepro should be held about a week before the shoot. At the very least, allow a day or two in-between prepro and shooting.

Shooting Board

The producer and director work out how they want to cover every shot in a more detailed blueprint than the original storyboard. This is called the shooting board. They want to cover each scene in a number of ways so that there are options when it comes to editing the commercial. The shooting board for just the first scene from the Fur in a Can storyboard is presented in Figure 16-1.

The director must strike a balance between adequate coverage of each scene and making sure that all the scenes are covered. The shooting board helps here too because it allocates a certain amount of time for shooting each scene.

There's often a tendency to make each scene perfect, to keep shooting take after take until it's as good as it can be. In principle, this is the way to do it. In reality, whether it's a feature film or a commercial, spending extra time on one scene means having less time to spend on the next. When too many scenes take too much time, the production runs late. At the end of the day, you're in the uncomfortable position of having to rush through the final scenes or incur overtime charges. So when your producer tries to move things along, he or she is doing a good job.

Sometimes, at the shooting board stage, or when you're on the set, a suggestion will be made to try something totally different. Often, the person who makes the suggestion is the director. You don't want to squelch the director's suggestions. You're paying for his or her expertise. And a good

Figure 16-1. Fur in a Can Shooting Board, First Scene

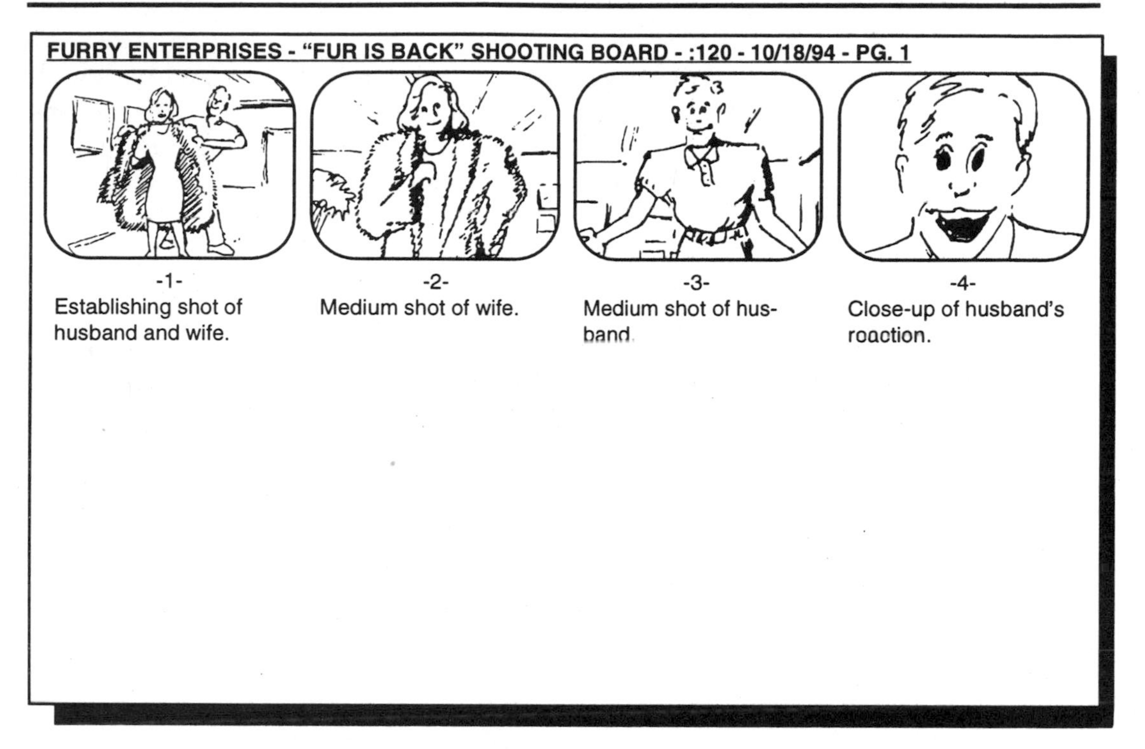

director will probably have many ideas. You'll agree with some and not with others. To complicate matters, the other members of the team may have their own ideas.

It's essential to come to a consensus at the shooting board stage. You don't want any ambiguity about how the scenes are going to be shot. If everyone can't agree, the only way out may be to cover it both ways and decide which version works best later on, in the editing room. This may be the most diplomatic way, but it has its price. It consumes time that could have been spent on other shots. You can't cover every scene different ways. At some point, you may have to make some hard decisions.

There's a saying in the advertising business, "No one ever got in trouble for shooting the board." However you finally agree to shoot the commercial, make sure you first cover it *as boarded*. Then, if there's time left, try something new. Don't do the impulsive thing that seems brilliant now but that you may regret tomorrow. And don't put yourself in the position of having to answer this legitimate question when you show the commercial to your boss: "What happened to my favorite scene? You *did* shoot that scene, didn't you?"

Shooting Matrix

If your production includes many versions to be tested, along with a shooting board, it's a good idea to have a shooting matrix. It can give everyone an invaluable picture of exactly what has to be covered during the shoot. A shooting matrix is usually not needed for general image commercials or in simple DR ones.

TABLE 16-2. SHOOTING MATRIX

Length	Commercial A	Commercial B	Commercial C
:120	Premium A Price A	Premium A Price A	Premium A Price A
:120	Premium A Price B	Premium A Price B	Premium A Price B
:120	Premium B Price A	Premium B Price A	Premium B Price A
:120	Premium B Price B	Premium B Price B	Premium B Price B
:120	Premium C Price A	Premium C Price A	Premium C Price A
:120	Premium C Price B	Premium C Price B	Premium C Price B
:60	Premium A Price A	Premium A Price A	Premium A Price A
:60	Premium A Price B	Premium A Price B	Premium A Price B
:60	Premium B Price A	Premium B Price A	Premium B Price A
:60	Premium B Price B	Premium B Price B	Premium B Price B
:60	Premium C Price A	Premium C Price A	Premium C Price A
:60	Premium C Price B	Premium C Price B	Premium C Price B

Your copywriter should create the shooting matrix and check it with the producer and the script supervisor before and during the shoot, to make sure nothing is omitted.

While the matrix is for everything that must be shot, it's not for everything that has to be edited. Much of the film will be left "in the can." It will either be used or discarded depending on the results of the test.

Imagine you decided to produce three commercials, each as a :120 and a :60. Suppose you wanted to test three different premiums and two price points. If you finished and tested each variation, you'd have 36 commercials (3 commercials x 2 versions x 3 premiums x 2 prices) and the shooting matrix in Figure 16-2. If it looks familiar, that's because we simplified it for on-air testing in Chapter 13.

CHECKLIST: Preproduction

	Yes	No
Determine budget?	☐	☐
Producer chosen?	☐	☐
View director reels?	☐	☐
Director selected?	☐	☐
Producer/director?	☐	☐
Preproduction meeting?	☐	☐
Union crew?	☐	☐
Right-to-work state?	☐	☐
Travel?	☐	☐
Shooting board?	☐	☐
Shooting matrix?	☐	☐
Consensus on coverage?	☐	☐
Consensus on interpretation?	☐	☐
Location?	☐	☐
Set?	☐	☐
Props?	☐	☐
Models?	☐	☐

Bidding the Job

How much *should* your commercial cost? That's like asking, "How long is a piece of string?" The question should be, what is the least you can pay without jeopardizing the image of your product or service and the communication of your commercial? Today, you may get by shooting on videotape for $20,000. Or you may have to spend $50,000, $100,000, or more. As of this writing, the average 30-second general image commercial costs more than $200,000. What you spend on production is a small percentage of what you'll spend on media, and media costs are a small percentage of the profits you hope to realize. So keep production costs in this perspective and read this chapter to find out how to get the most for your money.

Prebid Meeting

Before the job is bid, a prebid meeting should be held at which the producer explains how he or she plans to handle the shoot. This will help determine the cost of the production. If the producer is staying within budget, you have no problem. However, the producer may not be able to execute the commercial with the available dollars. In that case, changes must be made, either in the storyboard or in the way the board will be shot.

Bidding Protocol and Forms

How can you avoid a conflict of interest if one of the directors being bid is the producer sending out the bids? First, make sure all concerned agree on the specifications of the job at the prebid meeting. Next, send the same job specs to all directors and production companies. Last, make sure the bids are returned to the agency account executive or broadcast business manager.

Your agency will probably send a job specs sheet to the production companies. This is a one-page form that defines the scope of the project so that the production company can estimate it.

The production company will return a form that can run five to six pages, detailing, line by line, the personnel, equipment, and supplies they estimate will be required.

Producers who are not affiliated with an advertising agency may belong to the Association of Independent Commercials Producers, and use the AICP Form, which lists more than 250 line items. We have reproduced an actual AICP Form in Appendix B. Whatever form you use, it should be comprehensive.

Evaluating Bids

Using standardized forms lets the agency know precisely what each production company thinks it will cost to do the job. The forms are very detailed and can be several pages long. For the sake of simplicity, we've reproduced only a section of a completed bid form for Fur in a Can in Figure 17-1. For instance, we did not include the director's fee, which is a separate line item. Nor did we include the production company markup. The small section of the bid form we reproduced is from an imaginary company called ABC Productions, which believes the job can be done in one day.

XYZ Films, another imaginary production company, sees it as a two-day shoot. They fill out this same small section of the bid form quite differently, as shown in Figure 17-2.

Most of the costs double if it's a two-day shoot. Can it be done in one day without compromising quality and getting into costly overtime? An experienced producer is your best guide.

Besides the issue of one day or two, notice that the two production companies differ in three other areas. XYZ Films doesn't think they'll require an extra grip, one of the crew who moves equipment about. They also think they can get by with one less production assistant (P.A.) Finally, they don't plan on using any crane shots.

These are issues you probably won't want to get into. Your producer has the experience to know what it will really take to do the job correctly. If he or she thinks it needs two days, ABC Productions may be asked to bid it accordingly. On the other hand, if the producer thinks a crane shot is essential, that should be included in the XYZ Films bid.

Figure 17-1. Section of Completed Production Company Bid Form—1-Day Shoot

ABC PRODUCTIONS BID FORM

	Estimated			Actual		
	Days	**Rate**	**Total**	**Days**	**Rate**	**Total**
Camera Operator	1	800	800			
Ass't. Camera	1	425	425			
Loader	1	300	300			
Gaffer	1	425	425			
Key Grip	1	425	425			
Grip #2	1	375	375			
Grip #3	1	375	375			
Mixer	1	400	400			
Boom	1	400	400			
P.A.	1	125	125			
P.A.	1	125	125			
Camera Rental	1	1975	1975			
Lighting Rental	1	1500	1500			
Crane Rental	1	750	750			

As far as extra crew members are concerned, advertisers sometimes think they're saving money if they only have a skeleton crew. Depending on the commercial, this may or may not be true. In many cases, a larger crew may save money by finishing sooner, or to take our example, by shooting in one day instead of two.

Sharpening Pencils

The rates for most of the line items in a bid are standard. Equipment rentals are more or less the same. And union crew rates are exactly the same. So bids are often very close to each other. The differences show up mostly in the director's rate and the production company markup.

Figure 17-2. Section of Completed Production Company Bid Form—2-Day Shoot

XYZ FILMS BID FORM						
	Estimated			Actual		
	Days	Rate	Total	Days	Rate	Total
Camera Operator	2	800	1600			
Ass't. Camera	2	425	850			
Loader	2	300	600			
Gaffer	2	425	850			
Key Grip	2	425	850			
Grip #2	2	375	750			
Grip #3	2					
Mixer	2	400	800			
Boom	2	400	800			
P.A.	2	125	250			
P.A.						
Camera Rental	1	1975	1975			
Lighting Rental	1	1500	1500			
Crane Rental						

Your producer may or may not ask for a lower bid. Is there fat in the estimate? Or simply a fair profit? Are some of the items less than imperatives, but touches that enrich the production? Before you eliminate them, remember that when you make a stew but keep taking out ingredients, you wind up with consommé.

Awarding the Job

Some advertisers have a policy of automatically awarding the job to the lowest bidder. This isn't necessarily the best policy. As we've seen, the low bid may not have enough in it to do the job adequately. Assuming that the bids are all in the ballpark, go with the company the producer believes will do the best job. Any incremental costs will be money well spent.

Payment Protocol

Production companies expect to be paid 50 percent upon signing the contract. This is because they will immediately start to incur substantial out-of-pocket expenses. They will expect to be paid the remainder when the shooting is completed. Never put your advertising agency in the awkward position of having to float a no-interest loan for you.

Editors' Bids

Aside from selecting a production company, your producer will also have to choose an editor. The editor will also fill out a form that details his or her part of the job. Again, for the sake of simplicity, we've reproduced only a small section in Figure 17-3. Over the years, your producer probably has developed a working relationship with certain editors and would feel most comfortable using one of them for your job.

Figure 17-3. Section of Completed Editor's Bid Form

PDQ EDITING BID FORM						
	Estimated			Actual		
	Hours	Rate	Total	Hours	Rate	Total
Editor	25	100	2500			
Ass't. Editor	10	50	500			
Track Transfer	3	200	600			
Recording	4	200	800			
Mixing	3	200	600			
Masters	7	40	280			
Cassettes	3	35	105			
Off-Line	16	100	1600			
On-Line	4	500	2000			
Titling	2	500	100			

Agency Estimate Form

Advertisers don't ordinarily look at either the production company bid form or the editor's bid form. As you can see from the sections reproduced, they are far too technical to make much sense to a nonprofessional.

The agency will take the bottom line numbers from the production company and the editor, include the costs of casting, talent payments, and other necessary items, and total them. Traditionally, the agency marks up the subtotal by the standard 17.65 percent. Nowadays, more typical is a "commissioned account structure." The agency will not mark up the total but will be paid a flat production fee, plus out-of-pocket expenses, including travel and per diems, if required. This total will be the final number presented to you. The prototype filled-in form is shown as Figure 17-4. Figure 17-5 is a blank one you may find useful.

CHECKLIST: Bidding the Job

	Yes	No
Prebid meeting?	☐	☐
Producer knows selected director's work?	☐	☐
Producer has experience with production companies?	☐	☐
Producer knows recommended editor?	☐	☐
Job spec sheet to production companies?	☐	☐
Job spec sheet to editor?	☐	☐
Production bids evaluated?	☐	☐
Production company selected?	☐	☐
Editor's bid evaluated?	☐	☐
Editor selected?	☐	☐
Agency compensation method chosen?	☐	☐
Agency Estimate Form approved?	☐	☐

Figure 17-4. Completed Agency Estimate Form

TV PRODUCTION ESTIMATE

CLIENT: Furry Enterprises
PRODUCT: Fur in a Can
TITLE: "Fur is Back"
DATE: 10/18/94

Production Co.	**ABC Prod.**	**XYZ Films**	**PDQ Pictures**
Production Fee	35,353	42,022	38,678
Casting Fees	2,300	2,300	2,300
On Camera Talent	1,600	1,600	1,600
Voiceover Talent	800	800	800
Extras	700	700	700
Talent Travel	900	900	900
Talent Per Diem	400	400	400
Music	300	300	300
Sound Effects	250	250	250
Recording	725	725	725
Editorial Fees	12,067	12,067	12,067
Sub Total	**42,703**	**49,372**	**46,028**
Agency Markup/Fee	7,537	8,714	8,124
Shipping	200	200	200
Messengers	100	100	100
Art/Type	425	425	425
Sales Tax	283	283	283
Agency Travel	4,500	4,500	4,500
Agency Per Diem	3,500	3,500	3,500
TOTAL	**59,248**	**67,094**	**63,160**

AGENCY APPROVAL ____________________

CLIENT APPROVAL ____________________

Figure 17-5. Blank Agency Estimate Form

TV PRODUCTION ESTIMATE

CLIENT: ____________________
PRODUCT: ____________________
TITLE: ____________________
DATE: ____________________

Production Co.	
Production Fee	
Casting Fees	
On Camera Talent	
Voiceover Talent	
Extras	
Talent Travel	
Talent Per Diem	
Music	
Sound Effects	
Recording	
Editorial Fees	
Sub Total	
Agency Markup/Fee	
Shipping	
Messengers	
Art/Type	
Sales Tax	
Agency Travel	
Agency Per Diem	
TOTAL	

AGENCY APPROVAL ____________________
CLIENT APPROVAL ____________________

Casting Actors

In Chapter 16, we discussed signatories, right-to-work states, and other union topics that relate to the crew. They relate to the cast as well. There are also some other cast-related issues you should be aware of, including session fees, residuals, and the difference between principals and extras. This chapter will discuss them all, as well as the most critical matter—selecting the best cast. Depending on your commercial, you may need: On-camera talent, voiceover talent, extras, hand models, and special talent. Set aside ample funds for casting. The right talent can make your spot.

SAG and AFTRA Union Rules

Most commercial actors belong to two unions: the Screen Actors Guild (SAG) and the American Federation of Television and Radio Actors (AFTRA). If you're shooting on film, the union of responsibility will probably be SAG. If you're shooting on tape, it'll probably be AFTRA.

From a practical standpoint, the union rules are so close that we can safely lump them together. While some talented performers have not joined a union, by far the bulk of professionals—people who earn their living as actors—are members of the unions.

Union Radius of Authority

The union radius of authority may overlap into a right-to-work state. For instance, there is a Screen Actors Guild office in Washington, D.C. This office has a 100-mile radius of authority. This means that any member performing within this radius must abide by SAG rules. So even though Virginia is a right-to-work state, union rules apply in Richmond. The radius of authority differs from city to city. In this, as in all decisions concerning unions, your producer is your best guide.

Session Fees

Union performers are paid a fee for each version of a commercial they shoot. If you change one word, a price for example, that counts as another commercial, and they are entitled to another session fee. However, there are exceptions to the pay-per-version rule. Your producer will tell you if you can take advantage of them.

The basic union payment is called "scale." However, some actors who are much in demand may require double scale.

Extras, the people who can't be recognized and who do not speak, receive a standard day rate no matter how many versions they do of a single commercial.

Residuals

In addition to session fees, principal performers (but not extras) receive a payment every time the commercial airs. Residuals can be substantial if the spot rolls out. If your commercial is doing that well, residual payments should be looked at as a cost of doing business. Remember, you wouldn't be paying residuals if your commercial wasn't running. And you wouldn't be running it if it wasn't working for you.

Nonunion actors do not earn residuals. Also, their session fees are negotiable. But even if you can find ones good enough for the part, you will not be allowed to use them if your company, your ad agency, or your production company are SAG/AFTRA signatories.

Tag Rates

If you're using union talent, whether on camera or voiceover, only have them say the 800 number within the last 15 seconds of the spot, never sooner. You can *show* the number for as long as you want. If you rollout with numerous 800 numbers, you'll save a fortune on union announcer talent payments. This is because the talent will be compensated at a lower fee, called a tag rate. If you have them say the price earlier on, the union considers each price version as an entirely new commercial. So if you had eight telephone numbers—a normal number for testing—the union talent would receive session fees for eight commercials.

Casting Principals

Your agency will come up with a casting profile for each principal role. Everyone should agree on them before they go to the casting director. A typical casting profile reads like this:

> "A woman about 35 to 40 who could be your next-door neighbor. She is married and has teenage children. She is attractive but not sexy or glamorous. Intelligent and articulate, she doesn't know what to get her kids for Christmas."

The production team will probably look at 50 to 100 actors for each role. They may ask the ones they like to come to a second audition. If you have more than one person in your spot this will also give them the opportunity to mix and match roles. Finally, they'll select two or three recommendations and show you them on videotape.

What should you look for? First, that the talent fits the casting profile. Often, casting directors will put out a "cattle call" and instead of "a woman about 35 to 40 who could be your next door neighbor," half the people on the reel will be "a glamorous, upscale woman in her late 20s who lives in a penthouse." The problem comes in if one of these miscast women is also a superior actress. Everyone may forget she's not right for the role and recommend her. But the actors in your commercial must be the right ones to reach your target audience and enhance the image of your product.

Assuming the talent fits the casting profile, what should you look for? As with a director, talent. You want to see an intelligent reading of the role. (It's likely to be the *wrong* reading because the director isn't there.) The actor will probably do two or three takes. Look for a range of interpretations among them. Most important, do you believe what the actor is saying?

If you're not comfortable with the recommendations, you might want to look at some of the rejects. Before the two or three were presented to you, the initial 50 to 100 were culled down to about a dozen. Resist the impulse to look at all 50 to 100. You're paying professionals to do a very tedious job for you.

If you're still uncomfortable, you may have to do more casting. If your casting director isn't coming through, try another. If you've exhausted all the talent in your city, try another. (Note: Union actors travel first class.)

Callbacks

After the talent is narrowed down to two or three good actors, they will be called back for a second audition. There will also be a callback if your commercial requires a certain chemistry between actors and they didn't have an opportunity to play against each other in the first audition. This is usually the case because actors are auditioned in no particular order at 10- to 15-minute intervals.

For instance, Amy and Bill read their lines together, as did Cynthia and Dave. You like Amy and you like Dave. But the only way to see how they work together is to call them back and have them audition together.

It doesn't cost anything to ask a union actor to come to a callback or even a second callback. However, there is a charge for a third callback.

The best way to see a casting session is on video, as this is the closest to how the actors will be seen on television. If you attend a casting session, try to keep the number of observers to a minimum. Some actors can handle crowds better than others, which has nothing to do with their ability to perform in front of a camera. Also, you're not casting for a play, so don't look at the actors when they perform. Instead, look at the TV monitor.

The director will probably direct the final casting session. He or she will ask the actors to read the role a couple of different ways. Maybe even the wrong way. This is done to see if the talent can take direction and to get an idea of their range. They should be able to give different interpretations and subtle shades of emphasis.

In the end, the director will recommend the actors he or she thinks have the most potential to bring the part to life. Don't underestimate the value of a good director's advice when it comes to casting. Unless you have a good reason to disagree, go along with the director's recommendation. He or she has done this many times before.

Booking Talent and First Refusal

When the casting decision is made, the producer will tell the casting director to book the talent. This means that the actor(s) and you have entered into a contractual agreement. They agree to perform in the commercial. You agree to pay them for the day(s) they are booked. Even if they are eventually cut out of the commercial, they must be paid. And should you cancel the production, they are entitled to a kill fee. This is fair, because they may have turned down another job so they could do yours.

Sometimes when you try to book an actor, you find out you can't because he or she is on first refusal for another job. This means that the actor has been reserved for the other job but has not yet been booked. If the actor were booked for the other commercial, he or she *definitely* would not be available for yours.

But now that the actor has a definite offer to appear in your commercial, his agent will notify the other commercial producer, who will tell his client they must either book the actor for their commercial or release him so he can be in yours. This matter is usually resolved in 24 hours.

Finding out that the actor you believe can make your commercial is on first refusal can be depressing. But good actors are much in demand and often are in the final rounds on a number of productions. Even so, most often you'll be able to book first refusal talent.

Naturally, when you find out someone is on first refusal, you can protect yourself by putting your second-choice and third-choice talent on first refusal. You can do it anyway if you're not yet sure whom to choose. This is how the first refusal system perpetuates itself.

Not to complicate things, but there is also a second refusal. This means just what the name implies, being next in line after first refusal. Sometimes an actor will be on first refusal for one role and second refusal for another on the same day. So the procedure for resolving everything just takes a little longer.

If the actor you wanted was booked for his first refusal job and you still want him for yours, an option to consider is changing the date of your shoot. This may or may not be possible, depending on the schedules of the director, the production company, and the advertising agency.

Voiceover Talent

If you're doing a table top commercial, or an announcer is handling the voiceover section of the commercial, you'll have to cast for this part. It's important to get the right voice, so take the time to do it right.

Start with a casting profile. This one could work for a sports car magazine:

> "A man about 35 with high energy and high enthusiasm. He is very dynamic, the embodiment of the high-performance cars in the magazine."

A casting profile for a magazine on investing might read more like this:

> "A man about 50 with a deep, distinguished voice. He exudes the calm confidence of someone with money. His grammar and articulation say that he is very well educated."

You'll probably listen to announcer auditions on audiotape. If you go to a casting session, don't look at the announcer reading lines. The viewer will never see a face and you shouldn't let appearance affect your impression. If it helps, close your eyes while listening.

Extras

These are the people in the background of a scene. You can't quite make out who they are but they bring a feeling of reality to the production. Depending on the commercial, you may not require any extras, or you may need up to ten or more. For instance, if you're shooting a street scene, you'll need pedestrians.

Extras are paid a flat rate that is less than the on-camera rate. Also, extras don't collect residuals. If you're working with union talent, remember that extras must not be recognizable. The union rule states that if you (or their mothers) can recognize their faces, they become principals.

Special Talent

Stunt performers, body models, hand models, and the like are included in this category. It may seem that you would rarely need such a person. You may, however, consider using a hand model. If your product requires many closeups of someone holding it, it will simply look better in an attractive hand. Also hand models know how to open, move, and hold various types of products. This may seem trivial, but it's most important. One of the most critical areas on a shoot is close-ups. Getting the product into exactly the right place, take after take, not tilted up or down, nor to the right or left, not reflecting the lights, not with fingers covering the brand name, can be frustrating. Things can be a lot smoother when you're working with someone who's done it hundreds of times.

If you're using a celebrity, definitely use a hand model. You'll want to spend as much time as you can getting the celebrity to give you good on-camera lines. Don't waste valuable time trying to get a celebrity to properly handle the product when you can use a hand model.

Children

There are any number of marvelously talented, well-trained child actors. However, when you're working with children, keep three things in mind. First, if your commercial calls for a parent and a child, cast the child you want before the parent. It's always easier to find an adult that's right for the part—there are more of them. Second, your producer will be aware of the child labor laws in different states. These limit the number of hours a day a child may work. Finally, the younger the child, the more important it is to have a backup performer as insurance. The stand-in is paid even if not called on to perform.

Paying Union Talent

If you are using union talent, at the end of the shoot (or the recording session) they will have to sign various forms, which your producer will supply. These include the employment contract, production report, and completion report. As complicated as these are, the real difficulty comes in figuring out what the talent should be paid for the session and as residuals while the commercial airs. If your agency doesn't have a talent payments department, we recommend the use of a paymaster. This is a company that knows the union rules and regulations, does the math, and even cuts the checks for you. The paymaster gets 10 percent, and like a good accountant, is worth every penny.

If the shoot is not local, before they leave the set, the talent will also require cash payments for meals. Your producer will tell you how much. Also, talent travel and hotels will be prepaid by you. Again, your producer will handle the details.

CHECKLIST: Casting Actors

	Yes	No
Casting profile done?	☐	☐
Union talent?	☐	☐
Union radius of authority considered?	☐	☐
Scale performers?	☐	☐
Principals?	☐	☐
Comfortable with director's choices?	☐	☐
Extras?	☐	☐
Voiceover?	☐	☐
Special talent?	☐	☐
Children?	☐	☐
Follow child labor law?	☐	☐
Back-up children?	☐	☐
Talent booked?	☐	☐

Casting Celebrities, Clients and "Real People"

If you're not using professional actors in your commercial, you may be thinking of using celebrities or "real people." Or you may consider starring in your own commercial. This chapter will show you the advantages and disadvantages to all these approaches. It will also show you how to successfully work with celebrities.

Casting Celebrities

You will have to decide if celebrities are worth it to your product. In general image, direct response (DR) and infomercials, celebrities are *not* a guarantee of success. Sometimes celebrities are used simply because they bring instant recognition to a product. As we have seen, this is often the case in infomercials.

The best use of celebrities is to make them integral to the product. This is what *Sports Illustrated* did with their exercise videos with swimsuit models Cheryl Tiegs, Elle Macpherson, and Rachel Hunter.

Even if celebrities are not part of the product, a concept should be built around them. It was difficult to imagine anyone but Ray Charles singing, "You Got The Right One Baby, Uh-Huh." In fact, one of the spots in this campaign spoofed other entertainers auditioning for the role.

Similarly, Bob Vila, who hosts a TV show for do-it-yourselfers, was a good choice as the spokesman for the Time-Life Books series on home improvements. Here the use of the celebrity was driven by the concept, as it should be.

Why Celebrities Do Commercials

Sometimes celebrities do commercials for the money, which can be substantial. But it's important to remember that while celebrities like the money and want the money, they most often don't *need* the money. They feel no *extra* obligation to the client because of the amount of money involved. They are being paid what, to them, is their normal fee.

Sometimes celebrities do it for the exposure. The celebrity may think it's in his or her best interests to be associated with your product. Celebrities are constantly bombarded by offers to appear in commercials. Their agents and business managers tell them which ones they should accept.

Sometimes they do it because they like the storyboard. Or because they'll be cast with a friend of theirs. Or simply because they have nothing better to do that day.

You may never know why a celebrity agrees to do your commercial. But one thing is for sure. Once you decide to use them, you need them more than they need you. And you have little leverage over them. The key to successfully working with celebrities is using an experienced producer and director.

We've worked with many celebrities and had only positive experiences. But we've heard stories of celebrities who did one take and left, celebrities who walked off the set, celebrities who never showed up.

Before you throw your lot in with a celebrity, have your agency research him or her. They'll be able to tell you if the person you have in mind may be more trouble than he or she is worth.

Logistics and Timing

If possible, don't count on one particular celebrity agreeing to do your commercial. Generate a list of backups. The chances are, your first choice may not be able to do it. Even if he or she wants to, the schedule may make it impossible. They could be shooting a movie for the next 3 months. Or tied up with speaking engagements. Celebrities are busy people.

Allow plenty of time up front to negotiate the deal. Every step in communicating with a celebrity is likely to turn into four steps: first, the agent, next the business manager, then the attorney, and finally the celebrity. Why does it have to be so complicated? Because celebrities have a lot to lose and must always be on guard against unscrupulous types who would take advantage of them.

Be prepared to shoot the commercial where the celebrity wants you to. This may be the only feasible way to fit it into his or her schedule.

Negotiations

When you hire union talent, you pay standard, predetermined rates. With celebrities, the sky's the limit. There is simply no standard procedure for the payment of celebrities.

A large ad agency with an in-house casting department will have someone experienced in celebrity negotiations. Smaller agencies must employ a casting service to do this. In either case, it's a matter of starting out with trial balloons and evolving to a mutually acceptable figure. One negotiating tactic in direct response (DR) is to ask the celebrity to forego some of the up-front payment in exchange for a share of the back-end profit.

The Care and Feeding of Stars

Celebrities are accustomed to being treated as such. A relatively modest investment in pampering can pay a huge dividend on the set. You want your celebrity relaxed, comfortable and in good spirits. We suggest:

- Have a limousine pick the celebrity up at home, or at the airport or train station. This will also help ensure that your star shows up.
- Have him or her stay at the best room in the best hotel in town.
- Have a bouquet of flowers or a fruit basket delivered to the star's hotel room.
- If you haven't met the celebrity before (usually the case) invite him or her to dine with your team at a good restaurant. This is a good time to have the director go over the storyboard with the celebrity. He or she may not have focused on it until this moment.
- Have a wardrobe check. Your star may have brought appropriate attire. If not, your wardrobe person will go shopping for it. If something is bought for him or her, the star may want to keep it. If it's not a designer original, let him or her.
- Make sure the celebrity knows what time the limo will arrive on the day of the shoot.
- Make sure he or she knows how many hours you'll need him or her.
- Make sure the star knows how many versions he or she will have to do.

- Find out if the celebrity has any special requests for the shoot, such as a certain food or beverage. If possible, accommodate the request.
- Have a stand-in so your star doesn't wilt under the lights.
- Use a hand model for close-ups of product shots.
- Use a TelePrompTer. Don't assume the star will know his or her lines. Some will. Some won't.
- Have a private dressing room the celebrity can go to between takes.
- Have a copywriter and art director ready to quickly revise the storyboard if there's something the star can't or won't say or do.
- If you want souvenir photos, autographs, and the like, try to get them in during breaks in shooting. By the end of the day, the celebrity will be tired and ready to leave.
- Have a limo ready when the shoot is over.
- Celebrities love "freebies" as much as the next person.

Acting Is Reacting

It's important to use a director experienced in getting good performances from celebrities. A talented and experienced director will be able to coax virtually any nonprofessional into giving a believable "talking head" performance. All the director has to do is ask questions and have them give their answer to the camera.

It's another matter entirely to expect amateurs to know how to relate to other performers. Actors study for years to learn how to react to a line in a way that makes it seem as if they're hearing it for the first time and answering it in their own words. When it's not done right, the dialogue sounds leaden and unbelievable. Authors, musicians, stand-up comedians, etc. are *not* actors. Expecting them (and real people as well) to do more than they're capable of can be asking for trouble. Your director may well caution you against an overly ambitious storyboard.

Athletes

Professional athletes generally do well as nonprofessional actors. The qualities that led them to success on the playing field—practicing the same thing over and over and striving for perfection—tend to make them competent commercial performers. Also, after seeing their colleagues in the movies and on TV, many have studied acting.

Celebrity Do's and Don'ts

Unless they created their character, actors do not have the license to portray it in commercials. A sunglasses maker wanted Clayton Moore, the star in "The Lone Ranger" TV series, to be its corporate spokesman. The owners of "The Lone Ranger" objected, saying that Mr. Moore was profiting from their intellectual property. Their argument was, of all the possible actors to choose from, would Clayton Moore have been selected if he hadn't been "That Masked Man."

The lesson is: Be careful. If you hire Christopher Reeve, the star of the *Superman* movies, he can say your product is, "great, wonderful, and the best." But if he says it's "super," you may get a letter from the law firm that represents the producers of *Superman.* For a Northwest Airlines ad, he was a passenger who said, "It's a better way to fly," which was a clever way to capitalize on his fame while avoiding legal problems.

Another thing to avoid is copying the style or likeness of a celebrity. Copying without approval may invite litigation.

> An ad agency wanted to use Bette Midler in a commercial. But they couldn't come to terms and the negotiations broke down. The agency hired a "Bette Midler impersonator" and shot the commercial. Ms. Midler sued and won. The court ruled that Ms. Midler, like any famous performer, has a style that she developed and owns.

Casting Clients

There are two good reasons why clients perform in their own commercials: The first is because they want to be stars. Some clients can be particularly believable, such as Frank Perdue saying, "It takes a tough man to make a tender chicken," and who better to make that statement? Or Victor Kiam, who told us he liked Remington Electric Shavers so much "I bought the company." Or Dave Thomas, the founder of the Wendy's restaurant chain. The list goes on.

The second reason to appear in your own commercial is economics. You don't pay actors when you perform. Of course, this is not a factor for a company the size of Wendy's. But it might be for a start-up. And *you* get paid, which may have tax benefits, especially for entrepreneurs.

The real issue is not losing sight of the big picture. Ask yourself if you are aiding the possible success of your commercial by appearing in it.

Casting Real People

Real people can be particularly believable and will often say things a copywriter would never dream of. Also, you're allowed to *say* they're real people who believe in your product, not paid actors. But be aware of the fact that they represent two thorny problems, finding them and directing them.

Finding Real People

Finding professional actors is easy. Your producer just calls a casting agent. The casting agent calls the actors' agents. The actors' agents call the actors.

Some casting agents cast real people. Some specialize in real people. But the problem always is, whom do they call? Where do they find people who look right, talk right, and will say the right thing about your product?

A good way to find real people is to go where they go. A research company will accost people on the street or in a mall (with permission first, of course) and ask them a few research questions. If they seem like good prospects, they take their picture, or better yet, put them on videotape.

It may take a search of 100 people to find five to seven finalists. Of these, maybe two to three will end up in the commercial. So you should budget extra time and money when casting real people. You should do the same when it comes to shooting them. If you have the budget, you may want to save time and simply employ one of the firms that specializes in finding real people.

Directing Real People

Professional actors are expected to learn their lines. Real people shouldn't have lines, even something they've said. It's best to have a patient, skillful director ask them questions they can answer in their own words. This can be tricky and time consuming, as shown in the following short segment based on an actual transcript. (We've changed the product name.) The real person just said a wonderful line, "My head felt like a big bell, until I took 'Pain-Away' and the pain just went away." Unfortunately, the real person was scratching her nose when she said the line, so the director is trying to get her to repeat it:

DIRECTOR:	Could you say that again?
REAL PERSON:	What?
DIRECTOR:	What you just said.
REAL PERSON:	It hurt until I took the Pain-Away.
DIRECTOR:	You said something about a bell.
REAL PERSON:	Oh, yeah, my head felt like the inside of a bell…like a big church bell on Sunday morning.
DIRECTOR:	And then what happened?
REAL PERSON:	I told you. I took the Pain-Away and I felt better.
DIRECTOR:	OK, good. Tell me the whole thing, about the bell and then what happened.
REAL PERSON:	My head felt like a big bell so I took the medicine and the pain went away.
DIRECTOR:	Good. But you have to say the name of the product.
REAL PERSON:	I took Pain-Away and I feel better.
DIRECTOR:	Fine. Now put it all together ... the bell and the name of the product and how you felt after.
REAL PERSON:	You keep asking me to say the same thing.

One way around this sort of problem is to have your real people say and do only the easiest of things. Keep their lines simple and don't try to get them to react to other people's lines or even to move as they speak.

Hidden Camera

Another way to get a good performance is not to let real people know they're on camera until after the fact. This technique worked well for the "Candid Camera" television show. Use a "hidden camera" and you'll get realistic, off-the-cuff performances that could never be duplicated.

If you go this route, your preproduction will have to be even more detailed than usual, as in this example of a detergent manufacturer whose commercial concept was that women wouldn't switch brands even if bribed to do so.

The commercial went like this: A woman would be leaving a supermarket with her groceries. A man would stop her and say he's doing research. He'd ask if she'd bought detergent. She'd say yes and the man would ask if he could see her brand. He'd offer to exchange it for two boxes of a competing brand. The woman would refuse and the man would up the ante to three boxes. The woman still wouldn't go for it. She'd say something like, "My detergent is so good, it wouldn't matter if you gave me a ton of the other stuff, my family's clothes still wouldn't get as clean." This believable and hard-hitting commercial required a great deal of logistical planning, including:

1. Cooperation from the supermarket.
2. A spotter in the detergent aisle who radioed the description of every woman who bought the brand to the others.
3. A spotter at the checkout who radioed when the right woman was about to leave the store.
4. A production truck parked in the back of the lot where a long lens camera would have a clear view of the front of the store.
5. A second truck where women who said the right thing could be taken to sign a release if they agreed to be in the commercial.

If you're a signatory to the SAG/AFTRA contract, real people must be paid according to the union wage scale. (They don't have to join the union if they just do one commercial, which is what most real people ever do.) You must also get a waiver from the union to use nonunion people. If you're not a signatory, you can pay real people any amount you mutually agree to.

Talent Release Form

Whether you use celebrities or real people, they must sign a talent release form. You must have them do this even if you have a separate contract between parties. (Unless the wording of the talent release form is incorporated in the contract.) We can't overstate the importance of this. Without the signed talent release form, you do *not* have the legal right to air the footage you just shot. Make sure the talent understands that they are required to sign the form and have them do it *before* they leave the set. Figure 19-1 is a sample talent release form.

CHECKLIST: Casting Celebrities, Clients, and "Real People"

	Yes	No
Celebrities chosen?	☐	☐
Negotiations completed?	☐	☐
Timing considered?	☐	☐
Logistics OK?	☐	☐
Intellectual property an issue?	☐	☐
Client to star?	☐	☐
Real people to be used?	☐	☐
Real people found?	☐	☐
Director skilled with real people?	☐	☐
Hidden camera?	☐	☐
Talent Release Form signed?	☐	☐

Figure 19-1. Sample Talent Release Form

TALENT RELEASE FORM

I, ____________ , hereby represent that I appear in and approve a television commercial produced by (AGENCY NAME) on behalf of its client, (CLIENT NAME).

Furthermore, I do hereby irrevocably consent to the audio and/or visual use of my name by (AGENCY NAME) and (CLIENT NAME) and any of their subsidiary and affiliated companies and licensees for the purpose of advertising and trade in the United States and throughout the world in any media.

In the commercial, I make certain statements about (PRODUCT OR SERVICE BRAND NAME AND/OR CLIENT NAME). This will confirm that these statements are true and fair and accurate representations of my personal experience with (PRODUCT OR SERVICE BRAND NAME AND/OR CLIENT NAME).

I waive any inspection or approval of the finished advertisement and I release (AGENCY NAME) and (CLIENT NAME) and any of their subsidiary and affiliated companies and licensees of any liability for any claim of alteration, optical illusion, or faulty mechanical reproduction.

____________________ ____________________

(Signature) (Parent Signature if Minor)

____________________ ____________________

(Please Print Name) (Please Print Parent Name)

____

(Address)

____________________ ____________________

(City) (State) (ZIP)

____________________ ____________________

(Date) (Witness)

20 Production

All the people, equipment, and activity on a set can seem overwhelming. You may not be sure what to do, what to say, even where to sit. But it's important for you to be involved. This chapter will explain who the players are, what happens during shooting, and what your role should be.

The Day of the Shoot

You'll probably be asked to be at a studio or location early in the morning. You may be surprised to learn that other people must be there even earlier. The first call is for the crew, who must set up their equipment and make last-minute lighting adjustments, and for the talent, who must get into wardrobe and have their hair and makeup done. Clients usually arrive an hour or so later.

Don't be afraid to walk around and ask questions. Film production is a fascinating business populated with hardworking, talented, and interesting people. If you're shooting on 35mm with a full crew, it's also exactly the way they make movies in Hollywood. Your commercial is a mini movie.

The Crew

Your first time on a set, your first words will probably be, "Who are all these people?" The answer is, "People you're paying to work for you." You'll see dozens of people you've never seen before, most of them not looking very busy at the moment. You'll start to get an idea of why film production is so expensive, and you'll wonder *why* they're not busy. They're specialists in one craft and when they're not needed they wouldn't know how to help the specialists in another craft. They wouldn't be allowed to either, because they're in different unions. As you'll soon discover, there's a lot of downtime on a set. It's a good idea to know what these different professionals do and why each is essential to your production.

Director of photography. Whether on a set or on location, the D.P. is responsible for the lighting. He or she will create the right look, mood, and feeling for the production. Another name for D.P. is cinematographer.

Camera operator. The person who turns the camera on and off and looks through the lens during filming is the camera operator. In commercials, unlike features, the director or the director of photography sometimes operates the camera.

It takes more than one person to operate a modern motion picture camera. In addition to the operator, two crew members may be required to move the camera on a dolly, while another simultaneously adjusts the focus. Finally, another person changes the film.

Gaffer. This is the term given to the licensed electrician on the set. He or she and the assistants are responsible for all power to the lights, cameras, sound equipment, etc.

Grip. It may be apocryphal, but the story is this term refers to people with strong grips. In any case, it's an accurate description of the job. The members of the grip crew set up the equipment in the morning, move it about during the shoot, and put it away at night.

Sound. If you're shooting on videotape, the sound will be recorded directly onto the tape itself. If you're shooting on film, the sound will be recorded separately and combined with the pictures later on in postproduction. In either case, you'll most likely use a boom person, who holds a microphone on the end of a long pole, and a recording engineer, who listens to every take through earphones.

Script Supervisor. This person is worth his or her weight in gold. He or she will make sure your takes are to time (so you won't wind up with a too-long or too-short commercial) and will make sure you've shot every scene and every variation. (The worst feeling in the world is waking up in the middle of the night after the shoot and realizing you forgot to cover a scene.) At the end of shooting, the supervisor will hand over the script notes to the editor. The script notes will help the editor find the selected scenes within a dozen or more reels of film.

Script notes usually run to many pages. We've reproduced one typical page in figure 20.1. Notice that each scene is indicated, along with the number of each take that was shot for that scene. The timing of each take is noted, along with comments as to what was good or bad about it. The selected takes are indicated with a star and the very good ones with a circled star. Different script supervisors may use different-looking forms and have their own way of keeping notes and indicating selects. For instance, a "NG," "G" and "VG" code.

There shouldn't be anything arcane or esoteric to script notes. They should be easy for anyone with a basic understanding of production terminology to follow. After all, that's why they're done. Still, it's a good idea to chat with the script supervisor to make sure you understand the system and you can decipher the handwriting.

Hair and makeup. Whether you're shooting men or women, you'll want a professional to do their hair and makeup. Don't think your hairdresser or makeup artist can do the job. Theatrical makeup is different from ordinary makeup. Making people look good under stage lights and in front of a camera is not the same as making them look good for normal day or evening situations.

Wardrobe. If your production requires period costumes, or a particular style or look, a wardrobe consultant should acquire them. This person will go shopping and bring back a number of selections to choose from. All but the ones you use will be returned to the store. The wardrobe consultant will also be on the set during the shoot for fittings.

If your shoot only requires normal clothing, you might let the talent bring their own. But some people have strange ideas about fashion. A wardrobe consultant is worth the relatively small extra expense.

Props and models. If you're shooting a normal scene, such as a suburban bedroom or a kitchen, a prop house will rent you everything you need. However, if you require something specialized, you may have to employ a prop maker or a model maker. If you think of these people as artists and their creations as sculpture, you won't be too shocked at what they charge.

> A commercial featured two men debating. As the rhetoric heated up, they started pounding on their podiums. By the end of the commercial, the podiums were destroyed.

Figure 20-1. Script Notes

Script Notes

Date 7/19/94
Job # 7/19/94/101/FP
Prod. Co. XYZ Productions
Title "Fur Is Back"

Page # 1 of 11
Agency BVI
Client Furry Products
Product Fur in a Can

Scene	Take	Timing	Comments	
101	1	5:02	(Estab. shot)	Too long
101	2	4:49	(Estab. shot)	Boom in shot
101	3	3:48	(Estab. shot)	Bad read
101	4	3:36	(Estab. shot)	Bad camera move
101	5	4:02	(Estab. shot)	OK read
101	6	4:15	(Estab. shot)	VG read
101	7	4:27	(Estab. shot)	Bad coat move
101	8	4:09	(Estab. shot)	Exc. take
101	9	4:12	(Estab. shot)	Exc. take
101	10	3:53	(Estab. shot)	So-so
102	11	2:33	(Close-up)	Bad eyes
102	12	2:40	(Close-up)	Bad for sound
102	13	2:25	(Close-up)	VG read
102	14	2:12	(Close-up)	Bad for camera
102	15	2:35	(Close-up)	Exc. take
102	16	2:18	(Close-up)	VG read
102A	17	2:47	(Alt. copy)	Wrong copy
102A	18	2:52	(Alt. copy)	Bad read
102A	19	2:38	(Alt. copy)	Bad read
102A	20	2:35	(Alt. copy)	VG read
102A	21	2:41	(Alt. copy)	Bad eyes
102A	22	2:27	(Alt. copy)	Wrong copy
102A	23	2:39	(Alt. copy)	Exc. take
301	24	3:45	(Dog)	Bad dog move
301	25	3:37	(Dog)	Good dog move
301	26	4:14	(Dog)	Bad for camera
301	27	3:28	(Dog)	VG dog
301	28	3:22		Exc. dog

> A prop maker had to create break-away podiums and sections of podiums. Tops that could be ripped off. Sides that could be punched through. Everything had to look real, match up perfectly, and be perfectly safe to hit. In addition, each complete podium and each breakaway section had to have a backup.
>
> The prop maker and his assistant worked on the props for days before the shoot. They continued to work on them—gluing, ungluing, screwing, unscrewing—during the entire two-day shoot.

None of this comes cheap. This job ran into many thousands of dollars. So before you create a commercial built around props or models, be aware of what you're getting into. Does the concept live or die without it?

Food stylist. If you're shooting food, you'll need a food stylist. Preparing food to look good under lights and on film is a very specialized occupation. It's not the same thing as preparing food to eat. When you see what a food stylist does to make food look good, you won't want to eat it. There are many tricks to the trade. Don't have an ordinary chef attempt it.

Caterer. Everyone on a shoot, yourself included, is under intense pressure to do the best job in the limited number of hours available. Meals help to lessen the pressure and keep up the energy. Catering services that specialize in film production help make everyone feel nourished and content and that will go a long way toward helping your shoot go smoothly.

Craft unions have very precise schedules as to how many hours their members may work between meals. You don't want to violate these rules and incur "meal penalties." Follow your producer's advice to the letter. At the end of the shooting day, if you're running late and into overtime, it may be better to keep rolling and incur a meal penalty. Again, follow the advice of your producer.

On a union shoot, the crew always goes through the lunch line first. This is because the crew gets a certain amount of time for lunch, usually 1 hour. But the clock doesn't start ticking until the first crew member goes through the line. So if the crew has to wait 15 minutes for the client and agency people to go through the line, the 1 hour lunch break actually takes 1 hour and 15 minutes.

Animal trainer. If your commercial requires an animal, engage the services of a professional trainer. Don't think this is your chance to make Fido or Fluffy a star. Even if they're a good dog or cat, they're not accustomed to doing the same trick 20 or 30 times in a row. And they're certainly not accustomed to the commotion on a shooting set.

A trainer will usually have a backup animal, in case the first one isn't in good form that day. They'll look identical, so if the standby has to take over halfway through shooting, the viewer won't notice the difference.

Production assistants. Production assistants run errands. They're basically messengers, and their pay scale reflects it. They're trying to break into film work and are happy to just be on a set, gaining experience and making contacts. A production assistant is often called a PA.

The Actual Shoot

Video Playback

You'll probably be asked to sit with the agency team in front of a video-playback monitor. This is nothing more than a VCR that records each scene and lets you see it again on a television set.

Video playback is a great help in choosing takes, but it has its limitations. Whites appear too bright, and lights burn out the scene altogether. Darks appear totally black, and gray tones are lost altogether. So don't try to judge lighting or picture quality from the video playback. For that, you'll want to take a look through the camera lens and, after that, rely on the director of photography and the art director.

TelePrompTer

Actors are trained professionals. They should learn their lines. But real people, including celebrities, may not be able to. You can help them by having a large cue card just to one side of the camera. But then the viewer will see their eyes move as they read the cue card. A TelePrompTer is a better solution. This is the brand name of a device that projects the lines onto the camera lens without the lines themselves being filmed. The performer can read the lines while looking directly into the camera.

Setting up the Scene

For each scene, your director will probably follow these steps:

1. Lighting the scene;
2. Blocking out the performer's movement;
3. Camera angle and movement;
4. Reading the lines;
5. Refining the performance; and
6. Covering alternate angles.

Say it's the first scene of Fur in a Can, where the wife pirouettes to show off her new fur coat and her husband says, "You look stunning, but how can we afford it on our budget?"

While the director is rehearsing the actress, the actor might be getting the lines wrong and saying something like, "You look stunning, but can we afford it?" Your impulse might be to jump in and correct him. Resist that impulse! Give the director and the actress time to block out the physical movement of showing off the coat. Then the director will help the actor get the lines right, start them at precisely the right point in the pirouette, and, finally, put the emphasis where it belongs, on the words "stunning" and "budget." It might require 10, 20, or more takes to get everything to come together perfectly. But all you need is *one* good take.

A scene starts with the director or assistant director saying, "Roll sound," then, "Roll camera." This is the signal for the sound engineer and camera operator to turn on their equipment. When it is at the proper speed, in a second or so, they will call out "Speed!" Now the director will say, "Slate."

The Slate

A slate is a piece of board or plastic about 9 inches high and 12 inches wide. On it are written the names of the producer and director, the title of the commercial, the date, the reel number, the scene number, and take number.

Someone, usually the assistant camera person, holds the slate in front of the camera for a few seconds at the start of each take. This helps the editor locate individual takes later on.

In film, the slate has another function. Along the top of it is a piece of wood. It's hinged to one end of the slate so it can swing up like a little door. The slate person lifts up the piece of wood and then claps it down, making a sharp sound.

Now there's a visual and an audio cue at the start of each take. Because pictures and sound are recorded separately, this cue is essential for the editor to synchronize the take.

Nowadays, slates are likely to be electronic and connected to the camera and audio recorder. The slates generate time code numbers that conform to standards established by the Society of Motion Picture and Television Engineers (SMPTE). The SMPTE time code is recorded on both the frame and the soundtrack. Electronic bleeps have replaced clap sticks.

Action

After the slate has been removed, the director will call "Action," and the scene will be shot. At the end of the take, the director will call "Cut."

The director will ask the sound engineer and the camera operator if the scene was "good for them." The director will tell their comments, along with his or hers, to the script supervisor.

If the director thinks the take is a good one, he or she will ask to see it again on video playback. Video playback is also helpful for seeing what's wrong with a scene. We've had success letting actors look at their takes so they can see for themselves how to refine their performances.

Watch out for eating up too much time trying to get each scene to be a masterpiece. There's a lot to accomplish in the budgeted time. At some point, the director is going to have to move on to the next scene. A good producer will help determine when the point of diminishing returns has been reached on a scene.

Set Etiquette

If you have a question, comment, or concern, talk to the agency account person or the producer. Resist the urge to talk directly to the director and the talent. Too many instructions coming from too many people may be confusing.

When you make a suggestion and it's relayed to the director, don't expect it to be implemented in the very next take. The director may be working out some other detail first and not want to confuse the talent by asking them to do too much at once.

Only three people can cut a scene: the director, the camera operator, and the sound engineer. If you see something wrong with a take, your instinct may be to yell out "Cut." Don't! There will be an opportunity to do the take again. And the director may have another reason to keep rolling, possibly because the actor is getting into a rhythm.

Camera Framing for Supers

Make sure your camera framing allows enough room at the bottom of the screen for your supers. You don't want live matter competing for attention with your supers. Don't cover your product with supers or make your supers (especially the phone number) impossible to read. Figure 20-2, from the Fur in a Can storyboard, shows the right and wrong ways to do it.

"Cheating" for Changes

Don't have an actor say your price while he or she is facing the camera. If you want to change your price later, you'll have trouble synchronizing the

Figure 20-2. Right and Wrong Way to Frame for Supers

RIGHT

1 800 123 4567

WRONG

1 800 123 4567

Figure 20-3. "Cheating" for Changes

RIGHT	**WRONG**

Anncr: (VO) It's only $29.95.

Anncr: It's only $29.95

words with the lip movements. Instead, say the price (and anything else subject to change) as a voiceover, or "cheat" the scene with the speaker looking away from the camera (see Figure 20-3).

Finally, every scene will be covered to everyone's satisfaction. The director will end the shoot the way we end this chapter, by saying "It's a wrap."

CHECKLIST: Production

	Yes	No
Checked script supervisor?	☐	☐
Scene lit properly?	☐	☐
Camera angle & movement blocked out?	☐	☐
Lines read correctly?	☐	☐
Performance refined?	☐	☐
Alternate angles covered?	☐	☐
Storyboard covered	☐	☐
Shooting board covered?	☐	☐
Shooting matrix covered?	☐	☐
Framing for supers?	☐	☐
"Cheating" for changes?	☐	☐
Set etiquette followed?	☐	☐

Postproduction

You may think that after the shoot, most of the work is finished. But in reality, all the shoot did was give you the raw material from which to create the commercial. Think of sculpture. The shoot gave you the clay. Now you must mold it, crudely at first, then more precisely, adding here, trimming there, until the creation is complete. This chapter will take you through the process.

The Rough Cut

Immediately after the shoot, the creative team will do an off-line edit. In a few days, they will show you a rough cut of the spot. A rough cut is, as the name implies, a first assembly of the scenes. The picture quality will be less than perfect. Fades, dissolves, titles, and supers won't look quite right. There won't be any music, and the announcer voiceover lines will probably be read by the producer or the copywriter.

There's one thing you should concern yourself with in approving a rough cut, and that's if the best scenes have been chosen. If you feel a certain scene or scenes are not as strong as they could be, ask to see alternates.

Time Code

In the last chapter, we saw how electronic slates create a visual time code on the film. A time code can also be created after the fact and is then called a burn in or a window dub. The time code makes it much easier for everyone to keep track of scenes during the editing process. So when you look at the rough cut, expect to see these time code numbers at the bottom of the screen. Of course, they will be gone when the spot airs.

The time code consists of a series of eight numbers that are arranged in four groups of two. They look like this—**00 00 00 00**—and they work like the numbers on an automobile odometer. The numbers on the left hardly move at all while the ones on the right spin constantly.

Going from left to right, the first two numbers count hours. The second two count minutes. The third two count seconds. The final two—the ones at the right—count individual frames. Because there are 30 frames in each second of videotape, these frame counters only go up to 29. Then the seconds counter ticks off 1 second and the frame counter goes back to zero. It's difficult to see this when the tape is moving at normal speed but when it's slowed down it's easy to follow and understand. The example in Figure 21-1 shows an elapsed time of 1 minute, 17 seconds, and 12 frames.

Film-to-Tape Transfer

After you've approved the rough cut, the agency can finish the commercial. But if you shot on film, the next step is the film-to-tape transfer. This is where the selected scenes are transferred from film to videotape. At this point, the art director and producer will adjust the color and lighting balance between scenes. The procedure is slow and time consuming. Clients usually never attend.

Figure 21-1. Scene with Time Code

Recording and Mixing

The recording and mixing sessions are worthy of your time. Recording is, as the name implies, the recording of announcer copy. Because this is the real "sell" portion of the commercial, it's essential that it be perfect. The mix is where all the sound elements—voices, music, and sound effects—are mixed together and the levels equalized so that the final audio track is clear and easy to understand.

The mixing is done with large, high-fidelity speakers called studio monitors. This lets the sound engineer hear every word, sound, and musical note. But this isn't how the commercial will sound on a normal television set. So recording studios have a low-fidelity small speaker that approximates the quality of a loudspeaker on a TV set. The human voices will sound about the same. But the high and low music notes will be cut off. So music that seemed too loud on the large speakers may sound perfectly balanced with the voice track on the small speaker.

Music

You'll also want to be involved in the approval of the music for the spot. And it's virtually certain that you'll use music. While 30-second image commercials often do not, a 2-minute spot is usually helped by it. Music brings the spot to life, gives it velocity, and weaves a thread that ties the scenes together. Depending on your needs and your budget, you'll use published music, original music, or stock music.

Published Music

This is music the public knows. It could be classical, rock, or whatever works for your commercial. The more famous the composer or the selection, the more it will cost. Some music is not for sale at any price. Ask yourself if the concept of the commercial requires published music.

If you decide to use a prerecorded version of a famous composition, you must pay two fees: one for rights to use the composition, and a second for rights to the performance. If you have the sheet music recorded, you must pay the composer and the musicians you use, as well as the studio. If it is in the public domain, you must still pay the musicians.

Sometimes one person will own all rights to a particular composition.

> When a news magazine wanted to use "Turn, Turn, Turn" for a direct response (DR) commercial, it had to negotiate with the composer, Pete Seeger. He had all rights, including the performance by "The Byrds," which was the one the magazine wanted to use.

Original Music

There are two ways to buy original music. The first is to pick three composers and pay them each a fee for creating a demo. You will probably listen to the demos in the composers' mini studios. The composer who wins is paid an additional fee, previously agreed on, to finish the piece. This will be done in a fully-equipped studio. The demo may be used as the basis for the finished composition, as additional tracks are added. Usually these will be synthesized, however, a live musician may lay down a track if necessary.

A less-expensive way to buy original music is to choose one musician and work out a deal with him or her to create a demo or demos and finish the composition.

Stock Music

Stock music is music for which you pay neither rights nor musician fees. You select the composition you want by listening to selections in a stock music library, and record directly from the CD or DAT you select.

You are charged for stock music by the "needle drop." The phrase dates back to when recordings were played on phonographs with needles. Paying by the needle drop means that you are charged every time a piece of music is begun. So if you picked out a particular piece and used it in its entirety, you'd pay for one needle drop. However, if you opted to use various sections of that piece (or other selections, of course) you'd be charged every time the "needle dropped" in a new place.

Stock music is never exactly what you want. By its nature, it's a compromise. It may not start or end right for your commercial. It may not hit on the cuts. It may sound vaguely like something you've heard before. Still, if budget is a major concern, it's better than no music. With skillful editing, it can be made to fit the picture.

Final Conform

The last step in postproduction is the final conform, titling and special effects, such as dissolves, wipes, etc. The conform is where the rough cut, which was most likely done on disk or ¾-inch videotape, is used as the blueprint for transferring and assembling the original footage onto the 1-inch videotape that will be released to the TV stations. This is known as the on-line edit and, per hour, costs much more than off-line editing. So you want to be sure the commercial is exactly the way it's supposed to be before you begin on-line editing. This is also your last opportunity to see the commercial before it goes on air, so you'll certainly want to sign off on this step.

Supers

Supers can be set as typography, or generated electronically. They should all be in the same easy-to-read typeface. A few of the many to choose from include: Antique Olive, Avant Garde, Avenir, Bookman, Folio, Franklin Gothic, Futura, Garamond, Goudy, Helvetica, Korinna, News Gothic, Optima, Sabon, Times, Trade Gothic, or Univers. Avoid italics and obliques, as well as going too light, too bold, too condensed, or too expanded. It may help the legibility of the supers, particularly if the background is confusing, if a little drop shadow is added to them.

The most important thing to keep in mind is that the voice of the typeface—the way it speaks its words—is in keeping with the concept of the commercial. Notice the different voices of the typefaces below.

Make sure that all the mandatory supers are included in the spot, that they're large enough to see, in keeping with the concept, tone, and manner of the commercial, and on screen long enough to read.

Figure 21.2 Sample Typefaces

Bookman conveys the stability appropriate for financial services

Avant Garde might work well for a more informal product

Times is easy to read and does not take up much space

Any legal supers that you are required to show should be as small as you are allowed to make them and stay on only long enough to be read. Supers that help you sell—such words as "Free," "Guaranteed," "Special Offer" and so on—should be shown large and often. The most important super in any DR commercial is the 800 number and it should be large enough to be read 10 to 15 feet away from the screen.

In a 2-minute commercial the phone number should be on at least 45 seconds. This will give the viewer time to jot it down, or better yet, call while the spot is still on the air. The 45 seconds should come at the end of the commercial. In a 1-minute spot, try to show the phone number for at least 30 seconds.

Masters

When the commercial is assembled it will have everything it needs to go on air, except supers. This version is called the generic master. The generic master will be used to make a second-generation copy called the titled generic. The third-generation copy will include the phone numbers. This is the version that goes on air.

It may seem that working this way makes things three times as complicated. Actually, it's the quickest way to do the job. Instead of having to master each phone number version, the commercial is done once. Then it's relatively easy to create the titled generic and each phone version. Also, it makes it easy if it becomes necessary to change the generic master later on.

Things can get a bit tricky if, in addition to the phone numbers, other versions of the commercial are necessary. For instance, if two prices are being tested, it will be necessary to create two titled generics. It's important for the producer to make sure the editor knows exactly what has to be done and that they figure out the most efficient way to do it *before* the clock starts ticking in the on-line suite. An editing matrix, similar to a shooting matrix, may be helpful.

Bars and Slates

The editor will lay down 60 seconds of color bars before the start of each version. These bars are standard in the industry and will help the technicians at the station balance the colors on the commercial to their equipment.

After the bars, each version of the commercial gets a slate. This is not at all like the slate we talked about in the chapter on production. The purpose of this slate is so that TV stations can identify the commercial. The slate goes on before the opening of the spot. These days it's usually generated electronically. The slate will include the names of the editing company, the ad agency, and the client and product. It will list the name of the commercial, the length, the 800 number and the commercial code number. These last two will come from the media department. This information will also go on the outside of the box that holds each commercial. Make sure that each 800 number on the screen matches the number on the slate and on the box and that the commercial code numbers match as well.

The slate will also count down in cadence, in video and audio, from "10" to "2." This is to allow the technician in the TV station to start the spot at exactly the right moment. If he or she hits the "start" button at "2," the commercial will fade up right on cue, at the missing "0" mark.

Copyright

The copyright symbol—©, followed by the year and your corporate name on the slate are all you need to afford your commercial legal protection.

Dubbing and Shipping

For testing purposes, it's easiest to have the editing facility make the eight or so dubs of the finished commercials that will be sent to the stations or cable networks. However, if you require many dubs, it will probably cost you less to have a tape duplication house do it. Make sure you include clear instructions for shipping the right commercial to the right station. The agency and you will also want an omnibus reel that contains all the spots. This can be made in any format you desire.

Earlier we said that one of the advantages of digital is that unlimited copies of copies can be made with no degradation of the signal. Theoretically, that is not true of the analog 1-inch format. In actuality, going from the original camera material to the generic master to the titled generic to the 800 number version to a dupe presents no appreciable loss of quality. One-inch videotape is so good that quite a few more generations could be made before you would notice any deterioration of the video or audio.

CHECKLIST: Postproduction

	Yes	No
Off-line rough cut OK?	☐	☐
Film-to-tape transfer done?	☐	☐
Published music?	☐	☐
Original music?	☐	☐
Stock music?	☐	☐
Recording and mixing OK?	☐	☐
On-line edit and conform done?	☐	☐
All supers included?	☐	☐
Appropriate/legible typeface?	☐	☐
Phone number on long enough?	☐	☐
Bars & slates done?	☐	☐
Commercial code numbers OK?	☐	☐
Copyright done?	☐	☐
Clear dubbing instructions?	☐	☐
Clear shipping instructions	☐	☐
Omnibus reel?	☐	☐

22 Next Steps

Now that you've finished the book, we suggest you refer to it again as you move ahead with your direct response (DR) television project. Certainly look at the chapter checklists along the way.

If you're ready to choose your marketing partners, the list of "Associations and Organizations" (Appendix B) will point you in the right direction. If you want to learn more, refer to "Recommended Reading" (Appendix A). If you're unclear about any words in this book, just look them up in the "Glossary." And turn to the "Index" to find any particular subject.

Timing

If you follow every step in this book, the cameras won't start rolling for about 6 months to a year after you first consider selling on TV. That's how long it will take to do all the research and testing that will point you in the right direction. Only you can decide if that's too long. You don't want to be in the middle of a test while your competition is selling products on the air.

The only thing worse than doing too much development, research, and testing is doing too little, or none at all. How many strategies? How many concepts? How much testing? After 2 to 3 years of learning and success, you may feel confident enough to skip some steps. In marketing, as in war, somewhere between caution and recklessness is where you will find success.

Even if you've already settled on a product and a strategy, a full production schedule (see Figure 22-1) shows why it can take 6 months more before you're on TV. Even an abbreviated schedule, which might be adequate for a small-scale production, can take months (see Figure 22-2).

Figure 22-1

Full Production Schedule

Date	Action
Week 1	Client review of strategies
Week 2	Generate concepts
Week 3	Generate concepts
Week 4	Present concepts and revise if necessary
Week 5	Present final concepts
Week 6	Create storyboards
Week 7	Create storyboards
Week 8	Present storyboards and revise if necessary
Week 9	Revise storyboards
Week 10	Present final storyboards
Week 11	Produce animatics
Week 12	Produce animatics
Week 13	Produce animatics
Week 14	Research animatics
Week 15	Research animatics
Week 16	Pick final spot and revise based on test
Week 17	Preproduction
Week 18	Preproduction
Week 19	Preproduction
Week 20	Production
Week 21	Production
Week 22	Postproduction
Week 23	Postproduction
Week 24	Dub and ship
Week 25	On-air test
Week 26	On-air test
Week 27	Rollout

Figure 22-2

Abbreviated Production Schedule

Date	Action
Week 1	Client review of strategies
Week 2	Generate concepts
Week 3	Present final concepts
Week 4	Create storyboards
Week 5	Present final storyboards
Week 6	Preproduction
Week 7	Preproduction
Week 8	Production
Week 9	Postproduction
Week 10	Postproduction
Week 11	Dub and ship
Week 12	On-air test
Week 13	On-air test
Week 14	Rollout

Shooting on a Shoestring

Suppose you don't have the budget to do anything we recommend in this book? Say you have a product and just a few thousand dollars to invest in marketing it. You can't afford agency fees, focus groups, storyboards, directors—none of that.

We think you should find out if your product shows promise. If so, you may be able to interest banks or venture capitalists in backing you. Of all the options we discussed in Chapter 6, in the case of a minimal budget we recommend working with a local TV station. Have them help you create a simple commercial, shoot it, edit it, and *run* it. Now you'll have a record of results that you can show to potential investors.

The station will want to get paid, of course, but the key to keeping your out-of-pocket costs down is to share a percentage of the back end with them. The deal they're willing to cut with you will depend on how much potential *they* see in your product. There's not much risk to the station. They can do the project during downtime and air the commercial when they have nothing else to run. So the only out-of-pocket cost to you will be the talent—unless you act in your own commercial. (If you need a voiceover announcer, the station will be able to recommend someone.)

Still, you won't be the first person to suggest a back-end arrangement to them. So you'll have to show belief in your venture and have covered the business details. One of the most important is, where will the orders go and who will keep track of them.

You may think they can go to you. (You can have 800 number service in your home or business for as little as $50 a month.) But the station probably won't trust your record keeping and neither will a bank when you ask them for a loan based on results.

The station probably won't be equipped to handle the calls either. But they should be able to recommend a telemarketing company. Having an independent everyone trusts is worth every penny it'll cost you. Make sure the telemarketing company can also handle fulfillment and you'll have covered all the bases.

To keep costs low, negotiate with the telemarketing company. Let them know you're small and just starting out. Maybe they'll go for a partnership deal if they think your product has great potential. There are no rules. Everything is negotiable. And everyone wants to be in on the ground floor of the next big success story. (Be careful of giving away too many shares to too many people. There may not be enough of a profit margin left to make the project viable to you, let alone the bankers or investors who will want their share.)

In the end, if you have a product you want to sell on TV, but little or no money to do it, you're going to have to be persistent and you're going to have to be creative. But being persistent and creative is what business is all about, isn't it?

Good luck and good fortune.

Recommended Reading

Books

Advertising, Pure & Simple, Hank Seiden, AMACOM, NY
Eicoff on Broadcast Direct Marketing, Al Eicoff, NTC Business Books, IL
Direct Marketing Handbook, Ed Nash, McGraw-Hill, NY
Direct Marketing Success, Freeman F. Gosden, Jr., Wiley, NY
Ogilvy on Advertising, David Ogilvy, Vintage Books, NY
Positioning, Al Ries and Jack Trout, McGraw-Hill, NY
Profitable Direct Marketing, Jim Kobs, NTC Business Books, IL
Reality in Advertising, Rosser Reeves, Alfred Knopf, NY
Response Television, John Witek, NTC Business Books, IL
Scientific Advertising, Claude Hopkins, NTC Business Books, IL
Successful Direct Marketing Methods, Bob Stone, NTC Business Books, IL
Winning Direct Response, Joan Throckmorton, Prentice-Hall, NY

Directories & References

Broadcasting & Cable Market Place, R.R. Bowker Company, NJ. Published annually

The Direct Marketing Market Place, National Register Publishing Co., Wilmette IL. Published annually

Spot Television Rates and Data, Standard Rate & Data Service, Wilmette, IL. Published monthly

Standard Directory of Advertisers, The National Register Publishing Co., Wilmette, IL. Published annually

Standard Directory of Advertising Agencies, The National Register Publishing Co., Wilmette, IL. Published three times a year

Television & Cable Factbook, Warren Publishing Inc., Washington, DC. Published annually

Periodicals

Advertising Age, Crain Communications, Chicago, IL

ADWEEK, A/S/M Communications Inc., NY

ADWEEK'S Marketing Week, A/S/M Communications Inc., NY

ADWEEK'S Media Week, A/S/M Communications Inc., NY

Broadcasting, Cahners Publishing Co., Washington, DC

Direct, Cowles Business Media Inc., CT

Direct Marketing, Hoke Communications Inc. NJ

DM News, Mill Hollow Corp., NY

Electronic Media, Crain Communications, Chicago, IL

Inside Media, Cowles Business Media Inc., NY

Millimeter, Penton Publishing, Cleveland, OH.

Mix, Act III Publishing Inc. Emeryville, CA

Telemarketing, Technology Marketing Corp., CT

Associations and Organizations

American Association of Advertising Agencies (AAAA)
666 Third Avenue
New York, NY 10017

Association of Independent Commercial Producers (AICP)
136 West 21st Street
New York, NY 10011

Direct Marketing Association (DMA)
6 East 43rd Street
New York, NY 10017

National Infomercial Marketing Association (NIMA)
1201 New York Ave., NW
Washington, DC 20005

Pro Forma Client-Agency Contract

This Agreement is dated effective [DATE], by and between [AGENCY NAME], with offices at [AGENCY ADDRESS], and [CLIENT NAME], with offices at [CLIENT ADDRESS].

RECITALS

[CLIENT NAME] has contacted [AGENCY NAME] for the purpose of having [AGENCY NAME] create advertising. [AGENCY NAME] agrees to perform these services upon the terms and conditions of this Agreement.

NOW, THEREFORE, the parties hereto agree as follows:

1. SERVICES TO BE RENDERED BY [AGENCY NAME].

1.1 [AGENCY NAME] agrees to write, art direct, and produce direct response television advertising as required by [CLIENT NAME].

1.2 [AGENCY NAME] agrees to follow through the usual steps in producing the advertising, including reasonable client revisions to the script, preproduction, production, and postproduction, to a completed master tape. This includes the supervision of: casting, location scouting and selection, and/or set design and construction, props, hair, wardrobe, makeup, music, sound effects, rehearsals, lighting, shooting, film-to-tape transfer, off-line editing, on-line editing, titling, recording, final mix, final conform, and any and all other usual and necessary production requirements.

1.3 [AGENCY NAME] agrees to finish the commercials(s) in :120 and :60 lengths, and with all required alternate versions.

2. SERVICES TO BE RENDERED BY [CLIENT NAME].

2.1 [CLIENT NAME] agrees to pay all costs for production of the commercial(s), including outside suppliers and vendors, including rental of equipment, rental of studios, location fees, props, talent, etc., applicable taxes, storage fees, shipment of materials, and any and all of the usual or necessary expenses for work of this nature.

2.2 [CLIENT NAME] agrees to pay any sales tax associated with the creation, production, shipping, or storing of the commercial(s).

2.3 [CLIENT NAME] agrees to allow [AGENCY NAME] to exhibit the advertising in the pursuit of new business and to enter and exhibit it in advertising awards competitions.

3. PROPRIETARY RIGHTS OF [CLIENT NAME].

3.1 The final advertising will be the property of [CLIENT NAME].

3.2 Any research, data, reports, documents, databases, mailing lists, and other learning and information shall likewise be the property of [CLIENT NAME].

3.3 [AGENCY NAME] shall not use for its own benefit, or disclose to third parties, any data, no matter how obtained, that is in [AGENCY NAME]'s possession as a result of its performance of this Agreement, without [CLIENT NAME]'s prior express written permission unless the same is in the public domain.

4. CONFIDENTIALITY.

4.1 [CLIENT NAME] and [AGENCY NAME] each recognize, acknowledge, and agree that Confidential Information of each may be disclosed to the other in the course of performance under this Agreement. Each party agrees that the Confidential Information of the other shall be held and maintained in utmost confidence and trust as set forth herein. Each party covenants and agrees that it, its employees, and agents shall not, directly or indirectly, use, disclose, or exploit the Confidential Information of the other, except as authorized in writing by the owner of the Confidential Information or except as is necessary to perform under this Agreement. Each party agrees to allow access to Confidential Information on a "need to know" basis only.

4.2 Each party shall take all measures necessary, and as may be reasonably required, to carry out its obligations under this Section 4.

4.3 "Confidential Information" is information disclosed to [AGENCY NAME] by [CLIENT NAME], or to [CLIENT NAME] by [AGENCY NAME], or known to either party as a consequence of their association with each other about the other party's systems, customers, and business practices and affairs, including without limitation information relating to a party's plans, procedures, products, processes and services, pricing, marketing, and selling practices. Confidential Information does not include information that is publicly disclosed by the owing party, or rightfully received from a third party.

4.4 Confidential Information disclosed hereunder shall remain the property of the disclosing party. No license under any patent, copyright, trademark, or trade secret is granted nor implied.

4.5 Each party upon the termination of this Agreement, or at such earlier time as the other party may require, shall return all copies or tangible records of Confidential Information of the other party, or shall destroy all such copies of tangible records, if so requested. The party who initiates the termination shall pay for the costs incurred as a result of the above.

4.6 Each party hereto understands and agrees that in the event of a breach by that party of its representations or obligations with respect to the Confidential Information of the other party, irreparable harm will be caused and that monetary damages will not be an adequate measure of the harm suffered by the other party, and, in addition to such damages or legal remedies that the other party may have, the other party shall be entitled to obtain an injunction or other equitable relief against such party in any court of competent jurisdiction.

4.7 The representations and obligations of this section shall survive the termination of this Agreement.

5. REPRESENTATIONS AND WAIVER.

This Agreement contains the sole understanding between the parties hereto and shall not be modified except in writing. No waiver by either party or any breach of this Agreement by the other shall be deemed to be a waiver of any preceding or subsequent breach thereof.

6. INDEMNIFICATION.

6.1 [CLIENT NAME] shall indemnify and hold [AGENCY NAME] harmless and defend against:

a. Any and all claims, liabilities, and damages arising from the creation, use, presentation, broadcast, distribution, and publication of any advertising created by [AGENCY NAME], which is used, presented, distributed, or aired in accordance with the marketing programs of [CLIENT NAME].

b. Any and all claims, liabilities, and damages caused by the negligence of [CLIENT NAME], its partners, agents, or employees.

c. Any and all claims by government agencies relating to the creation, use, presentation, broadcast, distribution, and publication of the advertising.

d. Substantiation for all statements of fact, promises, superlatives, and competitive advantages made in the advertising.

e. Notwithstanding anything to the contrary in subsection 6.1a, b, c, and d, [CLIENT NAME] shall not be required to indemnify [AGENCY NAME] for or against any claims, liabilities, and damages arising out of any wrongful act or omissions of [AGENCY NAME], its principals, agents, vendors, suppliers, talent, employees, successors, or assigns, or which do not arise out of [CLIENT NAME]'s obligations under this Agreement.

6.2 [AGENCY NAME] shall indemnify and hold [CLIENT NAME] harmless and defend against:

a. Any and all claims, liabilities, and damages caused by the negligence of [AGENCY NAME], its partners, employees, or clients.

b. Notwithstanding anything to the contrary in subsection 6.2a, [AGENCY NAME] shall not be required to indemnify [CLIENT NAME] for or against any claims, liabilities, and damages arising out of any wrongful act or omissions of [CLIENT NAME], its principals, agents, vendors, suppliers, talent, employees, successors, or assigns, or which do not arise out of [AGENCY NAME]'s obligations under this Agreement.

7. **INDEPENDENT CONTRACTOR.** [AGENCY NAME] shall act as an independent contractor and not as an agent of [CLIENT NAME]. [AGENCY NAME] shall have no authority to act on behalf of [CLIENT NAME] or to bind [CLIENT NAME] in any way whatsoever.

8. **COMPENSATION TO BE PAID BY [CLIENT NAME] TO [AGENCY NAME].**

8.1 [CLIENT NAME] agrees to pay 50% of the total production estimate at the signing of this contract.

8.2 [CLIENT NAME] agrees to pay the remaining 50% of the total production estimate upon the delivery of the master tapes.

8.3 [AGENCY NAME] will supply [CLIENT NAME] with actual costs within ten (10) working days of the completion of the project and [AGENCY NAME] and [CLIENT NAME] mutually agree to a final reconciliation of costs, with each party agreeing to reimburse the other within thirty (30) days.

8.4 [CLIENT NAME] agrees to reimburse [AGENCY NAME] for all actual reasonable travel, meal, and lodging expenses incurred and documented for any trips required to service [CLIENT NAME] business, or reasonably complete a project.

8.5 Transportation costs to be reimbursed include air, train, bus, taxi, or car, and gasoline, tolls, tips, and parking fees. The actual cost under car rental agreements shall be reimbursed.

8.6 [CLIENT NAME] will reimburse [AGENCY NAME] for meals paid for by [AGENCY NAME] personnel, if incurred in connection with the performance of services under this Agreement, as well as lodging.

8.7 Business telephone calls made in connection with services performed for [CLIENT NAME] will be reimbursed.

8.8 For trips that extend beyond four (4) days, reasonable valet and laundry charges will be reimbursed.

8.9 [AGENCY NAME] will provide appropriate documentation of the expense incurred on behalf of [CLIENT NAME] when requesting payment and reimbursement.

8.10 [CLIENT NAME] will not reimburse [AGENCY NAME] for personal expenses incurred by [AGENCY NAME] personnel. If expenses of a personal nature (i.e., hotel shop purchases, sundry items, etc.) are charged against the room, the amount will be deducted from the invoice submitted to [CLIENT NAME].

8.11 [CLIENT NAME] agrees to compensate [AGENCY NAME] for services rendered in Section 1, at the rate of 17.65% markup of all production costs, 50% to be paid at the signing of this contract, with the balance to be paid upon delivery of the master tapes.

(-or-)

8.11 [CLIENT NAME] agrees to compensate [AGENCY NAME] for services rendered in Section 1, at a flat fee of [$$$$$], 50% to be paid at the signing of this contract, with the balance to be paid upon delivery of the master tapes.

(-or-)

8.11 [CLIENT NAME] agrees to compensate [AGENCY NAME] for services rendered in Section 1, according to actual hours spent by

[AGENCY NAME], at an hourly rate of [$$$] per person involved. [AGENCY NAME] agrees to submit weekly time reports and [CLIENT NAME] agrees to pay [AGENCY NAME] within thirty (30) days of receipt of same.

(and if applicable)

8.12 [AGENCY NAME] will plan, buy, and analyze media for [CLIENT NAME]. [AGENCY NAME] will receive the standard and customary 15% rebate from the broadcasters, television stations, and/or cable networks.

(-or-)

8.12 [AGENCY NAME] will plan, buy, and analyze media for [CLIENT NAME]. For performing these services, [AGENCY NAME] will receive from [CLIENT NAME] a flat fee of [$$$$$] per month.

(-or-)

8.12 [AGENCY NAME] will plan, buy and analyze media for [CLIENT NAME]. For performing these services, [AGENCY NAME] will be compensated by [CLIENT NAME] at an hourly rate of [$$$] per person involved. [AGENCY NAME] agrees to submit weekly time reports and [CLIENT NAME] agrees to pay [AGENCY NAME] within thirty (30) days of receipt of same.

9. TERM AND TERMINATION.

9.1 The term of this Agreement shall be for one (1) year commencing on the date set above. After one (1) year, the Agreement shall continue to remain in force indefinitely thereafter until either party terminates this Agreement upon ninety (90) days advance written notice to the other party of intent to terminate.

9.2 Upon notification by either party, [AGENCY NAME] shall, within five (5) business days of [CLIENT NAME]'s request, and at [CLIENT NAME]'s expense, deliver any information or material in which [CLIENT NAME] has proprietary rights and which is in the possession of [AGENCY NAME], to [CLIENT NAME] or to a third party as specified by [CLIENT NAME].

9.3 [CLIENT NAME] can elect to terminate this Agreement by written notice to [AGENCY NAME] if [AGENCY NAME] shall make an assignment for the benefit of creditors or file a voluntary petition in bankruptcy or to be adjudicated a bankrupt or insolvent or shall admit in writing its inabilities to meet its obligations as they mature, or if a permanent receiver for all or any portion of the property of either of the foregoing parties shall be appointed in any judicial proceeding or there shall be entered against it an order adjudicating it bankrupt or insolvent or an order appointing a liquidator, receiver, or trustee for it or all or substantially all of its assets or approving as property filed against it a petition seeking reorganization, arrangement, or other proceeding under any bankruptcy or other law for the relief of debtors, which order shall continue unstayed and in effect for, or which proceedings shall not be terminated and [AGENCY NAME] released from such proceeding, within thirty (30) days or if [AGENCY NAME] shall attempt to assign or encumber this Agreement or permit any other person, firm, or corporation to conduct the business or services provided for here.

9.4 In the event [CLIENT NAME] exercises its right of termination herein in Section 9, [AGENCY NAME] shall (i) upon the effective date of termination, terminate all work, take the steps to reduce the net, final costs under or associated with such other agreements and commitments [AGENCY NAME] may have entered into in connection with this Agreement, and (ii) be entitled to compensation for the work performed, and expenses incurred up to the time of termination, and be reimbursed for such costs of terminating said other agreements.

10. TIMELY PERFORMANCE.

10.1 Upon signing of this Agreement, [AGENCY NAME] shall perform everything agreed to in Section 1 in a timely manner, or as agreed upon by all parties involved. [AGENCY NAME] shall not be liable for any delays or disruptions in providing the services hereunder due to conditions beyond its control, due to acts of God, widespread power outages, strikes, acts of government authorities, including state of national emergency or war. In the event that any such condition occurs and shall continue for more than ten (10) business days, [CLIENT NAME] shall have the right to terminate this Agreement immediately without any further obligation to [AGENCY NAME].

10.2 In the event that the principals of [AGENCY NAME] shall die or suffer a mental or physical disability, and if such disability shall continue for more than ten (10) business days, [CLIENT NAME] shall have the right to terminate this Agreement immediately without any further obligation to [AGENCY NAME].

11. MODIFICATIONS.

11.1 If either party decides to modify this Agreement or change the Program Descriptions, that party shall give thirty (30) days advance written notice of the desired modification or change to the other party.

11.2 No modification or change to this Agreement shall be effective unless in writing, signed by both parties to this Agreement.

12. MISCELLANEOUS.

12.1 Entire Agreement. This instrument contains the entire Agreement between the parties hereto with respect to the subject matter set forth herein and may not be amended unless such amendment is in writing and signed by both parties.

12.2 Governing Law. This Agreement shall be governed by and interpreted under the law of the State of [CLIENT HOME OFFICE].

12.3 Notices. All notices or other communications provided for herein shall be in writing, given by delivery in person or by certified mail, return receipt requested, addressed to the parties at the following addresses:

If to [CLIENT NAME]: Attn: [NAME]
[TITLE]
[CORP. ADDRESS]
[CITY, STATE, ZIP]

If to [AGENCY NAME]: Attn: [NAME]
[TITLE]
[CORP. ADDRESS]
[CITY, STATE, ZIP]

12.4 Prohibition. Nothing herein shall prohibit [AGENCY NAME] from performing advertising services for any other person, firm, corporation, or entity.

12.5 Benefit. The services to be provided by [AGENCY NAME] are personal in nature and [AGENCY NAME] may not assign, encumber, or subcontract this Agreement or any of its rights or obligations hereunder without the prior written consent of [CLIENT NAME]. Subject to the foregoing, this Agreement shall be binding upon and inure to the benefit of the parties hereto and their successors and assigns.

12.6 Severability. The invalidity or unenforceability of any provision of this Agreement shall in no way affect the other provisions of the Agreement which shall remain in full force and effect.

13. RECORDS AND REPORTS

13.1 [AGENCY NAME] shall maintain complete and accurate records of all transactions handled in connection with the Agreement and it shall make these records available at all reasonable times upon reasonable notice for inspection by [CLIENT NAME] and persons designated, in writing, by [CLIENT NAME].

IN WITNESS WHEREOF, the undersigned have executed this Agreement effective on the day and year first above written.

[CLIENT NAME]	[AGENCY NAME]
______________________	______________________
By:	By:
[TITLE]	[TITLE]

AICP Form

FILM PRODUCTION COST SUMMARY

	Bid Date:		Actualization Date:	
Production Company:	R/Greeberg Associates		Agency:	
Address:	350 W. 39th St., NY 10018		Client:	
Telephone No:	(212)239-6767			
Production Contact:			Producer:	Tel:
Director:			Art Dir:	Tel:
Cameraman:			Writer:	Tel:
Set Designer:			Bus. Mgr:	Tel:
Editor:			Commercial Title:	No.
No. Pre Prod Days:	Days	Pre-Lite	1	
Build/Strike Days:	Days	Hours	2	
Studio Shoot Days:	Days	Hours	3	
No. Location Days:	Days	Hours	4	
Location Sites:			5	
			6	

SUMMARY OF ESTIMATED PRODUCTION COSTS		ESTIMATED	ACTUAL	
1. Pre production and wrap costs	Totals A & C			
2. Shooting crew labor	Total B			
3. Location and travel expenses	Total D			
4. Props, wardrobe, animals	Total E			
5. Studio & Set Construction Costs	Total F, G & H			
6. Equipment costs	Total I			
7. Film stock & printing ft. 35 mm	Total J			
8. Miscellaneous	Total K			
9 Sub Total A to K				
10. Director/creative fees(Not included in Direct Costs)	Total L			
11. Insurance				
12 Sub Total: Direct Costs:				
13. Production Fee				
14. Talent Costs and expenses	Totals M & N			
15. Editorial and finishing per:	Total O			
16 Special Effects Total				
17 Grand Total(Including Director's Fee)				
18. Contingency				

Comments:

PAGE 1

A: PRE-PRODUCTION/WRAP

B: SHOOTING CREW

	CREW	ESTIMATED					ACTUAL					ESTIMATED					ACTUAL			
		DAY	RATE	1.5	2	TOTAL	DAY	RATE	O/T	TOTAL		DAY	RATE	1.5	2	TOTAL	DAY	RATE	O/T	TOTAL
1	Proudcer										51									
2	Asst Director:										52									
3	Cameraman:										53									
4	Camera Operator:										54									
5	Asst Cameraman:										55									
6	Outside Prop:										56									
7											57									
8	Inside Prop:										58									
9											59									
10											60									
11	Gaffer:										61									
12	Best Boy:										62									
13											63									
14											64									
15											65									
16	Key Grip:										66									
17	Grip:										67									
18	Dolly Grip:										68									
19	Crane Grip:										69									
20	Mixer:										70									
21	Boom Man:										71									
22	Recordist:										72									
23	Playback:										73									
24	Make-up:										74									
25	Hair:										75									
26	Stylist:										76									
27	Wardrobe:										77									
28	Script:										78									
29	Home Ec.:										79									
30	Asst. Home Ec:										80									
31	VTR Man:										81									
32	EFX Man:										82									
33	Scenic:										83									
34	Telepr. Operator:										84									
35	Generator Man:										85									
36	Still Man:										86									
37	Loc. Scout:										87									
38	P.A.:										88									
39	Coord/Prod Mgr:										89									
40	Nurse:										90									
41	Craft Service:										91									
42	Fireman:										92									
43	Policeman:										93									
44	Wlfr:/Tchr:										94									
45	Teamster:										95									
46											96									
47											97									
48											98									
49											99									
50											100									
		SUB TOTAL A										SUB TOTAL B								
		PT/P& W										PT/P&W								
		TOTAL A										**TOTAL B**								

PAGE 2

PRE-PRODUCTION & WRAP/MATERIALS & EXPENSES				ESTIMATED	ACTUAL
101	Auto Rentals	No. of Cars	x Amount per Car		
102	Air Fares:	No. of People	x Amount per fare		
103	Per Diems:	No. of People	x Amount per day		
104	Still Camera Rental & Film				
105	Messengers				
106	Trucking				
107	Deliveries & Taxis				
108	Home Economist Supplies				
109	Telephone & Cable				
110	Casting	Call/Prep	Casting Call Backs		
111	Casting Facilities				
112	Working Meals				
113					
			Sub Total C		

LOCATION EXPENSES				ESTIMATED	ACTUAL
114	Location Fees				
115	Permits				
116	Car Rentals				
117	Bus Rentals				
118	Camper, Dressing Room Vehicles				
119	Parking, Tolls & Gas				
120	Trucking				
121	Other Vehicles				
122	Other Vehicles				
123	Customs				
124	Air freight/Excess Baggage				
125	Air Fares:	No. of people	Cost Per Fare		
126	Per Diems:	No. of man days	Amount per day		
127	Air Fares:	No. of people	Cost Per Fare		
128	Per Diems:	No. of man days	Amount per day		
129	Breakfast	No. of man days	Amount per person		
130	Lunch	No. of man days	Amount per person		
131	Dinner	No. of man days	Amount per person		
132	Guards				
133	Limousines(Celebrity Service)				
134	Cabs and Other Transportation				
135	Kit Rental				
136	Art Work				
137	Gratuities				
138					
139					
			Sub Total D		

PROPS AND WARDROBE & ANIMALS		ESTIMATED	ACTUAL
140	Prop Rental		
141	Prop Purchase		
142	Wardrobe Rental		
143	Wardrobe Purchase		
144	Picture Vehicles		
145	Animals & Handlers		
146	Wigs & Mustaches		
147	Color Correction		
148			
	Sub Total E		

PAGE 3

STUDIO RENTAL & EXPENSES-STAGE		ESTIMATED Days	Rate	Total		ACTUAL Days	Rate	Total
151	Rental for Build Days							
152	Rental for Build O.T. Hours							
153	Rental for Pre-Lite Days							
154	Rental for Pre-Lite O.T. Hours							
155	Rental for Shoot Days							
156	Rental for Shoot O.T. Hours							
157	Rental for Strike Days							
158	Rental for Strike O.T. Hours							
159	Generator & Operator							
160	Set Guards							
161	Total Power Charge & Bulbs							
162	Misc. Studio Charges(Cartage, Phone, Coffee)							
163	Meals for Crew & Talent(Lunch, Dinner)							
164	Craft Service							
165								
166								
167								
		Sub Total F						

SET CONSTRUCTION		ESTIMATED Days	Rate	O/T Hrs	Total	ACTUAL Days	Rate	O/T $	Total
168	Set Designers Name:								
169	Carpenters								
170	Grips								
171	Outside Props								
172	Inside Props								
173	Scenics								
174	Electricians								
175	Teamsters								
176	Men for Strike								
177	P.A.'s								
178									
179									
180									
		Sub Total G							
		PT/P &W							
		TOTAL G							

SET CONSTRUCTION MATERIALS		ESTIMATED	ACTUAL
181	Props(Set Dressing Purchase)		
182	Props(Set Dressing Rental)		
183	Lumber		
184	Paint		
185	Hardware		
186	Special Effects		
187	Special Outside Construction		
188	Trucking		
189	Messengers/Deliveries		
190	Kit Rental		
191			
192			
	Sub Total H		

PAGE 4

EQUIPMENT RENTAL		Days	Rate	ESTIMATED	ACTUAL
193	Camera Rental				
194	Sound Rental				
195	Lighting Rental				
196	Grip Rental				
197	Generator Rental				
198	Crane/Cherry Picker Rental				
199	VTR Rental With Playback X Without Playback				
200	Walkie Talkies, Bull Horns				
201	Dolly Rental				
202	Camera Car				
203	Helicopter				
204	Production Supplies				
205	Teleprompter				
206					
207					
208					
209					
210					
	Sub Total I				

STOCK 35 MM		ESTIMATED			ACTUAL		
FILM RAW STOCK DEVELOP & PRINT		FOOTAGE	$/FT	TOTAL	FOOTAGE	$/FT.	TOTAL
211	Purchase of Raw Stock: Footage		.49				
212	Developing footage amount		.18				
213	Printing Footage amount		.32				
214	Transfer to Mag.		.12				
215	Sync/Screen Dailies						
216	Prep for video transfer						
			Sub Total J				

MISCELLANEOUS COSTS		ESTIMATED	ACTUAL
217	Petty Cash		
218	Air Shipping/Special Carriers		
219	Phones and Cables		
220	Accountable Cash Expenditures Under $15 Each		
221	External Billing Costs(Computer Accounting, etc.)		
222	Special Insurance		
223	DGA P & W		
224			
225			
226			
	Sub Total K		

DIRECTOR/CREATIVE FEES		ESTIMATED	ACTUAL
227	Prep		
228	Travel		
229	Shoot Days		
230	Post-Production		
231			
232			
233			
	Sub Total L		

PAGE 5

TALENT		No.	Rate	Days	Travel	1.5 OT	2X OT	ESTIMATED	No.	Days	ACTUAL
234	O/C Principals										
235	O/C Principals										
236	O/C Principals										
237	O/C Principals										
238	O/C Principals										
239	O/C Principals										
240	O/C Principals										
241	O/C Principals										
242	O/C Principals										
243	O/C Principals										
244											
245											
246											
247	General Extras										
248	General Extras										
249	General Extras										
250	General Extras										
251	General Extras										
252	General Extras										
253											
254											
255											
256	Hand Model										
257											
258	Voice Over										
259	Fitting Fees S.A.G.										
260	Fitting Fees S.E.G.										
261											
262	Audtion Fees S.A.G.										
263	Audtion Fees S.E.G.										
264											
265											
	Sub Total										
266	Payroll & P/W Taxes										
267	Wardrobe Allowence No of talent & garments					fee per garment					
268											
	Sub Total										
269	Other										
270	Mark-up										
						Sub Total M					

TALENT EXPENSES				ESTIMATED	ACTUAL
271	Per diem:	No. of man days	amount per day		
272	Air Fares:	No. of people	amount per fare		
273	Cabs and other transportation				
274	Mark-up				
275					
276					
			Sub Total N		

PAGE 6

	EDITORIAL COMPLETION	Quantity	Units	Rate	ESTIMATED	ACTUAL
277	Editor		Days			
278	Editing Room		Days			
279	Assistant Editor		Days			
280	Conforming		Hours			
281	Projection					
282	Artwork for Supers					
283	Shooting Artwork					
284	Stock Footage					
285	Still Photos					
286	Optical					
287	Animation					
288	Stock Music					
289	Original Music					
290	Sound Effects					
291	Dubbing Studio		Hours			
292	Record Narration		Hours			
293	Transfer to cassette					
294	Mix		Hours			
295	Optical Tracks		foot			
296	Answer Prints		foot			
297	Interpositive/Dupe Neg		foot			
298	Contract Items					
	VIDEOTAPE FINISHING					
299	Off-Line Editing		Hours			
300	Film To Tape Transfer		Hours			
301	"Pin Registered" Trans/Composite		Hours			
302	On-Line Editing		Hours			
303	Additional VTR's		Hours			
304	ADO/Kaleidoscope		Hours			
305	Paint Box/Harry		Hours			
306	Abekas DDR		Hours			
307	Workprint to Cassette		Spot			
308	D1 Tape		Spot			
309	Tape		Spot			
310	Master & Safetys		Spot			
311	Cassettes		Spot			
312	Post Production Supervisor		Days			
313	Working Meals					
314	Shipping					
315						
316						
317						
318						
319						
320						
321						
322						
323						
324						
325						
326	Misc					
327	P & W					
328	SUB TOTAL EDITORIAL COSTS					
329	Editorial Handling Fee					
				Sub Total O		

PAGE 7

SPECIAL VISUAL EFFECTS

	CREW	ESTIMATED					ACTUAL			
		DAYS	RATE	OT 1	OT 2	TOTAL	DAYS	RATE	O/T $	TOTAL
330	FX Producer									
331	Production Manager									
332	Coordinator									
333	Dir. of Photography									
334	Asst. Camera									
335	Electrician									
336	Grip									
337	Rigger									
338	Model Wrangler									
339	Technical Director									
340	Computer Programmer									
341	SPFX Supervisor									
342										
343										
344										
345										
346										
347	M.C. Operator									
348	Production Assistant									
			SUB TOTAL P					SUB TOTAL P		
			PT/P& W					PT/P& W		
			TOTAL P					TOTAL P		

	STAGE COSTS	Quanity	$/Unit	ESTIMATED	ACTUAL
349	Stage Prep				
350	Prep O.T.				
351	Stage Shoot				
352	Shoot O.T.				
353	Stage Strike				
354	Strike O.T.				
355	Total Power Charges				
356	Misc Stage Costs				
			Sub Total Q		

	EQUIPMENT/RIGS/PROPS	Days	Rate	ESTIMATED	ACTUAL
357	Motion Control Camera				
358	Motion Control System				
359	Motion Graphics System				
360	Matte Camera System				
361	Lighting/Grip Equipment				
362	Generator				
363	VTR				
364	Motion Control Dolly/Track				
365	Production Supplies				
366	Special Rigs				
367	Rear Screen Projector				
368	Props				
369					
370					
			Sub Total R		

PAGE 8

PRODUCTION SUPPLIES		Quanity	Units	$/Unit	ESTIMATED	ACTUAL
371	Craft Services		Days			
372	Production Meals		Days			
373	Working Meals		Days			
374	Telephone, Telex, FAX		Weeks			
375	Couriers, Shipping		Weeks			
			Sub Total S			

MODEL/SPECIAL EFX CONSTRUCTION		Quanity	Units	$/Unit	ESTIMATED	ACTUAL
376	Model maker		Days			
377	Model Wrangler		Days			
378	Model Supplies		Allow			
379						
380						
381	Other		Allow			
			Sub Total T			

		ESTIMATED					ACTUAL			
ART DEPARTMENT		Quanity	Units	$/Unit	OT Hrs	TOTAL	DAYS	RATE	O/T $	TOTAL
382	Art Director		Days							
383	Artist/Animator		Days							
384	Assistant		Days							
385	Ink & Paint		Days							
386	Art Support/Strip-Up		Days							
387	Rotoscope		Days							
388	Photos/Stats		Days							
389	Art supplies		Days							
390	Typset		Days							
391	Storyboards		Days							
392	Research & Development		Days							
393										
394										
395										
396	Other		Allow							
				PT/PW				PT/PW		
				Sub Total U				Sub Total U		

ANIMATION		Days	Units	Rate	ESTIMATED	ACTUAL
397			Days			
398			Days			
399			Days			
400			Days			
401			Days			
402			Days			
403			Days			
404			Days			
405			Days			
406			Days			
			Sub Total V			

PAGE 9

FILM/PROCESSING		Footage	Cost/ft.	ESTIMATED	ACTUAL
407	Color Stock				
408	Process & Print				
409	Lab Rush Orders				
410	Registered Prints				
411	B/W Raw Stock				
412	B/W Prints				
413	Stock Footage				
			Sub Total W		

COMPUTER GENERATED IMAGERY		Quanity	Units	$/Unit	ESTIMATED	ACTUAL
414	Producer		Days			
415	Director		Days			
416	Animator 1		Days			
417	Animator 2		Weeks			
418	Technical Director					
419	Scanner Operator					
420	Animation Workstation					
421	Image Processing Workstation					
422	Input Output Scanners					
423	Rendering Workstation					
424	Research and Development					
425	Computer Output to Video					
426	Computer Output from Video					
427						
428						
429			Weeks			
				Sub Total X		

CGI INTERGRATION		Quanity	Units	$/Unit	ESTIMATED	ACTUAL
430	Live Action Matching		Days			
431	Motion Control Matching		Days			
432			Days			
				Sub Total Y		

PAGE 10

DIGITAL/VIDEO GRAPHICS		Quantity	Units	Rate	ESTIMATED	ACTUAL
433	Supervisor/Layout		hours			
434	Digital Video Suite(unsupervised)		hours			
435	Digital Video Suite(unsupervised O.T.)		hours			
436	Digital Video Suite(supervised)		hours			
437	Digital Video Suite(unsupervised O.T.)		hours			
438	Additional Abekas		hours			
439	Additional D1- DVTR		hours			
440	Additional D2- DVTR		hours			
441	GCG Kaleddoscope(per channel)					
442	Digital Paint System		hours			
443	Digital Paint System(Rotoscope)		hours			
444	Digital Conform		hours			
445	Special Color Correction					
446	Digital Noise Reduction		hours			
447	D-1 to 1" Video		hours			
448	D-1 to 3/4" Video		hours			
449	Audio Relay		hours			
450	Digital Video to Recording					
451	Conversion to PAL or SEACAM		hours			
452						
453						
454						
455						
456						
457						
458						
459						
				Sub Total Z		

DIGITAL/VIDEO GRAPHICS MATERIALS		Quantity	Units	Rate	ESTIMATED	ACTUAL
460	1/2" Cassettes		Cassettes			
461	1" Tape 30 minutes		Rolls			
462	1" Dubs		Spots			
463	3/4" Cassettes		Cassettes			
464	D-1 Cassettes (76 minutes)		Cassettes			
465	D-1 Cassettes(34 minutes)		Cassettes			
466	D-1 Cassettes(12 minutes)		Cassettes			
467						
468						
469						
470						
				Sub Total AA		

TRAVEL		Persons	Units	$/Unit	ESTIMATED	ACTUAL
471	Round Trip Airfares		Fares			
472	Per Diems		Days			
473	Lodging		Nights			
474	Auto Rentals, Cabs		Days			
				Sub Total AB		

PAGE 11

MISCELLANOUS		ESTIMATED	ACTUAL
475	Messengers		
476	Taxis/Cabs		
477	Shipping		
478	Working Meals		
479	Other		
480			
481			
	Sub Total AC		

ADDITIONAL		Quanity	Units	$/Unit	ESTIMATED	ACTUAL
482						
483						
484						
485						
486						
487						
488						
489						
490						
491						
492						
				Sub Total AD		

DIRECTOR/CREATIVE FEES		ESTIMATED	ACTUAL
493	Prep		
494	Shoot Days		
495	Post Production		
	PT/PW		
	Sub -Total AE		

496	Special Effects Sub-Total	(Except Digital Video Graphics & Materials)		
497	Mark-Up on Above	35%		
498	Director/Creative Fees	Sub Total AE		
499	Digital Video Graphics & Materials	Sub Total Z & AA		
500	Total Effects			

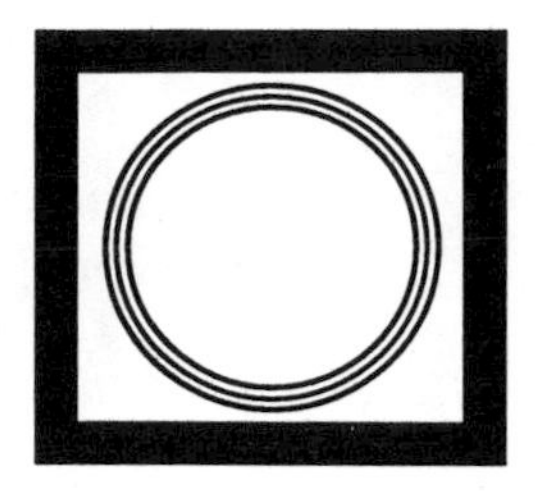

Glossary

One of the most frustrating experiences anyone can have is being in a situation where everyone except you is speaking in "techno jargon" — the buzz words indigenous to a particular profession, business, or industry. You don't want to appear unknowledgeable, or slow things down, by asking for definitions every few minutes. Yet, you know these words are important to understand.

The problem is particularly frustrating if you're new to direct response (DR) television, because so many professions — each with its *own* buzz words — are involved. And sometimes the words themselves can have different meanings depending on which DR professional is speaking. *Wrap,* for instance, means one thing in direct marketing and another in commercial production.

To help solve the techno-jargon problem, this Glossary includes the words you are most likely to hear in DR TV. Many have already been discussed in the book.

A

AAAA - (American Association of Advertising Agencies) An organization of advertising agencies that sets standards, procedures, and billing practices for the profession.

"A" county - A county that encompasses one of America's 25 largest cities. See *"B," "C,"* and *"D" counties.*

Academy leader - The standard film strip, developed by the Academy of Motion Picture Arts and Sciences, and attached to the beginning of a commercial, that lets a projectionist know when the film will begin.

Account executive - The person at an advertising agency who coordinates all other agency professionals on an account and acts as a liaison between agency and client.

"Action" - Said by the director to signal the start of a take.

Actor - A professional who is paid to take on a role and perform in a commercial.

ADI - (Area of Dominant Influence) The area covered by a particular TV station, as determined by the A.C. Nielsen Company.

ADO - The brand name of one type of electronic special effects device.

Advertising agency - A company that creates advertising, including commercials for its clients. See *creative boutique, full-service agency, media buying service,* and *research company.*

AFM - (American Federation of Musicians) The union responsible for professional musicians.

AFTRA - (American Federation of Television and Radio Actors) One of the unions responsible for actors. Generally, if a shoot is on videotape, the union is AFTRA. See *SAG.*

Agent - A person or company who represents professional actors and celebrities.

AICP - (Association of Independent Commercial Producers) An organization of producers not affiliated with advertising agencies.

AICP form - A standardized form for bidding on commercials used by producers not affiliated with advertising agencies.

Air date - The date on which a commercial first airs on a station. See *deadline.*

Allowable - The maximum amount of all costs, while maintaining a profit.

American Association of Advertising Agencies - See *AAAA.*

American Federation of Musicians - See *AFM.*

American Federation of Television and Radio Actors - See *AFTRA.*

Ampex - The brand name of a professional audio tape recorder used in a recording studio. See *Revox* and *Studer.*

Analog - Recording, whether audio or video, that makes an approximate copy of the original. See *digital.*

Angle - See *camera angle.*

Animatic - A test commercial that is a series of still drawings that are dissolved together to create a rough approximation of movement.

Animation - A motion picture that is a series of drawings, each one slightly different from the next, to create the illusion of movement.

Animation stand - A piece of equipment that supports a camera above animation cells and can move the camera in a very precise way. An animation stand is also used for animatics, titling, and sometimes for a product shot if the product is relatively flat, such as a magazine.

Apple - A box used in production as a stand to raise equipment or props.

Arbitron - A service that measures viewership of television programs.

Arriflex - The brand name of one type of motion picture camera. See *Mitchell* and *Panavision.*

Art director - The person who, together with a copywriter, generates a concept for a commercial and draws the pictures on the storyboard. In production, the art director works with the set designer, wardrobe and hair and makeup, the director of photography, and the director, to help achieve the desired "look" to the production.

As-produced storyboard - A storyboard that has been updated to include changes to dialogue and/or video done during production or post-production.

Association of Independent Commercial Producers - See *AICP.*

Audience - The number of people watching a TV show and their demographics and psychographics. See *clearance, frequency, reach* and *GRP.*

Audience flow - An increase or decrease in the number of people watching a show or an infomercial.

Audio - All the sound portions of a commercial.

Audio tape recorder - A device used for reproducing sounds on location or in a recording studio. See *Ampex, Nagra, Revox,* and *Studer.*

Audition - See *casting session.*

Automated telemarketing - Replacing a human telemarketer with a recorded message that prompts the caller to use the telephone touch pad to enter required information or select from a tree of services.

Avid - The brand name of a system for nonlinear, random-access computer editing.

Award - To give the job of producing a commercial to a particular production company. Jobs are usually awarded on a number of criteria, including the bid, the reputation of the company, the director's reel, etc.

B

"B" county - A county with a population over 150,000 that is not an "A" county. See *"A," "C,"* and *"D" counties.*

Back end - All the components of a direct marketing program that occur after the initial sale, including billing, bad debt, returns, etc.

Background light - Light(s) that illuminate the scene behind the foreground.

Backlight - Light(s) that illuminate the subject from behind, often used on the hair.

Back lot - In a large studio, where temporary exterior sets are constructed, or where there are permanent exterior sets that re-create extensive areas, such as a New York street scene, an old west town, etc.

Bars - See *color bars.*

Beauty shot - A scene with all the items offered for sale arranged in a pleasing way.

Beta - The brand name of a ½-inch videotape format.

Beta SP - A high-quality version of the Beta format.

Bid - 1. To ask a production company to generate an estimate of how much it will cost to produce a commercial. 2. The amount of money a production company believes it will cost to shoot a commercial. 3. The formal, itemized estimate a production company submits to an advertising agency.

"Bill me" - A method of ordering products where the customer is sent a bill for the order. The product may be sent before the bill, after the bill has been returned, or after the customer's check has cleared.

Bipack - Running two films through a camera or printer at the same time, so that one film reveals the other.

Blocking - The body movements and motions of the actor, as opposed to speech.

Blowup - A scene that has been enlarged.

Blue screen - See *matte shot.*

Book - To hire an actor to appear in a commercial. See *first refusal.*

Boom mike - A microphone that is attached to the end of a large pole and held above the actor. See *miked.*

Booth - A soundproof room in a recording studio. The booth is where the voiceover announcer records his or her lines.

Boutique - A limited-service advertising agency. Often used to describe one that supplies only creative services, which is called a creative boutique.

Break - A pause in filming. Breaks occur for such things as camera reloading, setting up for a new scene, lunch, dinner, etc.

Build - To create a setup to be shot. To physically construct a set. See *strike.*

Burke Test - A day-after recall test done by Burke Marketing Research, Inc. TV viewers are telephoned and asked what they remember about commercials they saw the night before.

Burn in - See *time code* and *visual time code.*

Buyer - See *media buyer.*

Buying service - A company that specializes in selecting and buying media.

Buyout - Paying for unlimited usage of an actor's services without having to pay residuals.

C

"C" county - A county with a population between 40,000 and 150,000. See *"A," "B,"* and *"D" counties.*

Cable - Television programming that is paid for by the viewer.

Cable buy - Airtime that is bought on cable networks. See *spot buy, national,* and *run of station.*

Call - The time of day when members of the cast and crew are to arrive at the studio or location for a shoot.

Callback - A second (or third) audition for actors.

Camera angle - Any of various ways of positioning a camera, vertically and horizontally.

Camera move - See *move.*

Cast - The performer(s) in a commercial.

Casting - Selecting the cast of a commercial.

Casting director - A person hired to select potential actors for a role and audition them.

Casting profile - A description of the role(s) to be played in a commercial.

Casting session - An audition for actors who want to perform in a commercial. It is arranged and conducted by a casting director. The session is videotaped so that the production team can screen the talent at their convenience.

CCC - See *continuing central character.*

Celebrity presenter - A famous person who endorses a product.

Chapman - The brand name of a type of crane.

Cheat - To take creative license with some aspect of film production. For example, when four people are seated at a dinner table in real life, they might be at right angles facing due north, south, east, and west. On camera, they would be in a semicircle facing east, southeast, southwest and west. The actors cheat the seating arrangement so that the camera does not shoot the back of anybody's head.

"Check the gate" - Sometimes said by the director to the camera crew during a change of film magazines, to be certain that no dirt or dust is on the gate.

Cherry picker - See *crane.*

Chyron - The brand name of an electronic title and super generator. See *title camera.*

Cinematographer - See *director of photographer.*

Cinema vérité - A style of filming that tries to create absolute reality by attempting to break down the imaginary "stage" that separates the camera and its subject. In cinema vérité, the camera is usually hand held, it moves to whoever is speaking without cutting, and the lights, camera, and crew may at some point be in the scene.

Clapstick - A hinged piece of wood on the top of a slate that is used to simultaneously make a noise and create a visual cue, thus establishing a sync mark at the start of a film take. See *in sync* and *out of sync.*

Claymation - A type of stop motion where flexible clay puppets are moved slightly each time the camera shoots a frame or two.

Clearance - See *commercial clearance.*

Closeup - (CU) A shot where the camera appears quite close to the subject. If the subject were a person, a closeup would be the person's head only.

Club - A direct marketing program where a customer receives an initial selection of the product at a reduced price in exchange for agreeing to buy more of the product over time. The customer makes a commitment to buy the product. See *continuity program* and *subscription.*

CMX - The brand name of a master control unit used in on-line editing.

COD - (Collect on delivery) A method of ordering products where the customer pays the person who delivers the product when the product arrives.

Color bars - A series of electronically generated colors that form a pattern on a TV screen and allow a technician to adjust the set to match what the colors should be.

Color correct - To retouch products that will be shot so that they appear on film or tape as they actually do in real life. To adjust the color and brightness of film or tape.

Commercial clearance - In direct response, a commercial that ran on air. If a commercial aired, it is said to have cleared.

Communication strategy - See *selling strategy.*

Computer animation - Animation that is created on a computer.

Concept - The translation of a communication strategy into an idea that is the basis for a commercial.

Confidence Level - The degree to which results of a test can be expected to be duplicated. Direct marketers usually work at the 95 percent confidence level. See *statistically significant.*

Conform - A final computer-controlled edit on 1-inch videotape that matches the off-line edit on videotape or film.

Consumer intercept - A type of research where pedestrians in shopping malls or other public places are screened and then asked questions about a product or service. Usually called *mall intercepts.*

Continuing central character - A series of commercials built around the ongoing presence of a personality, whether human, animal, or animated.

Continuity - Making sure there is a logical sequence from shot to shot, and from scene to scene. Also, making sure that there are no anachronisms, non sequiturs, inconsistencies, discrepancies, or impossibilities in the commercial. Continuity is particular critical when a scene is shot for more than one day. This is when the script supervisor must make sure wardrobe, hair, makeup, props, lighting, etc. are consistent throughout. A break in continuity could result in a mistake such as earrings mysteriously changing from pearls to gold in the middle of a scene, or an ashtray magically jumping from one side of a table to the other. See *hot set.*

Continuity program - A direct marketing offer structure where a customer receives a product but is not obligated to buy it. If the customer decides to buy it, then he or she pays for it. If not, the customer returns it. See *club, negative option* and *positive option.*

Control - In direct response, the commercial that is currently achieving the best results. The control is the standard against which any new commercial must be tested. If a new commercial does better, it will probably become the new control.

Conversion rate - In a lead-generation program, the percentage of prospects that eventually buy the product or service. See *CPI.*

Cookie - A screen with holes or patterns cut in it to create a shadow pattern on a subject when placed in front of a light. See *flag.*

Copywriter - The person who, teamed with an art director, generates a concept for a commercial, and who writes the storyboard. In production, the copywriter works with the script supervisor to make sure the lines are covered, and with the director to make sure the interpretation of the lines is correct.

Cost Per Inquiry - See *CPI.*

Cost Per Order - See *CPO.*

Coverage - How many ways a particular scene will be shot. While it is desirable to cover a scene many ways, such as CU, MS, dolly shot, etc., coverage must always be a balance between having adequate material for editing, versus the cost of film, the time budgeted for the shoot, and the fatigue level of the performers.

CPI - (Cost per inquiry) The amount it costs in media to run a commercial divided by the number of leads generated. For example, if $1,000 spent on media generated 100 leads, the CPI would be $10 (1,000 ÷ 100 = 10). An attempt is then made to convert the leads into sales. See *conversion rate.*

CPO - (Cost per order) The amount it costs in media to run a commercial divided by the number of orders generated. For example, if $1,000 spent on media generated 50 orders, the CPO would be $20 (1,000 ÷ 50 = 20).

Crane - A device that can raise and lower a camera during a take.

Crane shot - A take made with the use of a crane.

Crawl - Superimposed type that moves across the screen. The closing credits of a feature film are usually a crawl.

Creative - Relating to all aspects of the development of a commercial and/or to the actual commercial itself. A commercial considered to be innovative.

Creative boutique - An advertising agency that specializes in the creative product and does not offer full agency services, such as media, research, etc.

Creative department - In an advertising agency, the department that writes, art directs and produces television commercials, as well as advertising for other media.

Creative strategy - See *selling strategy.*

Crew - All the crafts people who work on a commercial.

Cue - A signal given to an actor or to a member of the crew to do something at a certain time during a take.

Cut - An instantaneous change from one scene to another. See *dissolve* and *fade.*

"Cut" - Said by the director to signal the end of a take.

Cutaway - To go from the main scene to another scene that helps the flow of the story or adds to the drama. For instance, if a scene were of a person reading a book, a cutaway could be to a page in the book.

Cycle - A certain amount of time a commercial may be aired without having to pay union talent an additional fee. A normal cycle is 13 weeks. See *AFTRA* and *SAG.*

D

"D" county - A county with a population under 40,000. See *"A," "B,"* and *"C" counties.*

D-1, D-2, D-3, etc. - Digital videotape formats.

Dailies - In film, the shots taken the previous day. Also called rushes.

Dayparts - The 24-hour day divided into six segments: early morning (6 a.m. - 9 a.m.); daytime (9 a.m. - 5 p.m.); early fringe (5 p.m. - 8 p.m.); prime time (8 p.m. - 11 p.m.); late fringe (11 p.m. - 1 a.m.); and late night (1 a.m. - 6 a.m. or sign off). Audiences, programming, and commercial rates are different for each daypart.

Daytime - Televison programming that takes place from 9 a.m. to 5 p.m. See *dayparts.*

Deadline - The date on which a TV station must receive materials in order to make a certain air date. See *air date.*

Dead spot - A section of audio track that sounds peculiar because it is absolutely quiet, instead of having a faint background ambiance. See *room tone.*

Deal - In direct response, the financial component of the offer, particularly if it is a price-off, a special, a sale, or includes a premium.

Delivery time - How long it will take for the product to arrive. This must be stated or shown in the commercial, and must be a reasonable amount of time, such as 30 days, 4-6 weeks.

Demo - (Demonstration) Showing how a product works.

Demographics - The age, sex, education, and income level of a group of consumers. See *psychographics.*

Demo reel - (Demonstration reel) See *sample reel.*

Depth interview - See *mall intercept.*

DGA - (Directors Guild of America) The union that represents feature film and commercial directors.

Diffuser - Any of several gels used in front of lights, and/or filters used in front of camera lenses, to soften lighting.

Digital - Recording, whether audio or video, that reproduces the original as a series of numbers (digits) that can be understood and manipulated by a computer. See *analog.*

Director - The person responsible for the actions and speech of the actors during a shoot.

Director of photography - The person responsible for the lighting during a shoot. Also called a cinematographer.

Direct response - The business of selling products or services directly to the customer without the use of stores, middlemen, etc.

Direct response agency - An advertising agency that specializes in direct response, as opposed to general image advertising.

Dissolve - To overlap the fade out of one scene onto the fade in of the next. See *cut* and *fade.*

DMA - (Direct Marketing Association) An organization of advertising agencies, clients and vendors involved in direct response.

Dolly - A device that supports a camera and lets it move during filming.

Dolly shot - See *move.*

Double exposure - To shoot a scene, rewind the camera, and shoot another scene on the same film. Literally, to expose the film twice, so that two images appear on the screen simultaneously, creating a particular effect.

Double scale - An actor who requires twice the standard union wage to appear in a commercial. See *AFTRA, SAG,* and *scale.*

Drift - To move the camera in or out on a scene almost imperceptibly.

Dry test - Offering on air a product, service, or premium that does not exist in order to gauge consumer reaction. Sometimes done but not legal.

Dub - A copy of a commercial.

Dubbing service - A company that quickly and relatively inexpensively can make multiple copies of commercials to send to various TV stations.

E

Early fringe - Television programming that takes place from 5 p.m. to 8 p.m. See *dayparts.*

Early morning - Television programming that takes place from 6 a.m. to 9 a.m. See *dayparts.*

Edit - To assemble the various scenes that were shot into a commercial.

Edit on disk - To transfer takes from a film shoot onto video disk to do a rough cut.

Edit on film - To select takes and do a rough cut on film.

Edit on tape - To transfer takes from a film shoot onto videotape to do a rough cut.

Editor - The person who edits a commercial and generally is responsible for postproduction.

800 number - A toll-free telephone number often used to place an order in direct response.

EQ - (Equalization) To set a standard level for all parts of an audio recording. To balance out the various frequencies of the recording.

Establishing shot - A shot where the camera is as far away from the subject as possible while including everything that sets the scene.

Execution - The tangible advertising that results from following a given strategy. The actual commercial a viewer sees.

Exterior - (EXT) A scene filmed outside. See *interior.*

Extra - An actor who appears in a commercial but who does not speak and whose face cannot be recognized.

Extreme closeup - (ECU) A shot where the camera is very close to the subject. If the subject were a person, an extreme closeup would be a part of the head only, such as the mouth or eyes.

F

Fade - A slow transition from one scene to another. Fade in is to dissolve from black to a scene. Fade out is to dissolve from a scene to black. See *cut* and *dissolve.*

Fast motion - Action on film that appears faster than in real life. To achieve fast motion the camera is run at a slower speed than normal. See *slow motion.*

Fatigue - The tendency of a commercial to lose its effectiveness over time.

FCC - (Federal Communications Commission) The U.S. Government agency responsible for monitoring all aspects of the television broadcasting industry.

Field - A measurement of the area a scene occupies. A guide as to how much a scene may be enlarged. See *blowup.*

Fill light - The light(s) that fills in the shadows. See *key light, back light,* and *background light.*

Film - A chemical medium for shooting and recording commercials. See *tape.*

Film-to-tape transfer - To transcribe scenes of a commercial shot on film onto videotape.

Filter - Any of several types of devices that are placed in front of a camera lens and/or lights to create a diffused look or other effect.

First refusal - A way of reserving actors for a shoot on a given day before booking them. According to union rules, an actor must notify whoever put him or her on first refusal before accepting another job that conflicts with the first refusal. If the actor is not booked for the first refusal job, he or she is free to accept the second job.

Fisher - The brand name of a type of dolly.

Fish eye - A extreme wide-angle lens that forces the edges of a shot to curve toward the center.

Fixed spot test - A way of testing commercials where each one runs on the same TV shows on consecutive days. When a fixed spot test is completed, each commercial will have run on every show, and each commercial will have had the same amount of media dollars spent on it. See *matched market test.*

Flag - A screen that blocks the light on a particular area. See *cookie.*

Flare - A subject, usually metallic or glossy, that acts like a mirror, reflecting too much light. A flare most often occurs when the subject is moved.

Flashback - A scene of something that occurred in the past.

Flatbed - A type of editing machine where the film travels horizontally, as opposed to a *Moviola,* where the film travels vertically. See *Kem* and *Steenbeck.*

Focus group - A type of marketing research where approximately ten consumers are asked a series of questions by a trained moderator. Focus groups are often recorded and usually observed by clients from behind a one-way mirror.

Following shot - A take where the camera follows the subject's movement.

Frames per second - (FPS) The number of individual pictures taken by a camera each second it is running. Normal speed in film is 24 frames per second, in video it is 30 frames per second.

Framing - The composition of a scene, the "picture" the camera sees.

Free-lancer - A person who does not work for a company, but who offers his or her services on a project-by-project basis.

Freeze frame - To stay on one frame in a take so that all motion stops.

Frequency - The number of times a commercial airs each week. Frequency is more related to general image advertising than to direct response. See *audience, clearance,* and *GRP.*

Front end - In direct response, relating to the order. See *back end.*

FTC - (Federal Trade Commission) The U.S. Government agency responsible for truth in advertising.

Fulfillment - In direct response, relating to sending the customer what was ordered.

Fulfillment center - A company that specializes in storing, packing, and shipping direct response products in response to orders.

Fullcoat - A magnetic tape track with all the sound elements recorded on it.

Full-service agency - An advertising agency that offers a complete range of services, including creative, account management, media, research, production, etc.

G

Gaffer - The person responsible for everything electrical on a shoot.

Gate - The part of a motion picture camera where the film passes in front of the lens. See *"check the gate."*

Gel - A transparent film placed in front of a light to create a particular color or effect.

General - Advertising that attempts to influence consumer attitudes toward a product or service that is not sold through direct response. Also called general image.

General agency - An advertising agency that specializes in general image advertising, as opposed to direct response.

Generation - In film or tape, relating to the distance a copy is away from the original. A master would be the first generation; the first dub would be the second generation; the second dub would be the third generation, etc.

Generator - An electric power plant, mounted on a truck, that is transported to locations to supply power for the lights, cameras, etc.

Generic master - A first-generation commercial on 1-inch videotape without any titles or supers. See *titled generic.*

Gennie - See *generator.*

Green screen - See *matte shot.*

Grip - The crafts people responsible for moving and setting up equipment on a shoot.

Group shot - A take that includes a number of people.

GRP - (Gross rating points) A measure of the media weight supporting a given commercial. The GRP is the *frequency* multiplied by the *reach* (GRP = F x R).

H

Hair & makeup - The person responsible for the actors' hairstyles and theatrical makeup on a shoot.

1/2" - A videotape format that is ½-inch wide. It includes Beta, Beta SP, VHS, and SVHS, which are analog, and D-1, D-2, and D-3, which are digital.

Hand held - A camera that is supported by the camera operator, as opposed to being mounted on a crane, dolly, or tripod.

Hand model - A model with particularly attractive hands who is used to hold the product in closeups.

Head - The opening frames of a take, which may be used in their entirety or cut, to help achieve a smooth transition between scenes. See *tail*.

Head sheet - A photograph of an actor. The back usually lists the actor's credits and training.

Heavy-up - To increase media spending. This may be done because a particular station is generating orders, or because of seasonality, such as heavying-up on a gift item in the weeks before Christmas.

Hidden camera - A commercial technique where a real person does not know he or she is being filmed.

High 8 - An 8 mm videotape format normally not used for commercials.

HMI - A very large, very bright light, used to simulate daylight.

Holding fee - The amount of money required to prohibit a performer from acting in a competitor's commercial while the original commercial is not being aired.

Hot - 1. In audio, when a component of the mix, usually the music, is too loud in relation to the other components. 2. In video, when a certain part of a scene, or the entire scene, is too bright.

Hot set - A set where nothing is to be touched or moved, to maintain continuity between days of shooting.

Hot spot - A small area in a scene that is too bright.

I

IA - (International Alliance of Theatrical Stage Employees and Motion Picture Machine Operators of the United States and Canada) The IA is the union responsible for all crafts people on a shoot, such as the grip, gaffers, camera operators, etc.

Image - 1. In film, what the camera captures. 2. In advertising, the feelings in a person the product elicits, the emotional reasons to buy it, as opposed to the logical reasons for buying it. See *strategy, USP,* and *positioning.*

Impressions - The number of times an individual sees a particular commercial.

Inbound telemarketing - Incoming telephone calls made to a telemarketing center, fulfillment center, or research company. See *outbound telemarketing.*

In-depth research - Any of several techniques that employ formal, structured questionnaires to achieve quantitative results. See *consumer intercepts,* and *in-home interviews.*

Infomercial - A long-form (28-minute) television commercial.

In-home interviews - A technique where a researcher goes into subjects' homes, administers a formal questionnaire, and observes the subjects' lifestyles.

In sequence - See *shooting schedule.*

In sync - (In synchronization) Audio and video that occur at exactly the same time on film. See *out of sync.*

Integrated marketing - A marketing campaign where direct marketing is used in conjunction with other marketing efforts, such as general image advertising, sales promotion, and/or package-logo-product design.

Interior - (INT) A scene filmed indoors. See *exterior.*

International Alliance of Theatrical Stage Employees and Motion Picture Machine Operators of the United States and Canada - (IATSE and MPMP) See *IA.*

Interpretation - The way lines are read. The feeling, mood, and emotion an actor and a director bring to the role.

In the can - Scenes that have been shot but are not included in the final edited version of the commercial.

J

Jingle - A song created to help sell a product or service.

Jump cut - A scene that does not flow smoothly from the previous one, usually because the focus of attention shifts from one part of the frame to another. For example, if an actor is on the right of one scene and then appears on the left of the next.

K

Kem - The brand name of a flatbed film editing machine. See *Moviola* and *Steenbeck.*

Key light - The main (modeling) light(s) used on a subject. See *fill light, back light,* and *background light.*

L

Laboratory - (Lab) Where motion picture film is developed, usually overnight.

Late fringe - Television programming that takes place from 11 p.m. to 1 a.m. See *dayparts.*

Late night - Televison programming that takes place from 1 a.m. to 6 a.m. See *dayparts.*

Leader - A section of film or video that starts at 10 and declines to 2 at the rate of one number per second before going to black. A leader is used to help a projectionist know when the actual commercial starts. See *academy leader.*

Lexicon - The brand name of an electronic device that can shorten the running time of a commercial up to 10 percent. With a Lexicon, a commercial that times out at up to 2 minutes and 12 seconds could be shortened to 2 minutes.

Lift - In direct response, something that increases the response rate.

Light meter - A device used by the director of photography to check the illumination on the subjects as each scene is set up and after any change in lighting.

Limbo - A background that is simply a neutral color and does not appear to be any particular place or setting.

Limited use - A commercial that is only to run in certain areas or for a certain length of time.

Lines - The words in a script that are spoken by an actor.

Lip sync - In on-camera scenes, audio and video occurring at the same time.

Live callback - An audition where actors are asked to perform before a group of people.

Local - A commercial that runs in just one market, such as Miami or San Jose. See *regional* and *national.*

Location - A place, other than a studio, where a commercial is filmed.

Location scout - The person who finds a location for filming and who arranges rental fees and permits, if required.

Lock off - A camera that does not move throughout a scene or an entire commercial.

Logo - A visual symbol that represents a product or service.

Long shot - A shot where the camera is relatively far away from the subject. If the subject were a person, a long shot would be of the entire body.

Loop - To combine a short section of video or audio track so that it repeats itself and appears to be longer.

Lot - See *back lot.*

M

Mag track - (Magnetic track) Magnetic tape that is used to record the audio portions of a commercial.

Make good - When a TV station does not run a commercial as promised, it will make good and run it at another time.

Mall intercept - A type of research where shoppers in a mall are asked questions about a product, service, strategy, concept, or commercial.

Mandatories - Anything that because of legal reasons or client dictates, must be included in a commercial.

Margin - After a sale, the amount of money left as profit after all costs and expenses have been subtracted. Also called profit margin.

Mark - The place where an actor starts or stops a particular movement or action.

Marketing objective - The goal of a marketing campaign, which should always be expressed in numbers so that success or failure can be measured.

Marketing product - A product whose existence or superiority is not the result of technology, but a new combination of ingredients, new packaging, a new design, etc. For example, peanut butter and jelly in one.

Marketing strategy - The way in which all the components of the marketing mix will be used to achieve a marketing objective.

Market test - A test in a particular market. See *fixed spot test* and *matched market test.*

Markup - A percentage, charged by a production company and an advertising agency, over the actual cost of production, and that represents their profit margin.

Master - The first-generation 1-inch videotape of a commercial with all the titles and supers. The master is usually duplicated for insurance against loss or damage and this second-generation tape is called a protection master. The master is then sent to a dubbing service to make multiple copies, which are sent to TV stations for airing. See *generic master.*

Match dissolve - To end one scene with a similar scene, so that the images blend together and the audience is not immediately aware of the change.

Matched market test - A form of on-air test where a commercial that is run in one market is tested against another commercial run in a similar market. See *fixed spot test.*

Matrix - A grid that shows, graphically, every version of every commercial that is to be tested.

Matte shot - A special effect where the subject is filmed against a blue or green background. During film processing the colored background is removed, and the subject is printed onto film of a different background, for example, a tropical rain forest. The final product makes it appear as if the subject were shot on location in a tropical rain forest.

Media - The business of selecting stations on which to run commercials, negotiating rates with stations, buying air time, and analyzing the results of the buy.

Media buyer - The person who negotiates price with and contracts for commercial air time with TV stations.

Media buying service - A company that primarily or exclusively deals in media. See *creative boutique, research company,* and *full-service agency.*

Media planner - The person who decides which combination of TV stations, programs, and dayparts will make the most efficient use of a media budget.

Medium shot - (MS) A shot where the camera appears to be fairly close to the subject. If the subject were a person, a medium shot would be from about the waist up.

Miked - A small microphone and a transmitter that are hidden in a performer's clothing. See *boom mike.*

Mini rollout - Less than a full rollout of a commercial.

Mitchell - The brand name of one type of motion picture camera. See *Arriflex* and *Panavision.*

Mix - To blend together all the sound elements of a commercial, including voices, music, sound effects, and room tone.

Mixed crew - A crew that includes union and nonunion members.

Mixed track - An audio track that has been mixed.

Mix session - The process of creating a mix in a sound studio.

Mix to pix - Fitting the audio of a commercial to the video, as opposed to fitting the video to the audio.

Moderator - A trained researcher who conducts focus group sessions.

Monitor - A high-definition TV screen used in an editing studio.

Montage - Combining many visual elements in one scene.

Morphing - A commercial technique that digitally transforms one object into another.

Mortise - A small section of a scene that shows another scene. Often used to show a product shot in a live action scene or a closeup of a face in a product shot.

MOS - A portion of a film shot without sound, with wild sound added later. See *sync sound.*

Move - Any of the various ways a camera can travel during a take. Dolly in is to move the camera toward the subject. Dolly out is the reverse. Truck (also called dolly left and dolly right) is to move from side to side in relation to the subject. Pan is to rotate the camera from side to side. Tilt is to rotate the camera up or down. More than one move may be used in one take.

Moving shot - Any scene where the camera physically moves.

Moviola - The brand name of a vertical format of film editing machine.

MRI - (Mediamark Research, Inc.) A research company that profiles demographic and marketing segmentations of media audiences.

MSA - (Metropolitan statistical area, formerly SMSA, standard metropolitan statistical area) An urban area, as designated by the U.S. Census Bureau, served by a certain number of TV stations.

Multiple exposure - Various pictures appearing in one scene.

Multi track - In audio, the process and equipment used for recording and/or mixing where different voices, instruments, etc., have their own discrete sound track. Depending on the complexity of the project, as many as 64 tracks may be used.

Music library - A place where stock music selections are catalogued and can be auditioned. See *original music* and *published music.*

N

Nagra - The brand name of a sync audio tape recorder used during filming.

National - A commercial that runs on stations all over the country. See *local* and *regional.*

Negative option - A direct marketing continuity program where the product continues to be sent — and the customer is billed — until the customer asks for it to stop. See *continuity program* and *positive option.*

Network - A group of TV stations across the country that run the same programming. ABC, CBS, and NBC are networks.

Network buy - Airtime that is bought on an entire television network, which is never done in direct response. See *cable buy* and *spot buy.*

Nielsen - (A.C. Nielsen Company) 1. A service of the company that rates viewership of TV shows. 2. A service of the company that ranks products by sales and market share.

900 number - A telephone number service that is charged to the caller's telephone bill.

Nonlinear random access - Editing on a computer. This allows for instant access to anyplace in the commercial, compared to real-time editing on film or videotape.

Nonunion - A cast and/or crew that does not belong to a union. See *union.*

Normal - A lens that most closely approximates the human eye, from 40 mm to 50 mm. See *prime lens, zoom lens, fish eye, telephoto,* and *wide angle.*

No seam - Fabric or paper on a roll that can be pulled down and toward camera, like a window shade, and create a surface with no horizon line or angles. A surface on which a subject may be shot. See *sweep.*

O

OC - See on *camera.*

Off camera - Video that the camera does not see. Audio that is off camera is called voiceover.

Off line - Rough editing that is usually done in an editing suite with limited equipment and at less cost than final editing, which is done on 1-inch videotape and on an on-line editing system.

Offer - In direct response, the product or service being sold and any additional components of it, such as a free premium. See *deal.*

Offer build - A direct response technique where the deal keeps getting better and better throughout the commercial so that at the end it seems irresistible.

Offer structure - The way in which a direct response product or service is offered for sale to the public. One of several systems or techniques used in direct response selling. See *club, continuity program, one step, sequential marketing, subscription,* and *two step.*

On air test - To test a commercial on television. See *fixed spot test* and *matched market test.*

On camera - (OC) Everything that is seen by the camera and every line that is spoken on camera.

1" - One-inch videotape. The highest-quality videotape and the format on which most television stations and networks accept commercials.

One light - The first, quick print of film, literally done with one light, and with no attempt to be faithful to the true colors of the film. See *dailies.*

One step - A direct response program that asks the customer to buy the product or service after seeing the commercial. A one-step program does not offer free information, a brochure, a catalog, etc. See *two step.*

:120 - (One twenty) Literally 120 seconds, a 2-minute commercial, which is the standard length for direct response.

On line - Final editing that is done on 1-inch videotape in a state-of-the-art, expensive editing suite. On line means that the equipment is controlled by computers.

Opticals - (Optical effects) Blowups, dissolves, wipes, fades, mortises, etc.

Original music - Music that is composed, scored, and performed specifically for a commercial. See *published music* and *stock music.*

Outbound telemarketing - Outgoing phone calls from a telemarketing service or a research company. See *inbound telemarketing.*

Out of sequence - See *shooting schedule.*

Out of sync - A scene where the spoken words do not match up to the lip movement. The audio is either starting or ending at a different time than the video. See *in sync.*

Outs - Takes or portions of takes that have been discarded.

Outtake - A take that is not used in the final edit.

Over scale - Actors who require more than normal union wages to perform in a commercial.

Over-the-shoulder shot - A take that shows the shoulder and the back of the head of one person and the face of another.

Ownable - An advertising message, symbol, concept, image, positioning, or *USP* that is so closely identified with a particular brand that the competition can never challenge or erode it. For example, "The Marlboro Man," "Miller Time," "The Heartbeat of America ... Today's Chevrolet," "Merrill Lynch Is Bullish on America," and "Own a Piece of the Rock."

P

PA - (Production assistant) A person learning the production business, and who runs general errands on a shoot.

Paintbox - The brand name of an electronic special effects device that lets the user literally paint a scene on film.

Pan - See *move.*

Panavision - The brand name of one type of motion picture camera. See *Arriflex* and *Mitchell.*

Parity claim - An advertising statement that, because of clever wording, seems to say the product is superior to the competition, but in reality only says no other product is better. For example, the Quaker Oats slogan, "Nothing is better for thee than me," leaves open the possibility that other cereals may be as nutritious as Quaker Oats. Or, "Nothing outlasts the Energizer," which tries to deal with the fact that battery technology is the same among brands. See *preemptive* and *superiority claim.*

Paymaster - A company that handles session fees and residuals for AFTRA and SAG actors.

Per diem - An amount paid for living expenses while on location. In the case of advertising agency and production company personnel, and a nonunion cast and crew, negotiated with the client beforehand. In the case of a union cast and crew, set according to union rules.

Per inquiry - See *PI.*

Photoboard - Still photos of actual scenes from the commercial along with the actual dialogue. See *storyboard.*

PI - (Per inquiry) An arrangement between an advertiser and a TV station where there is no charge for running a commercial. The station runs the spot at its discretion and the advertiser pays if orders are received.

Pick-and-pack - A way of warehousing and fulfilling multiple-component orders. The components are stored separately until it is time to select and package them.

Pickup - A take or scene that is to be redone or acquired from another source.

Planner - See *media planner.*

Playback - 1. To see, on a video playback system, the last take or last few takes shot, to get an idea of how they came out. 2. To hear, in a recording session, the last take or last few takes recorded.

Players - The performers in a commercial.

Positioning - In advertising, the place the product or service occupies in the consumer's mind, as opposed to other products or services in the category. See *image* and *strategy.*

Positive option - A direct marketing continuity program where the product is not sent until the customer asks for it.

Postproduction - Everything related to producing a commercial that takes place after the shooting. See *preproduction* and *production.*

Pre-bid meeting - A meeting between a client and an advertising agency to set the cost parameters for the commercial. Topics include: film vs. tape, union vs. nonunion, location vs. set, etc. When these are agreed upon, the job is bid to production companies.

Pre build - The time required to construct a set before the actual shooting day.

Preemptible - TV commercial airtime that is sold at highly discounted rates because it is subject to replacement by commercials that have paid a higher rate. Standard practice for direct response television.

Preemptive - An advertising promise that infers brand superiority because no other product has made a similar claim. Being first with an advertising claim that blocks out the competition from making similar claims or staking out a similar position. For example, "The night belongs to Michelob." See *parity claim* and *superiority claim.*

Pre light - The time required to arrange the basic lighting of a set before the actual shooting day.

Premium - Something given away free with the purchase of a product.

Pre-post test - A type of testing that attempts to measure consumer proclivity to purchase a product after seeing a commercial, compared to before seeing it.

Preproduction - Everything related to producing a commercial that takes place before shooting. See *production* and *postproduction.*

Preproduction meeting - A meeting before a shoot among the client, advertising agency, and production company. Topics include: final cast, wardrobe, script, props, set, location, logistics, and the way the commercial is to be shot.

Primary research - Research that is commissioned, conducted, analyzed, and paid for by a marketer or an advertising agency. See *secondary research.*

Prime lens - A camera lens with one fixed focal length, such as 50 mm. A prime lens is more accurate than a zoom lens but not as versatile.

Prime time - Televison programming that takes place from 8 p.m. to 11 p.m. See *dayparts.*

Principal - An on-camera actor who performs in a commercial. If a SAG or AFTRA player says one word of dialogue and/or can be recognized in one scene, he or she is considered a principal and must be paid accordingly.

"Print" - In film, said by the director when a particular take is considered a good one and will be developed and printed.

Print - A copy of a commercial.

Producer - A person whose job is to oversee all aspects of transforming a storyboard into a commercial.

Producer/director - A person who assumes the roles of both a producer and a director during commercial production.

Production - The process of transforming a storyboard into a commercial. See *preproduction* and *postproduction.*

Production assistant - See *PA.*

Production company - A company that produces commercials.

Production values - The aesthetics of a commercial, which are influenced by the quality of the actors' performances, the directing, lighting, editing, music, etc., as well as by the quality of the original stock, the props, sets, studios, equipment, etc.

Product shot - A scene that features the product.

Propmaster - The person responsible for acquiring and handling props on a shoot.

Props - The items used to dress a set to make it appear realistic.

Protection master - A dupe of a master.

Psychographics - The goals, values, ambitions, and beliefs of a group of consumers. See *demographics.*

Published music - Music that has been professionally recorded, released, and performed for audiences. See *original music* and *stock music.*

Q

Qantel - The brand name of one type of electronic special effects device.

Qualitative - Broad-based research that seeks a direction, an area, or a feeling to pursue. See *quantitative.*

Quantitative - Narrow-based research that seeks definitive, statistically significant answers to specific questions. See *qualitative.*

Quick cut - A change of scene of short duration.

R

Rack focus - A scene where the camera quickly changes focus from the foreground to the background, or vice versa.

Rate card - See station rate card.

Ratings - The average number of viewers of a particular station or show.

Raw stock - See *stock.*

Reach - The number of people who watch a TV station at any given time of day. See *audience, frequency,* and *GRP.*

Real person - An ordinary person, not an actor or a celebrity presenter, who testifies positively about a product or service in a commercial.

Recording - The process of copying sounds on magnetic tape.

Recording engineer - The technician responsible for the quality of a recording or mix session. Also, the person who uses various equipment and techniques to change and/or improve the audio.

Recording studio - The place where recording and mixing take place.

Reel - A sample of commercials done by a particular advertising agency, director, or production company.

Reflector - A large silver or white board used to aim sunlight or artificial light toward a subject.

Regional - A commercial that runs in a certain part of the country, such as New England. See *local* and *national.*

Rehearsal - Practicing a scene before shooting it on film or tape.

Research - To determine, by scientific methods, consumer attitudes, behavior, and preferences. Also, to determine the likelihood of success of a particular strategy, concept, storyboard, and/or commercial. See *testing.*

Research company - A company engaged in setting up research projects and analyzing the results of those projects.

Research department - In an advertising agency, the people responsible for setting up research projects and analyzing the results of those projects. Sometimes a research department will use the services of an outside research company.

Residuals - Payments made to union talent every time a commercial runs. See *AFTRA* and *SAG.*

Response rate - How well a commercial performs. The number of viewers who call to order.

Reveal - To move the camera in a way that shows someone or something that was in the scene all the time.

Revox - The brand name of a professional audio tape recorder used in a recording studio. See *Ampex* and *Studer.*

Right-to-work state - A state where a worker need not be in a particular union to engage in a trade, craft, or profession.

Ripple dissolve - A wave-like transition between scenes, usually done to convey a dream sequence or the passage of time.

Rollout - To go from a test of a successful commercial to broadcasting on a large scale.

Room tone - The natural ambient sound in a studio or location. See *dead spot.*

Rough cut - The first crude assembly of a commercial without dissolves, effects, a mixed track, titles, supers, etc.

Run of station - A commercial that a TV station may run whenever it has available airtime, as opposed to being booked to run during a particular show or daypart. See *dayparts.*

Rushes - In film, the scenes filmed the previous day. Also called *dailies.*

S

Sample reel - A collection of commercials. Producers, directors, production companies and advertising agencies, as well as free-lance copywriters and art directors, use sample reels to solicit new clients.

SAG - (Screen Actors Guild) One of the unions responsible for actors. Generally, if a shoot is on film, the union is SAG. See *AFTRA.*

Scale - The basic rate a union actor is paid to appear in a commercial. See *over scale.*

Scene - All the action and dialogue that occur in one camera location.

Scratch track - A rough recording of the audio track, usually done by the producer, on the rough cut. The scratch track has no music or sound effects and is not mixed.

Screen Actors Guild - See *SAG.*

Screen Extras Guild - See *SEG.*

Script - The commercial, written as a manuscript or in screenplay form. See *storyboard.*

Script notes - A written record of each take, indicating its number, its length, and if there was anything particularly good or bad about it.

Script supervisor - The person responsible for keeping script notes, checking the length and accuracy of takes, and maintaining continuity during shooting.

Seasonality - The time of year when a certain type of product, or direct response commercials in general, perform better. The time of year when a product sells, such as lawn seed or Christmas trees.

Secondary research - Obtaining information by studying outside sources and studies, such as government data, industry directories, trade publications, etc. See *primary research.*

SEG - (Screen Extras Guild) The union responsible for extra actors. In New York City, SAG is responsible for extras. See *AFTRA* and *SAG.*

Segue - Sound that carries over from one cut, fade, or scene to another, to help make a smooth transition.

Selects - Takes that have been printed or takes that have been chosen from the dailies.

Selling strategy - The main argument(s) for buying a product or service. Sometimes called communication strategy or creative strategy. See *image, positioning,* and *USP.*

Sequential marketing - A type of integrated marketing that tries to teach a consumer the benefits of a product or service over a period of time. Sequential marketing is often used where the decision to buy involves much consideration, and where the product or service is expensive and technologically complex. See *integrated marketing.*

Session fee - The payment made to an actor for the time spent during the actual shoot, as opposed to residuals.

Set - An artificial environment that looks like a real place through the camera lens.

Set designer - A person who creates a set and furnishes it with props.

Setup - A particular arrangement of the camera and lights.

Shoot - Relating to the actual production, filming, or taping.

Shooting board - A detailed blueprint of all the scenes in a commercial, the order of shooting, and all the ways each scene will be shot. See *coverage* and *storyboard.*

Shooting day - The number of hours a union cast and crew will work before incurring overtime. For a union cast, a shooting day includes travel time to and from the location, meal breaks, wardrobe fittings, and hair and makeup. For a union crew, a shooting day includes travel time to and from the location, meal breaks, setting up cameras and equipment, striking, and wrapping.

Shooting schedule - The order is which scenes will be filmed during a shooting day. If the scenes are to be shot in the order in which they will appear on film, the shooting is *in sequence.* If the scenes are not to be shot in the order in which they will appear on film, which is the usual case, the shooting is *out of sequence.*

Shot - A scene filmed in a particular way.

Side-by-side - Something that is next to something else on screen, and often a way of showing a direct comparison between products. See *split screen.*

Signatory - A company or individual that has signed the SAG and/or AFTRA contracts, which means agreeing to only use SAG and AFTRA talent in commercial production.

Simmons - (SMRB - Simmons Marketing Bureau, Inc.) A market research firm that correlates brand preferences among audiences for different print media and broadcast programs.

16mm - A film format. Usually used for budget productions and documentaries. Sixteen millimeter captures approximately 25 percent of the information of 35mm.

:60 - (Sixty) A 1-minute commercial. Used often in direct response, especially on cable and when it is difficult for a :120 to achieve commercial clearance.

Slate - 1. A board on which is written the title of the production, the director, the cameraperson, the scene number, and the take number. The slate is held in front of the camera before each take. See *clapstick.* 2. A notice that comes on screen before a commercial, listing: the client, commercial name, commercial number, advertising agency, production company, producer, and date.

"Slate" - Said by the director to signal the start of each new take.

Slice of life - A commercial technique where two people have a conversation in which the first has a problem. The second explains how the product can solve the problem. At the beginning of the commercial the first person may be doubtful but by the end he or she has been converted to belief in the product. Slice of life is often used by packaged goods advertisers.

Slow motion - Action on film or video that appears slower than real life. To achieve slow motion the camera is run faster than normal. See *fast motion.*

Slug - A piece of film, usually white leader, put in the place where a scene will eventually go.

Small speaker - A speaker used in a recording studio that approximates the relatively low-fidelity, monaural speaker in a normal TV set, as opposed to the high-fidelity, stereo speakers used for mixing. The small speaker is used to hear what the mix will sound like in "real life."

Smoke - A harmless chemical used to fog up a scene, softening the light and creating a particular mood and feeling.

SMPTE - (Society of Motion Picture and Television Engineers) The association of professionals who set the engineering and technical standards for all aspects of film and video production and transmission.

SMSA - See *MSA.*

Snorkel - A lens that can weave around objects.

Society of Motion Picture and Television Engineers - See *SMPTE.*

Soft cut - A transition between scenes that is quicker than a cut but slower than a dissolve.

Soft focus - To throw a scene slightly out of focus, thus softening its look.

Sound effects - Any parts of the audio track that are added after the on-camera recording. Footsteps, a door closing, a phone ringing, are examples of sound effects.

Soundstage - A stage that is soundproofed, so that on-camera sound may be recorded there.

Sound studio - See *recording studio.*

Sound track - The audio portion of a commercial.

Special effects - (SFX) Various techniques used to create a reality on film where there is none in the real world, or where filming reality would be expensive or dangerous. Special effects include: explosions, spaceships, dinosaurs, superhumans, the supernatural, the hereafter, etc.

"Speed" - Said by the sound engineer and camera operator to the director, signaling that their respective equipment is up to sync speed and ready for the take to begin.

Splice - To physically join together two scenes on film.

Splicer - An apparatus that joins two pieces of film.

Split screen - A film technique where the left side of the screen shows one scene and the right side shows another. Often used in side-by-side demonstrations.

Spot - A commercial.

Spot buy - Airtime that is bought only for certain shows, stations, and/or dayparts, as opposed to a network buy, which is never the case with direct response. See *cable buy* and *run of station.*

SRDS - (Standard Rate & Data Service) - A book, used by media buyers and planners, that lists various advertising media, their costs, and requirements.

Stage - The place where a commercial is filmed. See *soundstage.*
Stand-in - A person who takes the place of an actor during setting up

lights, blocking action, and working out camera moves. A stand-in is often a PA, but if the actor is a celebrity, he or she may be an extra of approximately the same size and coloration as the celebrity.

Start mark - A mark made on film that shows where the corresponding audio and video begin.

Station rate card - The official price of airtime on a given station. The actual price paid is usually less.

Statistically significant - Research or test results that can accurately predict the behavior of larger populations because the research had a large enough sample size and/or a large enough difference between two numbers. See *confidence level.*

Steadicam - The brand name of a counterbalanced mount for hand-held cameras that helps to smooth out and steady the camera as it is moved.

Steenbeck - The brand name of a flatbed film editing machine. See *Kem* and *Moviola.*

Stock - Film or videotape that has not been used yet.

Stock footage - Scenes shot by others that can be rented for use in a commercial. Examples of stock footage include: wars, the first moon walk, panoramic views of mountains, famous landmarks, airplanes taking off and landing, etc.

Stock music - Prerecorded music rented from a music library. See *original music* and *published music.*

Stop motion - A type of filming where a frame or a few frames are shot and then the camera is stopped while the subject is slightly moved. Then the camera shoots another frame or frames. This technique can animate objects, such as showing a chair moving around a room. It can also give humans a stylized way of moving.

Storyboard - Drawings of the scenes to be included in the commercial and the proposed dialogue. See *photoboard.*
Strategy - See *communications strategy* and *marketing strategy.*

Strike - To undo a setup after it has been shot. To physically disassemble a set. See *build.*

Studer - The brand name of a professional audio tape recorder used in a recording studio. See *Ampex* and *Revox.*

Subscription - A direct marketing offer structure where the consumer pays for a product which, by its nature, is created and delivered at intervals, such as weekly or monthly. The customer is under no obligation and may cancel at any time. A subscription is most often thought of in relation to magazines and newspapers but is used for other types of products as well. See *club* and *continuity program.*

Super - Any type that is superimposed over the picture, such as an 800 number, the price of a product, etc.

Superiority claim - An advertising claim that the product is the best, or excels in some way. For example, the Tide slogan, "The Best Detergent on American Soil." See *parity claim* and *preemptive.*

Support - A commercial used to assist advertising in another medium, as opposed to being the primary selling medium. For example, a commercial used as support for an ad in Sunday supplements.

Sweep - The floor of a set, whether tabletop or a stage, that curves upward toward the background and flows into the rear wall so that no horizon line can be seen. See *no seam.*

Sweeten - To add sound effects to an audio track.

Synchronizer - A device used by a film editor that runs audio and video tracks at the same time and at the same speed.

Sync sound - (Synchronous sound). On-camera sound that is recorded at exactly the same speed as the picture. See *in sync, out of sync,* and *wild sound.*

Swish pan - An extremely rapid camera move.

T

Table top - Any small-scale production that uses small props and no on-camera actors.

Tag - The last 15 or 20 seconds of a direct response commercial. A local message or a different ending of a commercial.

Tag rate - According to AFTRA and SAG rules, a performer who does a variation in copy is paid less if the change is a tag, made during the last 15 to 20 seconds of the commercial, than if the change occurs during the main body of the commercial.

Tail - The closing frames of a take, which may be used in their entirety or cut, to help achieve a smooth transition between scenes. See *head.*

Take - Each performance of a particular scene. The take is recorded by placing the slate board, which has the take number written on it, in front of the camera before shooting each take.

Talent - The performers, whether on-camera or voiceover, in a commercial.

Talent release - A form real people must sign if they are to appear in a commercial. The talent release states that they agree to be in the commercial, what their compensation is, and that they believe what they say about the product or service.

Talking head - A commercial where an on-camera presenter speaks to the audience.

Tape - (Videotape) An electronic medium for shooting commercials. See *film.*

Teamsters - The union responsible for drivers of vehicles to and from locations.

Technological product - A product whose existence or superiority is a result of an invention or improvement in chemistry, electronics, physics, botany, etc. For example, CD players, shampoo and conditioner in one, time-release medication. See *marketing product.*

Telemarketing - Various marketing functions, such as research, order entry, handling consumer complaints, etc., that are done over the telephone. See *inbound telemarketing* and *outbound telemarketing.*

Telemarketing center - A department or company that does telemarketing.

Telemarketing script - A structured text that allows a telemarketer to close sales, capture information, and address a menu of questions and/or concerns about the product or service.

Telephone survey - A research technique where consumers are called and asked questions about a product, service, or commercial.

Telephoto - A lens of about to 75 mm to 500 mm or more. A telephoto lens has a narrow field of view, brings objects closer and reduces the distance between distant objects. See *normal, fish eye,* and *wide angle.*

TelePrompTer - The brand name of a device that projects a script on a camera lens. The talent can look into the camera while reading the script; however, the camera does not film it.

Test - Whenever one commercial, price, offer, or premium is compared to another.

Testimonial - A type of commercial where someone claims to have used the product or service and had a favorable experience with it. A testimonial may use an actor, a celebrity presenter, or a real person.

Testing - To determine, by scientific methods, consumer reaction to finished commercials, as well as to prices, offers, premiums, etc. See *research.*

Test market - An ADI where a commercial is run for a limited time, usually two weeks, to see how it performs.

35mm - The highest-quality film format. Used for feature films and often for commercials.

3/4" - A format of videotape used extensively for casting and copies of 1-inch material.

Three shot - A take that includes three people.

Tight shot - See *closeup.*

Tilt - See *move.*

Time code - A series of numbers on videotape that cannot be seen but are recognized by editing equipment and that help an editor locate scenes and frames within them. See *visual time code.*

Time lapse - A type of filming where individual frames are shot at relatively long intervals. This technique compresses time for events of long duration, such as the opening of a flower, into a few seconds.

Title - Any words, numbers, etc. that appear on a plain background, as opposed to being superimposed over a picture. See *super.*

Title camera - A camera mounted on a frame so that it faces down and can be moved. Below it is a flat bed on which items to be filmed are placed. A title camera is ordinarily used for flat art, supers, and 800 numbers that have been set as typography. See *Chyron.*

Titled generic - A second-generation commercial on 1-inch videotape with all titles and supers except for different 800 numbers. See *generic master.*

Title safety - The edges of a title or super that can be expected to not be cut off on a normal TV set. Title safety is always inside TV safety.

Track - 1. In audio, the sound portion of a film or video. Any discrete recording of the audio track, such as the voice track, the music track, the sound effects track. 2. Any subdivision of the music track, for example, the guitar track, the drum track, etc. 3. In shooting, parallel rails along which a dolly travels along during a moving shot.

Trim - Any part of a take that is discarded. See *head* and *tail.*

Tripod - A stationary, three-legged support for a camera.

Truck - See *move.*

TV safety - The edges of a scene that can be expected to not be cut off on a normal TV set. TV safety is always outside title safety.

Two shot - A take that includes two people.

Two step - In direct response, requiring two steps to make the sale. The first step does not ask the customer to buy anything, but simply to request more information, which is usually free. The second step attempts to close the sale.

U

U-Matic - The brand name of $^{3}/_{4}$-inch videotape, players, and recorders.

Under crank - To operate a camera at a slower-than-normal speed, which makes the action appear to move faster than normal.

Union - An organization of people engaged in a particular craft, trade, or profession, which protects their rights and establishes the criteria under which they will work. See *AFTRA, IA, SAG, Teamsters, union crew, union talent,* and *nonunion.*

Union crew - A crew that belongs to the IA, and/or to the Teamsters. The IA is the union responsible for all crafts people on the shoot, such as the grip, gaffers, camera operators, etc. The Teamsters is the union responsible for drivers, who transport equipment, people, portable dressing rooms, etc. to and from locations.

Union talent - Actors and actresses that belong to AFTRA and/or to SAG. Most belong to both.

Up-selling - Attempting to persuade a caller to order higher-priced products, additional products, or to continue in a direct marketing program for a longer period of time.

USP - (Unique Selling Proposition) An advertising philosophy developed in the 1950s by Rosser Reeves for Ted Bates & Company. A good USP tells the customer something that makes him or her want to buy the product and that is, or seems to be, an exclusive feature of the product.

V

Vampire video - A commercial where some aspect of the production is so interesting and entertaining that viewers forget who the advertiser is.

Version - A direct response commercial with a particular price, offer, and/or premium.

Video - The portions of a commercial that relate to what the camera sees. See *audio.*

Video disk - An editing format that uses laser disk technology similar to a home CD.

Video playback - See *playback.*

Videotape - See *tape.*

Viewer interest test - A type of focus group research where people are shown a commercial and express their interest by pressing buttons or turning a dial that registers a real time graph.

Vignette - A short, usually humorous, and exaggerated visualization. Often, a series of these are used in a vignette commercial.

Visual time code - A series of numbers that have been superimposed on videotape to help an editor locate scenes and frames within them. See *time code.*

Voiceover - Audio portions of a commercial where an actor is not seen.

W

Wardrobe - The clothes worn by an actor.

Wardrobe supervisor - The person responsible requiring for selecting, acquiring, and fitting clothing or costumes for actors in a commercial.

Wide angle - A lens of about 25 mm to 35 mm. See *normal, telephoto,* and *fish eye.*

Wild sound - Sound that is recorded without being in sync with the picture. See *sync sound.*

Wipe - An effect where a scene appears to move across the screen and erase the previous scene.

Wrap - 1. In direct marketing, a "bookend" commercial that comes on immediately before and immediately after a general image commercial, thus enveloping it. 2. In production, the end of shooting, either for the day or for the production. The wrap often happens in stages. For example, if the live action is finished but the product shots remain, the director will say: "Wrap talent, sound, hair and makeup, and wardrobe."

Z

Zoom - To change focal length during a shot, either getting closer to or farther away from the subject.

Zoom lens - A lens that can change its focal length, for example, from 35 mm to 120 mm. A zoom lens is more flexible than a prime lens, but not as precise.

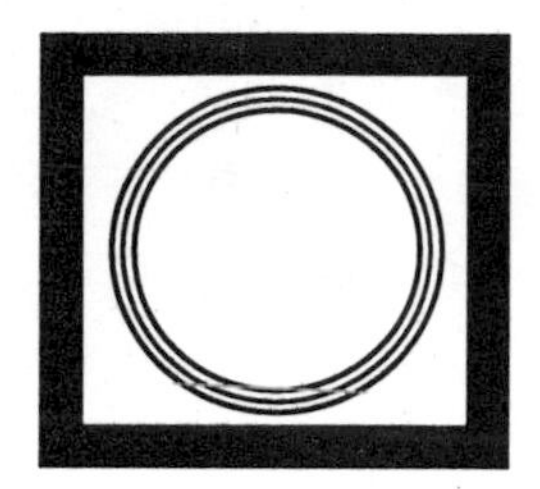

Index

A

B

C

D

E

F

G

H

I

J

L

M

N

O

P

Q

R

U

W

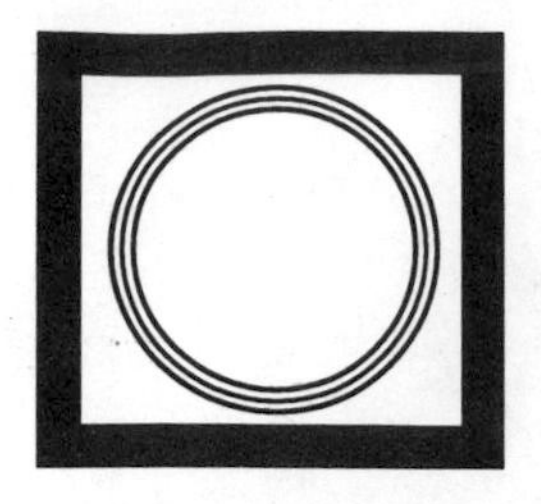

About the Authors

Frank R. Brady

Frank's early career included work at some of the top general image agencies in New York City, including BBD&O, Ogilvy & Mather, and Papert, Koenig & Lois. He also wrote for Dentsu in Tokyo, Japan. Frank got into direct response when he joined Wunderman Worldwide, where he rose to Associate Creative Director. He held a senior creative position at Dimac Direct and was creative director at Saatchi & Saatchi Direct.

J. Angel Vasquez

Angel Vasquez started his career in general advertising by spending five years at Ogilvy & Mather. He moved from O&M to a special creative group at D'Arcy, MacManus & Masius, and then to Wyse. He joined Wunderman Worldwide where he expanded his expertise in direct marketing and became proficient in both disciplines.